25 YEARS: THE NFL SINCE 1960

Ted Brock
and
Larry Eldridge, Jr.

  A National Football League Book

F A Fireside Book
Published by Simon and Schuster, Inc.
New York

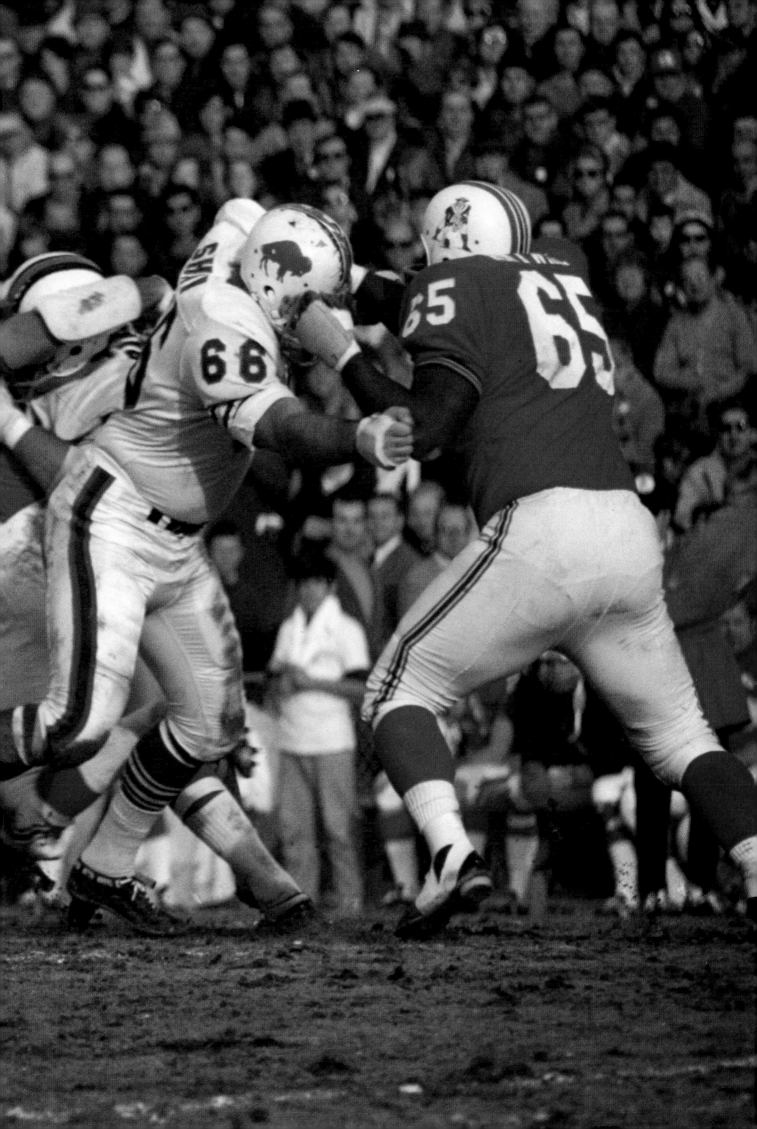

CONTENTS

Designed by Cliff Wynne

Creative Director: David Boss
Editor: John Wiebusch
Managing Editor: Chuck Garrity, Sr.
Assistant to Designer: Sandy Sumida Tokunaga

FIRESIDE and colophon are registered trademarks of
Simon & Schuster, Inc.
The names, helmet designs, and uniforms of the NFL Member
Clubs are registered in the U.S. Patent & Trademark Office.
The title "25 Years: The NFL Since 1960" is a trademark of
National Football League Properties, Inc.
Manufactured in Japan
Printed and bound by Dai Nippon, Tokyo, Japan
1   2   3   4   5   6   7   8   9   10
Library of Congress Cataloging in Publication Data
ISBN: 0-671-60441-4
ISBN: 0-671-60440-6 Pbk.

PHOTOGRAPHY
Legend: L-left; R-right; T-top; M-middle; B-Bottom; TL-top left; ML-middle left; BL-bottom left; TR-top right; MR-middle right; BR-bottom right.

ABC-TV 40TL; Bob Allen, 50B, 52BL, 69BR; Bill Amatucci 47TL; Arthur Anderson 58TR, 93, 143TL; Fred Anderson 52T, 54MR; Charles Aqua Viva 20T, 26B, 36B; Associated Press Wirephoto 120B; Morris Berman for the *Pittsburgh Post-Gazette* 21; John E. Biever 44T, 51T, 60TR, 131TL; Vernon Biever 17T, 25BL, 26T, 32TL, 33T, 34T, 40ML, 41B, 43B, 79, 82, 88, 90B, 98, 99TL-TR, 104, 105T-BR-BL, 109TR-M, 131TR; David Boss 24B, 28B, 43ML, 46MR, 52M, 54ML, 64TR, 67B, 68TL, 70B, 71, 77, 85, 94B, 106B, 107TL-BR, 151; Cliff Boutelle 38T; Bill Bridges, *Life Magazine* 149; Chance Brockway 109TL; Brockway-Emmons 90T, 108; Dick Burnell 47BR; Greg Cava 144L, 147BR; Cincinnati Bengals 34B; Coca-Cola 59; Tom J. Croke 63B; Dave Cross 65BL, 66TR, 70T, 136TL-TR, 137B, 140, 141L; Scott Cunningham 8; Dallas Cowboys 129; Detroit Lions 81; Daniel Dmitruk 48ML; Miguel Elliot 66B, 146L-R, 147TL-TR; Gin Ellis 56T; Malcolm Emmons 31T, 32M, 35BR, 41M, 46ML-B, 73, 75, 86, 87, 109B, 110T, 115, 130; Nate Fine 35TL, 60BL, 66M, 70M, 125T-B, 138B, 139TL-BL, 144R, 145TL, 150; Paul Fine 22TR, 48TR; James Flores 78T; L.D. Fullerton 53BL; George Gellatly 152; George Gojkovich 64B, 66TL; Pete J. Groh 63TR; Rod Hanna 37T-B, 65TR-BR, 118, 119T-B; Ken Hardin 32TR; Jocelyn Hinsen 47M; Harry Homa 35TR; Industrial Photography, Inc. 48MR; Walter Iooss 83; Don Lansu 51B, 63TL, 69T, 154; Laughead Photographers 13M, 100, 101TL; Ross Lewis 1, 49M; Ed Mahan 55B; Tak Makita 60TL, 133TL, 136TM; Bill Mark 30T, 31BL; Jack Martin 42ML; John E. Martin 42B; Fred Matthes 63M; John McDonough 55T, 84, 158-159; Al Messerschmidt 141R; *Miami Herald* 28T; Minnesota Vikings 15T, 31BR; NBC-TV 111B; NFL Properties 101BR; New Orleans Saints 39BL; Oakland Raiders 89; Pro Football Hall of Fame 12B, 102; Dick Raphael 4-5, 42MR, 50T, 113TR-B, 119M, 120T-M, 121, 128TL-TR; Russ Reed 20B, 49B, 52BR, 110B, 111T-M, 113TL, 116, 117TL-TR, 126B; Frank Rippon 27B, 122TL-TR-B, 123TL-TR, 142, 143B; George Rubarge 65TL; Fred Roe 2-3, 17B, 114, 131B; Ron Ross 64TL, 132, 133TR-B; Manny Rubio 7, 54B, 92, 160; Dan Rubin 14T-M, 18T, 15BR, 19ML, 40TR; Russ Russell 124, 138T, 139R; Jules Schick 23B, 99BR; Carl Skalak, Jr. 48TL, 80; Barton Silverman 112; Bill Smith 69BL, 137T; Robert L. Smith 17ML, 19T, 25T, 36T, 41T, 46T, 50M, 58ML; Chuck Solomon 94T; William Snyder, *Miami News* 62; Jay Spencer 44B; Sam Spina 68TR; Mike Spinelli 126TL; Paul Spinelli, 145TR-B; *Sports Illustrated* 49T, 103; R.H. Stagg 76; Barry Staver 78B; Vic Stein 13T, 19MR-B, 53BR, 107TR; Rick Stewart 157; Tony Tomsic 15BL, 18B, 60BR, 74, 91; Corky Trewin 143TR; Bob Verlin 29BR; *United Press International* 106T, 153R; University of Arkansas 17MR; Herb Weitman 32B, 38B, 43TR, 45TL-TR-BL-BR, 53MR, 61, 66TM, 67T, 95, 96, 148, 155; Lou Witt 16, 23T, 26M, 27T, 101TR, 134T-B, 135T-B; Washington Redskins 22TL; Michael Zagaris 51M, 56ML, 57, 58TL-MR, 126TR, 127T-B.

PART I

25 YEARS: A CHRONOLOGY

Think of where you were. . . and what you were doing. . . when Jim Marshall picked a fumble off the ground at San Francisco's Kezar Stadium and ran all the way. . . the wrong way. Or when Commissioner Pete Rozelle had to suspend play in the final College All-Star Game with 1:22 left to play in the third quarter because a thunderstorm was about to wash out the city of Chicago. Or when Marcus Allen made a U-turn to a 74-yard touchdown run in the Los Angeles Raiders' 38-9 romp over Washington in Super Bowl XVIII.

Maybe you can remember where you were. Probably you can't. You know it's all back there, though—a treasury of personalities and events, weaving its way forward with momentum that began in 1920, in Canton, Ohio, squarely in the country's midsection. The history of the National Football League is a swarm of interaction, on and off the field of play. Untangling the league's last 25 years, let alone its first 65, has its limits. What to say? Whom to single out? Whom to cheer, jeer, mourn, salute?

Americans share the NFL. They take the seasons and tumble them around in their minds and talk about the plays and the games and the developments off the field. A radio talk show, the neighborhood tavern, the back fence—the medium or the venue doesn't matter. Everyone has his or her version of how it went: Morrall shoulda thrown to Orr; Sipe shouldn'ta thrown to Ozzie. Chandler's field goal was no good; Renfro had possession, with both feet in the end zone. *Ad infinitum.*

Is it presumptuous to select the "high spots" of the NFL's last 25 years? Just remember, this is "pop history," not such a distant relative of what you're apt to hear at, say, a regular meeting of Howard Blindauer's Morning Coffee Club in downtown Green Bay on some cold, clear Monday in mid-November.

NFL co-founder George Halas (far left) and Washington Redskins owner George Preston Marshall (second from right) helped congratulate 33-year-old Pete Rozelle (center) moments after he had been elected NFL Commissioner.

1960

You had to feel happy for the Philadelphia Eagles. Celebrating their victory in the NFL Championship Game, they hugged each other, mugged for photographers, tossed back their sweaty heads, and poured the sweet beverage of triumph into faces streaked with the mud of Franklin Field.

You had to feel happy for the Eagles, because it was the first chance you'd had for a decade ...and the last you'd have for a couple more.

After winning NFL titles in 1948 and 1949, they had spent the 1950s as also-rans, sometimes close but more often distant. After a 10-4 second-place finish in 1961, the Eagles struggled for most of the next 18 years, finally emerging in 1980 with an NFC championship and a trip to Super Bowl XV. But go back to the postgame revelry of 25 years ago. . . .

If a single player captured the spirit of the 1960 NFL Championship Game—and the pivotal quality of pro football in the early 1960s—it was Chuck Bednarik, the last of the 60-minute men, a combination center-linebacker.

Two years later, Bednarik would end his playing career. From then on, there were one-platoon guys. Sure, there were rarities during the next two decades. Roy Green, the defensive back the St. Louis Cardinals turned into an eventual league-leading wide receiver in 1980, was one. Green is versatile, but he never goes the full four quarters. For two-way, 60-minute men, Chuck Bednarik was it. From Bednarik on, pro football turned to specialization. Coaching staffs would grow to twice their 1960 size. Players' roles would refine themselves to undreamed-of precision as the game turned to finesse.

"The Foolish Club" of AFL owners posed for this group photo with Commissioner Joe Foss (seated, right). Next to Foss is Houston owner K.S. (Bud) Adams. Standing, from left: William H. Sullivan, Jr., Boston; Calvin W. Kunz, Jr., Denver; Ralph Wilson, Jr., Buffalo; Lamar Hunt, Dallas; Harry Wismer, New York; Wayne Valley, Oakland; and Barron Hilton, Los Angeles.

Out of the night came the newly relocated Cardinals, pro football's oldest franchise, representing St. Louis for the first time in a 43-21 road victory over the Los Angeles Rams. The Cardinals had moved from Chicago, where they had begun as the Morgan Athletic Club in 1899.

In the visitors' locker room at Franklin Field on that final day of the 1960 season, Packers head coach Vince Lombardi dealt with an emotion he'd be feeling for the last time: defeat in an NFL Championship Game. Lombardi's Green Bay teams of the 1960s would be NFL champions in 1961, 1962, 1965, 1966, and 1967, and in the latter two would graduate to a new level of competition, an event initially called the AFL-NFL World Championship Game by the league office. In the media, the games were known as Super Bowls I and II.

"AFL" of course stood for American Football League. Born: 1960. Teams: Boston, Buffalo, Dallas, Denver, Houston, Los Angeles, New York, Oakland. Commissioner's resume: perfect. Joe Foss, a heavily decorated World War II fighter pilot and a national hero, chaired a group of owners that very early had dubbed itself "The Foolish Club."

While the new league's eight teams purchased uniforms and dived into the talent market for bodies to fill them, the NFL took on new leadership. Pete Rozelle, general manager and vice president of the Los Angeles Rams, was elected Commissioner. His charge: a league that since its founding in 1920 had evolved from 13 clubs to as many as 22, and after four decades, was back to 13, divided into two conferences.

Rozelle's predecessor was Bert Bell, a Main Line Philadelphia aristocrat whose death came at Franklin Field in 1959 as he watched the Eagles play the Pittsburgh Steelers from the end-zone stands.

Rozelle's ascension at age 33 to what some considered an interim role as Commissioner came after an arduous 23-ballot selection meeting among the league's owners; he was a compromise candidate nominated to break a hopeless stalemate.

The Dallas Cowboys' original brain trust included, from left, head coach Tom Landry, secretary-treasurer Bedford Wynne, vice president-general manager Tex Schramm, and president Clint Murchison, Jr.

The NFL's modest expansion from 12 to 13 teams in 1960 was its first in 10 years. In 1950, it had absorbed the Cleveland Browns, San Francisco 49ers, and Baltimore Colts from the fallen four-year-old All-America Football Conference.

The new team played in Dallas, wore blue stars on its white helmets and jersey shoulders, and called itself the Cowboys. Its head coach, Tom Landry, had been a player (mainly a defensive back) and a coaching colleague of Lombardi with the New York Giants, under Jim Lee Howell. (Another new NFL franchise, to be located in Minneapolis-St. Paul, was awarded in 1960 to be activated in 1961.)

Although the frustration of the Cowboys' early years would give rise to the familiar outcry for the coach's dismissal, Dallas owner Clint Murchison's response would be to provide a new 10-year contract for Landry. To this day,

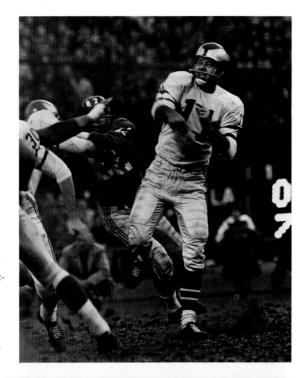

Quarterback Norm Van Brocklin, shown in the first of two back-to-back victories over the New York Giants, led Philadelphia to the NFL title in 1960, passing for 2,471 yards and 24 touchdowns.

The Dallas Cowboys may not have won a game in their initial season, but they claimed 1960's major moral victory by tying the Giants 31-31. Linebacker Jerry Tubbs pursued New York's Joe Morrison (40), who looked for help from guard Jack Stroud (66).

Landry is the only coach the Cowboys have known.

In its first game, played at the Cotton Bowl September 29, Dallas got a 345-yard passing performance from diminutive Eddie LeBaron, the former Washington Redskins quarterback. But Pittsburgh quarterback and native Texan Bobby Layne threw four touchdown passes and kicked all five extra points as the Steelers defeated the Cowboys 35-28. The Cowboys, 0-11-1 in their first season, were NFL cellar material. Off the field they faced an AFL competitor, the Dallas Texans, at the box office. Likewise, the New York Giants and Los Angeles Rams found themselves "sharing" their cities' pro football marketplaces with the New York Titans and Los Angeles Chargers of the AFL.

The AFL immediately threw a new wrinkle into pro football's relationship with television,

selling ABC the rights to its games for $2 million. In the unique package, the eight teams shared the revenue equally.

The AFL got its start on Friday night, September 9, at Boston University Field. Denver Broncos flanker Al Carmichael (formerly of Green Bay) caught a 59-yard pass from Frank Tripucka and scored the first touchdown in league history. Later, their teammate Gene Mingo returned a punt 76 yards for a touchdown, giving Denver a 13-10 victory over the Boston Patriots.

AFL founder Lamar Hunt's team, the Dallas Texans, was at the Los Angeles Coliseum the next evening to face Barron Hilton's Chargers, named after his newly initiated "Carte Blanche" credit card but symbolized by a white horse on the club's logo and lightning bolts on their helmets. Mixed metaphors and all, the Chargers defeated the Texans 21-20 as NFL castoff quarterback Jack Kemp passed for one touchdown and ran for another, both in the fourth quarter. (The Chargers' biggest asset probably was its coaching staff, headed by Sid Gillman, who lured a group of assistants whose names would became prominent during the next 24 years—Chuck Noll, Al Davis, Jack Faulkner, and Don Klosterman.)

The AFL completed its three-day grand opening on Sunday, September 11. At Kezar Stadium in San Francisco, Houston Oilers quarterback George Blanda, formerly of the Chicago Bears, threw four touchdown passes in a 37-22 victory over the Oakland Raiders, whose quarterback, rookie Tom Flores, completed only 13 of 32 passing attempts. At the Polo Grounds in New York, owner Harry Wismer's Titans spotted the Buffalo Bills a field goal in the first quarter, then held Buffalo quarterbacks Bob Brodhead and Tom O'Connell to 26 passing yards, winning 27-3.

When the Oilers had identified themselves as the class of the new league (their 6-3 record in late season belied their offensive might, and offense was the end-all in the early years of the AFL), the late Tex Maule wrote in *Sports Illustrated:* "The question is: how good are the Oilers [and, for that matter, how good is the rest of the league]? Unquestionably, the Oilers are better than Missouri or Minnesota or Mississippi. They are smarter and more versatile than these college teams; but they are not as good as the Dallas Cowboys, the newest and weakest team in the National Football League. The Cowboys, who are smarter and more versatile than

than the Oilers, would beat them, and easily."

The Oilers didn't have the Cowboys on their schedule in 1960, of course; the two teams wouldn't play a regular-season game until 1970. Tex Maule must have had at least a silent chuckle when the Cowboys won that one 52-10. But that's getting ahead of the story. In the first AFL Championship Game, against the Chargers, Houston's Blanda passed for 301 yards and three touchdowns. Oilers halfback Billy Cannon, the 1959 Heisman Trophy winner from LSU whose signing under the goal posts immediately following the Sugar Bowl had been an early AFL public relations coup, was the title game's most valuable player. His 88-yard touchdown reception from Blanda provided the decisive points as the Oilers defeated the Chargers 24-16.

Conversations around the hot stove burned into the night. NFL, AFL, what was your pleasure? Fun times lay ahead.

1961

Movement and change marked the early months of the AFL's second year, the NFL's forty-second.

San Diego got a franchise in the new league, as the Chargers moved south from Los Angeles. In the NFL, the Washington Redskins moved into newly constructed D.C. Stadium (later to be named in memory of slain presidential candidate Robert F. Kennedy). Art Modell purchased the Cleveland Browns. The San Francisco 49ers, enamored of their Shotgun formation and its prerequisite that a quarterback be able to run, traded Y.A. Tittle to the New York Giants for guard Lou Cordileone. The deal was a godsend for the Giants, as Tittle led them to three consecutive championship games.

In 1961, Norm Van Brocklin (shirtsleeves) became a head coach, leading the new Minnesota Vikings to an opening-day victory over Chicago. Among the celebrants were quarterback Fran Tarkenton (10), general manager Bert Rose, halfback Tommy Mason (eyes closed, on Tarkenton's right), and halfback Hugh McElhenny (between Van Brocklin and Rose).

1960 NFL

EASTERN CONFERENCE						WESTERN CONFERENCE					
	W	L	T	Pct.	Pts.	OP		W	L	T	Pct.	Pts.	OP
Philadelphia	10	2	0	.833	321	246	Green Bay	8	4	0	.667	332	209
Cleveland	8	3	1	.727	362	217	Detroit	7	5	0	.583	239	212
N.Y. Giants	6	4	2	.600	271	261	San Francisco	7	5	0	.583	208	205
St. Louis	6	5	1	.545	288	230	Baltimore	6	6	0	.500	288	234
Pittsburgh	5	6	1	.455	240	275	Chicago	5	6	1	.455	194	299
Washington	1	9	2	.100	178	309	L.A. Rams	4	7	1	.364	265	297
							Dallas Cowboys	0	11	1	.000	177	369

NFL Championship: PHILADELPHIA 17, Green Bay 13

1960 AFL

EASTERN DIVISION						WESTERN DIVISION					
	W	L	T	Pct.	Pts.	OP		W	L	T	Pct.	Pts.	OP
Houston	10	4	0	.714	379	285	L.A. Chargers	10	4	0	.714	373	336
N.Y. Titans	7	7	0	.500	382	399	Dall. Texans	8	6	0	.571	362	253
Buffalo	5	8	1	.385	296	303	Oakland	6	8	0	.429	319	388
Boston	5	9	0	.357	286	349	Denver	4	9	1	.308	309	393

AFL Championship: HOUSTON 24, L.A. Chargers 16

Far left: From 1957-1965 and beyond, Cleveland's Jim Brown was pro football's quintessential ball carrier. Left: In Philadelphia, the retirement of Van Brocklin left room for Sonny Jurgensen to set NFL records of 3,723 yards passing and 235 completions, and to tie a third with 32 touchdowns.

Denver Broncos receiver Lionel Taylor caught 100 passes in 1961, a pro football record. Note also Taylor's leggings, the infamous vertically striped socks; the Broncos destroyed their entire collection a year later in a public bonfire.

The NFL got its fourteenth franchise with the birth of the Minnesota Vikings. The state's last NFL team had been the Minneapolis Red Jackets (1929-30), whose combined record of 2-16-1 netted them two next-to-last place finishes.

Norm Van Brocklin, who had retired following his championship victory as the Philadelphia Eagles' quarterback, was the new club's head coach. The Vikings chose their first players as the Dallas Cowboys had—from a list submitted by the league's 13 other teams. But they had an advantage over the Cowboys; they also were able to take part in the annual college draft. Minnesota's draft class was headed by Tulane halfback Tommy Mason and Georgia quarterback Fran Tarkenton. Never one to avoid a macho challenge, Van Brocklin, the fiery "man's man" quarterback, subtly shifted gears and became Van Brocklin the drill sergeant, labeling his garage-sale bunch "the thirty-six stiffs."

In their maiden game, the "stiffs" upset Chicago 37-13. Tarkenton, whose serpentine scrambles in the seasons ahead would madden Van Brocklin as much as they enthralled spectators, passed for four touchdowns and ran for a fifth.

The NFL didn't know it yet, but here was its inventive, improvising, can-do, overachieving quarterback for the 1960s and 1970s, inaugurating his career with a team that would win only 2 of its next 13 games.

While the Vikings struggled, the Green Bay Packers drove to an 11-3 record and a championship-game victory over the New York Giants. The 1961 title game represented the coronation of the Packers' dynasty. Lombardi's "run to daylight" theme was predicated on a swift, strong offensive line. At its core were guards Jerry Kramer and Fred (Fuzzy) Thurston, men who made daylight for fullback Jim Taylor and multipurpose halfback Paul Hornung. Quarterback Bart Starr, reliable and serviceable and sometimes even spectacular, was in his sixth season, well-matured for the adventures ahead. Against the Giants on the last day of the year, Hornung set an NFL Championship Game record by scoring 19 points in a 37-0 rout.

Also notable in the statistical review of 1961 were the accomplishments of two players whose offensive prominence spanned, when combined, almost two decades: Cleveland fullback Jim Brown (1957-1965) and Philadelphia (and later Washington) quarterback Sonny Jurgensen (1957-1974). Brown, the league's leading rusher for the fifth time in his five-year career, tied his own single-game mark with 237 yards against the Eagles. Jurgensen set an NFL single-season record by passing for 3,723 yards.

The AFL style of play, meanwhile, got its "look" from the likes of Denver receiver Lionel Taylor, whose pro football-record 100 catches hid beneath his team's 3-11 showing. Just to show that this was a league that lived by the pass, Houston's George Blanda threw seven touchdown passes, tying a pro-football record, in a 49-13 victory over the New York Titans. Then, just to show that this was a league that refused to be labeled easily, Blanda and the Oilers held off the transplanted Chargers for a 10-3 victory in the AFL Championship Game.

Mark 1961, too, as a memorable year in pro football's successful marriage to television. The game had grown more and more salable to the major networks since the late 1950s, when the Baltimore Colts' sudden-death overtime victory against the New York Giants in the 1958 NFL Championship Game mesmerized millions tuned to the CBS telecast. Commissioner Rozelle, himself, challenged by the potential impact of television on his sport, began to lobby. So, in 1961, came Senator Emanuel Celler

(D-New York) with a bill legalizing single-network package sales by professional sports leagues. President John F. Kennedy signed it into law; by January, 1962, the NFL and CBS had agreed on a two-year contract calling for total rights fees of $4,650,000 annually.

The Green Bay Packers dominated pro football in the 1960s, thanks in large part to the power of the "Packer Sweep," built around fullback Jim Taylor (31) and pulling guards Jerry Kramer (64) and Fred (Fuzzy) Thurston (63).

1961 NFL

EASTERN CONFERENCE						WESTERN CONFERENCE					
	W	L	T	Pct.	Pts.	OP		W	L	T	Pct.	Pts.	OP
N.Y. Giants	10	3	1	.769	368	220	Green Bay	11	3	0	.786	391	223
Philadelphia	10	4	0	.714	361	297	Detroit	8	5	1	.615	270	258
Cleveland	8	5	1	.615	319	270	Baltimore	8	6	0	.571	302	307
St. Louis	7	7	0	.500	279	267	Chicago	8	6	0	.571	326	302
Pittsburgh	6	8	0	.429	295	287	San Francisco	7	6	1	.538	346	272
Dallas Cowboys	4	9	1	.308	236	380	Los Angeles	4	10	0	.286	263	333
Washington	1	12	1	.077	174	392	Minnesota	3	11	0	.214	285	407

NFL Championship: GREEN BAY 37, N.Y. Giants 0

1961 AFL

EASTERN DIVISION						WESTERN DIVISION					
	W	L	T	Pct.	Pts.	OP		W	L	T	Pct.	Pts.	OP
Houston	10	3	1	.769	513	242	San Diego	12	2	0	.857	396	219
Boston Patriots	9	4	1	.692	413	313	Dallas Texans	6	8	0	.429	334	343
N.Y. Titans	7	7	0	.500	301	390	Denver	3	11	0	.214	251	432
Buffalo	6	8	0	.429	294	342	Oakland	2	12	0	.143	237	458

AFL Championship: Houston 10, SAN DIEGO 3

1962

Head coach Jack Faulkner's idea of burning the Denver Broncos' ghastly, vertically-striped brown and yellow stockings at a public bonfire may have been as much witchcraft as it was public relations. The Broncos jumped from 3-11 to 7-7, good enough for a second-place Western Division finish in 1962. But Faulkner's magic extended to only 2 of the next 18 games, and the Broncos let him go after the first 4 games of 1964.

The Texans gave the city of Dallas a goodby gift in 1962, defeating Houston for the AFL title in sudden-death overtime (see page 100) before moving to Kansas City to become the Chiefs.

If the Oilers' habitual appearance in the AFL finale suggested stability, that notion was easily shaken by the reminder that they had done it under three different head coaches—Lou Rymkus, Wally Lemm, and Frank (Pop) Ivy. Before the decade was over, the team made three more coaching changes, switching to Sammy Baugh in 1964, Hugh (Bones) Taylor in 1965, and back to Lemm in 1966. An Oilers executive once left the following instructions with his secretary: "If the head coach calls while I'm out, be sure to get his name."

Nineteen-sixty-two also was the year the AFL got its first 1,000-yard rusher, Carlton (Cookie) Gilchrist of the Buffalo Bills. It was the first year in American pro football for the

Above left: Carlton (Cookie) Gilchrist joined the Buffalo Bills in 1962 after eight years in Canada and became the AFL's dominant running back. Above right: Arkansas halfback Lance Alworth was drafted by Oakland and traded to San Diego in 1962. He reached the Pro Football Hall of Fame in 1978. Below: In 13-degree cold, buffeted by gusts of 40 miles per hour, Green Bay defeated the New York Giants 16-7 for the NFL title at Yankee Stadium.

6-foot 2-inch, 243-pound fullback, after eight seasons in the Canadian Football League.

Off the field, the AFL's charges of NFL monopoly and conspiracy—in the areas of expansion, television, and player signings—fell flat in a U.S. District Court. Competition for college talent tilted heavily in the NFL's favor at the outset of 1962.

NFL rules makers ordained that a 15-yard penalty would be assessed whenever a player tackled another by the facemask.

Green Bay repeated as NFL champion, powered by Jim Taylor's league-leading 1,474 yards

ord-tying seven touchdowns as the New York Giants defeated the Washington Redskins and Sonny Jurgensen 49-34. Tittle's generation slipped a little further into the NFL's past with the retirements of Chuck Bednarik and Bobby Layne. There went the last of the two-way players and the last of the get-it-done-on-the-field-and-raise-hell-afterward quarterbacks. In fact, the most colorful of them all.

1963

In 1962, Commissioner Pete Rozelle had been given major credit when the NFL set an attendance record. This year, Rozelle acted and spoke in terms that went straight to the sensibilities of the fan in the street. He placed indefinite suspensions on the careers of Green Bay halfback Paul Hornung and Detroit defensive tackle Alex Karras, both of whom had admitted betting on numerous NFL games. Five other Detroit players (John Gordy, Gary Lowe, Joe Schmidt, Wayne Walker, and Sam Williams) were fined $2,000 each for betting on games other than their own. Other, more subtle signs of the NFL's assertiveness came in the area of public relations, with the establishment of the Pro Football Hall of Fame in the league's birthplace, Canton, Ohio, and the founding of NFL Properties as the licensing and publishing arm of the league.

The Hall of Fame opened with 17 charter inductees, including Jim Thorpe, Red Grange,

Above: Y.A. Tittle's seven touchdown passes in a 49-34 victory over Washington gave the New York Giants' quarterback a share of the NFL record. On this play, he had protection from guard Mickey Walker.
Right: Art Modell, who had purchased the Cleveland Browns in 1961, replaced coach Paul Brown with Blanton Collier in 1963.

rushing and an NFL-record 19 touchdowns. The former statistic grew in stature a few seasons later when it was noted that this was the only time Cleveland fullback Jim Brown had yielded the rushing title in his nine-year career.

In a wild shootout between two of the period's great quarterbacks, Y.A. Tittle threw a rec-

1962 NFL

EASTERN CONFERENCE

	W	L	T	Pct.	Pts.	OP
N.Y. Giants	12	2	0	.857	398	283
Pittsburgh	9	5	0	.643	312	363
Cleveland	7	6	1	.538	291	257
Washington	5	7	2	.417	305	376
Dallas Cowboys	5	8	1	.385	398	402
St. Louis	4	9	1	.308	287	361
Philadelphia	3	10	1	.231	282	356

WESTERN CONFERENCE

	W	L	T	Pct.	Pts.	OP
Green Bay	13	1	0	.929	415	148
Detroit	11	3	0	.786	315	177
Chicago	9	5	0	.643	321	287
Baltimore	7	7	0	.500	293	288
San Francisco	6	8	0	.429	282	331
Minnesota	2	11	1	.154	254	410
Los Angeles	1	12	1	.077	220	334

NFL Championship: Green Bay 16, N.Y. GIANTS 7

1962 AFL

EASTERN DIVISION

	W	L	T	Pct.	Pts.	OP
Houston	11	3	0	.786	387	270
Boston Patriots	9	4	1	.692	346	295
Buffalo	7	6	1	.538	309	272
N.Y. Titans	5	9	0	.357	278	423

WESTERN DIVISION

	W	L	T	Pct.	Pts.	OP
Dallas Texans	11	3	0	.786	389	233
Denver	7	7	0	.500	353	334
San Diego	4	10	0	.286	314	392
Oakland	1	13	0	.071	213	370

AFL Championship: Dallas Texans 20, HOUSTON 17, sudden death overtime

Bronko Nagurski, Sammy Baugh, and George Halas. The latter name had become synonymous with the Chicago Bears—as owner, player, and coach. Fittingly, Halas topped off the year of his enshrinement by leading his team to the NFL championship. The Bears defeated the New York Giants 14-10 on frozen Wrigley Field (see page 102), and Halas walked off with the last of his eight NFL titles as a head coach.

(see page 102)

The mark of that Chicago team was defense, and the Bears' 14-10 throttling of Tittle and the Giants' league-leading offense was footnoted by the team's awarding the game ball to a young defensive assistant coach named George Allen. In 1966, Allen would begin a five-year, 49-19-4 tenure as head coach of the Los Angeles Rams, who during the 1963 season had coincidentally laid the defensive cornerstone that would serve them well into the 1970s. Ends Lamar Lundy and David (Deacon) Jones joined tackles Roosevelt Grier and Merlin Olsen, the latter a baby-faced, soft-spoken giant in his second year. Together they terrorized quarterbacks in particular and offenses in general, inspiring a new round of NFL group nicknames with the one football fans remember best

Top: In 1963, Buffalo's Cookie Gilchrist scored one of an AFL-record five touchdowns, part of a pro football-record rushing day of 243 yards, in a 45-14 victory over the New York Jets.
Above left: Jim Brown set a single-season rushing record of 1,863 yards.
Above right: Don Shula became head coach at Baltimore.
Left: The Los Angeles Rams' defensive line, a.k.a. The Fearsome Foursome (from left): Lamar Lundy, Roosevelt Grier, Merlin Olsen, and David (Deacon) Jones.

of all. They were The Fearsome Foursome.

In the Eastern Division, Cleveland finished only a game behind the Giants. The Browns, named for Paul Brown, the man who had coached them since their inception in 1946, became a namesake without an original when he was fired in January, 1963. But they continued to thrive competitively under new coach Blanton Collier, and their 10-4 record was driven in part by their reliable engine, Jim Brown. His 1,863 yards rushing was an NFL single-season record and included games of 232 yards against Dallas and 223 against Philadelphia.

The AFL wrapped up its season with a mighty display of offense by Sid Gillman's San Diego Chargers. Led by all-purpose back Keith Lincoln (206 yards rushing, a touchdown run of 67 yards, seven receptions for 123 yards, and 349 yards overall), the Chargers overpowered Boston 51-10 in the friendly, if primitive, confines of Balboa Stadium. The Patriots had won the dubious right to come west by breaking a 7-6-1 first-place tie with Buffalo, defeating the Bills 26-8 on the snow-covered field of Buffalo's War Memorial Stadium.

The two most notable events of the 1963 AFL season were the purchase of the New York

Titans by W. A. (Sonny) Werblin and the Oakland Raiders' hiring of former Chargers assistant Al Davis as head coach.

Werblin, formerly the president of Music Corporation of America, immediately changed his club's nickname from Titans to Jets and dressed its players in green and white instead of the original navy blue and gold. But despite a special draft of players made available by other AFL franchises, the Jets finished last in the Eastern Division with a 5-8-1 record.

Oakland, which had finished 1-13 in 1962, (they were a "walking, screeching band of ineptitude," said Patriots head coach Mike Holovak) got in on the special draft, too. But the Raiders' advantage turned out to be the uncanny football acumen of their new coach. Davis parlayed quarterback Tom Flores, center Jim Otto, receiver Art Powell, and league-leading rusher Clem Daniels into an attacking style that yielded a 10-4 record, one game behind eventual champion San Diego. (Flores, who later would take the Raiders to Super Bowl XV and XVIII victories as their head coach, had been a charter member of the team in 1960. After missing 1962 because of illness, he came on in 1963 to replace Davis's initial quarterback, Cotton Davidson.)

The era of Silver and Black, Pride and Poise, and Commitment to Excellence—catchwords used by the Raiders during the next two decades as they assembled professional sports' best overall record—had begun. If the NFL had struck a theme of assertiveness, the AFL had seen to it that the battle was more than joined.

Below: San Diego's Keith Lincoln (22) went on an offensive rampage in the 1963 AFL title game.

Right: New Oakland head coach Al Davis (center) and his assistants, from left: Ollie Spencer, John Rauch, Tom Dahms, and Charlie Sumner.

Opposite page: Morris Berman's classic photograph of Y. A. Tittle at Pittsburgh, 1964, bloodied and finally bowed as he personifies the downward trend of the Giants.

1963 NFL

EASTERN CONFERENCE	W	L	T	Pct.	Pts.	OP	WESTERN CONFERENCE	W	L	T	Pct.	Pts.	OP
N. Y. Giants	11	3	0	.786	448	280	Chicago	11	1	2	.917	301	144
Cleveland	10	4	0	.714	343	262	Green Bay	11	2	1	.846	369	206
St. Louis	9	5	0	.643	341	283	Baltimore	8	6	0	.571	316	285
Pittsburgh	7	4	3	.636	321	295	Detroit	5	8	1	.385	326	265
Dallas	4	10	0	.286	305	378	Minnesota	5	8	1	.385	309	390
Washington	3	11	0	.214	279	398	Los Angeles	5	9	0	.357	210	350
Philadelphia	2	10	2	.167	242	381	San Francisco	2	12	0	.143	198	391

NFL Championship: CHICAGO 14, N.Y. Giants 10

1963 AFL

EASTERN DIVISION	W	L	T	Pct.	Pts.	OP	WESTERN DIVISION	W	L	T	Pct.	Pts.	OP
Boston Patriots	7	6	1	.538	317	257	San Diego	11	3	0	.786	399	255
Buffalo	7	6	1	.538	304	291	Oakland	10	4	0	.714	363	282
Houston	6	8	0	.429	302	372	Kansas City	5	7	2	.417	347	263
N.Y. Jets	5	8	1	.385	249	399	Denver	2	11	1	.154	301	473

Eastern Division playoff: Boston 26, BUFFALO 8
AFL Championship: SAN DIEGO 51, Boston 10

1964

America's rival pro football leagues were having some fun now, and if you didn't believe it, you could check the windows up and down the

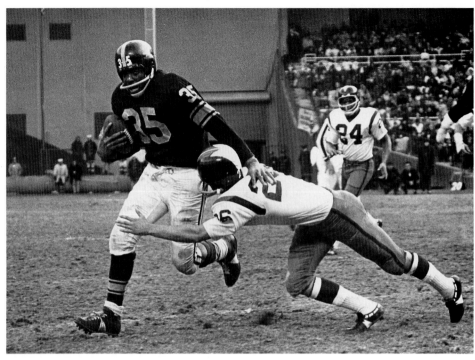

Left: The Giants traded future Hall of Fame linebacker Sam Huff (70) to Washington in 1964, touching off a furor among New York fans. Huff had gained a measure of fame as the star of a CBS-TV documentary on the mayhem of pro football. Right: Pittsburgh's John Henry Johnson, 35, ran for 1,048 yards in 1964.

block on Sunday afternoons for television's unmistakable, bluish glow. The NFL's new, bigger-than-ever two-year deal with CBS, consummated after a cloak-and-dagger, sealed-bid auction among the three major networks, meant more than $1 million a year for each team, an unheard-of sum. Meanwhile, Sonny Werblin orchestrated a five-year package for the AFL with rejected NFL suitor NBC that assured each team roughly $900,000 a year. "That does it," said Pittsburgh Steelers owner Art Rooney. "They no longer have to address us as 'Mister.' "

Television provided another new twist, this one the technical brainchild of CBS director Tony Verna. He had introduced it, actually, during the 1963 Army-Navy game. After Army's Rollie Stichweh ran for a touchdown late in the game, viewers were treated to a second showing of the play. *Instant replay!* At last, television had lifted the penalty for going to the refrigerator.

CBS's new toy came along just in time to review a play that Minnesota defensive end Jim Marshall probably wished never had been seen the first time. Houston writer Mickey Herskowitz recalled the episode years later in *PRO!* magazine:

". . .yet, despite his greater achievements, Marshall always will be remembered around the NFL as Wrong Way Marshall. In 1964, he scooped up a fumble in San Francisco, carried it 66 yards into the end zone, and then joyfully flung the ball toward the stands. It was the line-

man's dream come true. Alas, he had run into the wrong end zone for a safety. He sensed something was wrong when the 49ers began to congratulate him.

"Later, a booster club in Dallas honored Marshall with its Bonehead of the Year Award. He caught the wrong plane and flew to the wrong city—but it was all part of the act."

Marshall played on, and retired at age 41 in possession of a record that may never be broken, 282 consecutive games over a 19-year career. He was part of the Purple People Eaters, Minnesota's answer to the Rams' Fearsome Foursome. The other Eaters were tackles Alan Page and Gary Larsen and end Carl Eller.

In the mercurial AFL, Sonny Werblin's upgrading of the Jets took the team to multi-purpose Shea Stadium, situated in the midst of the recent New York World's Fair in Flushing Meadow, Queens. The move signaled a succession of similar transfers, taking pro football out of such aging venues as San Francisco's Kezar Stadium, home of the 49ers from 1946-1970 and the Oakland Raiders in 1960-61. (The Raiders' early odyssey took them from Kezar to Candlestick Park and eventually to Oakland's Frank Youell Field, a municipal sandlot exposed to the treacherous Nimitz Freeway, prior to their arrival at the new Oakland-Alameda County Coliseum in 1966.)

Houston's George Blanda attempted a record 505 passes in 1964 (68 of them in a loss to Buffalo), and end Charley Hennigan caught 101 of them for another record. The Oilers, however, slipped to 4-10, poorest in the Eastern Division. Buffalo (12-2) defeated San Diego (8-5-1) in the AFL Championship Game, 20-7.

Power shifted radically in the NFL's Eastern Division, as the New York Giants, about to bid farewell to two honored veterans, quarterback Y.A. Tittle and defensive end Andy Robustelli, sank to a 2-10-2 last-place finish. Cleveland, flourishing under the coaching of Blanton Collier, the passing of Frank Ryan to rookie split end Paul Warfield and flanker Gary Collins, and Jim Brown's seventh rushing title in eight years—went 10-3-1 for first. Western Division champion Baltimore, led by the passing of quarterback Johnny Unitas and an NFL-record 20 touchdowns by halfback-flanker Lenny Moore, was heavily favored in the title game. But Ryan, comfortable in cold and windy Cleveland Stadium, came out after a scoreless first half and threw three touchdown passes to Collins. The Browns scored a 27-0 upset, earning the largest winners' shares to date, $8,052 per man.

Unitas was the NFL's most valuable player in 1964, in the midst of a career that still ranks as the finest ever among professional quarterbacks. In 1956, the Pittsburgh Steelers had drafted him in the ninth round, out of Louisville. "Too dumb," Steelers coach Walt Kiesling told owner Art Rooney in training camp. The Browns gave Unitas a look, too, and told him to wait a year. So he took a job as the "monkey," or high man, on a pile driver setting the foundations for a tinning mill in Aliquippa, Pennsylvania. He was playing sandlot football for $6 a game when the Colts telephoned and invited him for a tryout. (The cost of the call was 80 cents, although NFL folklore at one time had it down to about a quarter.)

Unitas was not physically imposing. His shoulders slouched, and his marble-white skin covered a lean, almost gaunt frame. Could this physique be equipped with history's best passing mechanism?

He had many gifts. He had a deceptive delivery. He was the master of looking one way, staring down a cornerback, and throwing somewhere else. His arm put the ball where he wanted it to go, especially when he wanted it to go deep, with almost inhuman consistency.

Raymond Berry, Unitas's favorite receiver and still fourth on the all-time NFL list with 631 catches, once said, "I'm not sure he ever had a bad game. Maybe he had a bad half."

But the quality that made Unitas the com-

plete quarterbacking package was his leadership.

"John would sometimes make calls in games against us that just didn't make any sense at all," said Los Angeles Rams defensive tackle Merlin Olsen. "But everybody on his team believed they were brilliant calls, and they made the plays work. So they became brilliant calls. Another quarterback could have called the same plays and ten guys would have looked at him like he was from Mars. And the plays wouldn't have worked."

In the context of the rivalry between the NFL and AFL, Unitas alone sometimes was suggested as the difference between the two leagues. "No, we don't have Johnny Unitas," said Lou Saban, head coach of the AFL's Buffalo Bills, "but there are thirteen teams in the National Football League that don't have him, either."

The Steelers, whose rejection of Unitas was

Above: Houston's Charley Hennigan, shown here in his team's final preseason game, set a pro football record in 1964 with 101 receptions.

Left: Jerry Wolman (left), who had purchased the Philadelphia Eagles in 1963, signed new head coach Joe Kuharich to an eyebrow-raising 10-year contract.

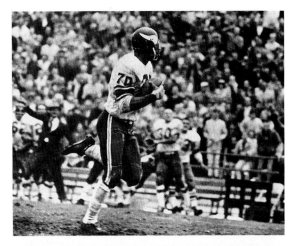

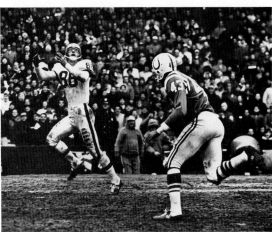

Top: What's wrong with this picture? Answer: Jim Marshall. In a 1964 game at San Francisco, the Minnesota defensive end recovered a fumble and took off, unchecked, for the goal line . . . the wrong goal line.

Right: In the 1964 NFL title game, Cleveland's Gary Collins broke clear for an 18-yard scoring pass from Frank Ryan, his first of three in a 27-0 upset of Baltimore.

Below: One week later, Ryan's shoulder was separated when he was tackled by Baltimore's Gino Marchetti in the West's 34-14 Pro Bowl victory.

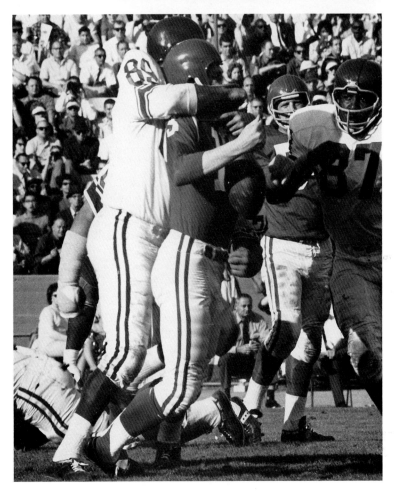

just one of many regrets, finished 1964 with a 5-9 record, not far ahead of the slumbering Giants. But the Steelers had a running back whose accomplishments have weathered time's abrasions on the record book. In 1964, John Henry Johnson's contribution to the NFL was a total of 1,048 yards rushing. He was 35 at the time.

1964 NFL

EASTERN CONFERENCE						WESTERN CONFERENCE					
	W	L	T	Pct.	Pts. OP		W	L	T	Pct.	Pts. OP
Cleveland	10	3	1	.769	415 293	Baltimore	12	2	0	.857	428 225
St. Louis	9	3	2	.750	357 331	Green Bay	8	5	1	.615	342 245
Philadelphia	6	8	0	.429	312 313	Minnesota	8	5	1	.615	355 296
Washington	6	8	0	.429	307 305	Detroit	7	5	2	.583	280 260
Dallas	5	8	1	.385	250 289	Los Angeles	5	7	2	.417	283 339
Pittsburgh	5	9	0	.357	253 315	Chicago	5	9	0	.357	260 379
N.Y. Giants	2	10	2	.167	241 399	San Francisco	4	10	0	.286	236 330

NFL Championship: CLEVELAND 27, Baltimore 0

1964 AFL

EASTERN DIVISION						WESTERN DIVISION					
	W	L	T	Pct.	Pts. OP		W	L	T	Pct.	Pts. OP
Buffalo	12	2	0	.857	400 242	San Diego	8	5	1	.615	341 300
Boston Patriots	10	3	1	.769	365 297	Kansas City	7	7	0	.500	366 306
N.Y. Jets	5	8	1	.385	278 315	Oakland	5	7	2	.417	303 350
Houston	4	10	0	.286	310 355	Denver	2	11	1	.154	240 438

AFL Championship: BUFFALO 20, San Diego 7

1965

The NFL could point proudly to a class of rookies that included halfback Gale Sayers and linebacker Dick Butkus of Chicago, flanker-kick returner Bob Hayes of Dallas, and running back Ken Willard of San Francisco. Sayers highlighted his first season by tying an NFL record with six touchdowns in the Bears' 61-20 rout of the 49ers on a rain-soaked field in Chicago.

The center of attention, however, was an AFL rookie: Alabama quarterback Joe Namath, who signed with Sonny Werblin's New York Jets for more than $400,000. By outbidding the St. Louis Cardinals, who refused to offer Namath a no-cut contract, the Jets landed the most publicized blow in the six-year interleague rivalry.

The NFL's off-the-field highlight was a new television contract with CBS that called for $18.8 million a year, plus $2 million for the championship game. In the league expansion "game," the score was 1-1, as the NFL announced plans to add a franchise in Atlanta, the AFL in Miami.

For the second straight year, Buffalo dominated San Diego in winning the AFL Championship Game, this time 23-0. The Chargers' Paul Lowe, who had led the AFL with 1,121 yards in the regular season, was limited to 57 by Bills coach Lou Saban's tough defense.

In the NFL, Jim Brown's ninth and final season ended with another rushing title (1,544 yards), and Cleveland again won the Eastern Division. But there were audible tremors coming from Dallas. The Cowboys finished second at 7-7 with help from Olympic 100-meter champion Bob Hayes at flanker, quarterback Don Meredith's 22 touchdown passes, and computer-advised "sleeper" draftees such as defensive tackle Jethro Pugh from Elizabeth City (North Carolina) State, an eleventh-round choice.

Western Division champion Green Bay held Brown to 50 yards in chilly weather, and on a muddy field that had to be cleared with shovels and snow plows, the Packers scored a 23-12 victory for their third NFL championship of the decade. Paul Hornung, finishing his second season since being reinstated from his 1963 gambling suspension (Detroit's Alex Karras also was reinstated after a year's exile), rushed for 105 yards and was supported by Jim Taylor's 96.

Green Bay and Baltimore had tied for the Western Division championship with 10-3-1 records. The Packers won the playoff 13:39 into sudden-death overtime on a field goal by Don Chandler (see page 104). Both teams played that day with substitute quarterbacks. The Packers' Zeke Bratkowski filled in for Bart Starr, who was hurt on the game's first play,

Above: The first start of Joe Namath's career came at Buffalo in week 3 of 1965, as the Bills defeated the New York Jets 33-21.
Left: At rain-soaked Wrigley Field, Chicago's Gale Sayers scored a record-tying six touchdowns against San Francisco.

Left: Bears linebacker Dick Butkus, along with Sayers, was a first-round draft choice in 1965. He wrought terror in the middle for nine years, and entered the Hall of Fame in 1978.
Right: Olympic champion Bob Hayes, Dallas's rookie flanker, sprinted into the NFL in 1965.

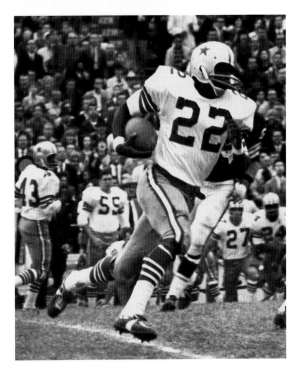

Above: CBS's Ray Scott interviewed Jim Taylor (31) and Paul Hornung (5) after the two Green Bay backs had combined to upstage Jim Brown in the Packers' 23-12 NFL title victory over Cleveland in 1965. Right: Hot prospect Tommy Nobis discussed the AFL-NFL battle for his services with NBC's George Ratterman. Below: Buffalo quarterback Jack Kemp, shown handing off to fullback Billy Joe, was named the most valuable player in the Bills' 23-0 victory over San Diego for the 1965 AFL title.

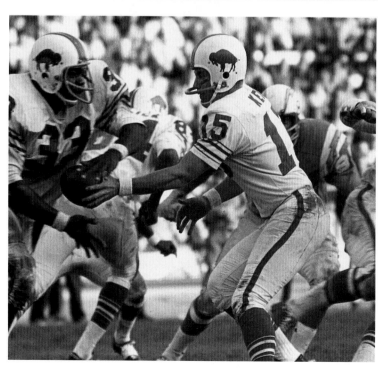

while Tom Matte, a halfback who had played quarterback at Ohio State, directed the Colts. Johnny Unitas and Gary Cuozzo, Baltimore's starting and second-string quarterbacks, were injured and unable to play the Colts' regular-season finale against Los Angeles. While Green Bay was being tied by San Francisco, Matte started against the Rams and, wearing a wristband equipped with a list of plays, led the Colts to a 20-17 victory. He led all rushers that day with 99 yards, and set up the winning field goal.

1965 NFL

EASTERN CONFERENCE						WESTERN CONFERENCE					
	W	L	T	Pct.	Pts.	OP	W	L	T	Pct.	Pts.	OP
Cleveland	11	3	0	.786	363	325	Green Bay	10	3	1	.769	316	224
Dallas	7	7	0	.500	325	280	Baltimore	10	3	1	.769	389	284
N.Y. Giants	7	7	0	.500	270	338	Chicago	9	5	0	.643	409	275
Washington	6	8	0	.429	257	301	San Francisco	7	6	1	.538	421	402
Philadelphia	5	9	0	.357	363	359	Minnesota	7	7	0	.500	383	403
St. Louis	5	9	0	.357	296	309	Detroit	6	7	1	.462	257	295
Pittsburgh	2	12	0	.143	202	397	Los Angeles	4	10	0	.286	269	328

Western Conference playoff: GREEN BAY 13, Baltimore 10, sudden death overtime
NFL Championship: GREEN BAY 23, Cleveland 12

1965 AFL

EASTERN DIVISION						WESTERN DIVISION					
	W	L	T	Pct.	Pts.	OP	W	L	T	Pct.	Pts.	OP
Buffalo	10	3	1	.769	313	226	San Diego	9	2	3	.818	340	227
N.Y. Jets	5	8	1	.385	285	303	Oakland	8	5	1	.615	298	239
Boston Patriots	4	8	2	.333	244	302	Kansas City	7	5	2	.583	322	285
Houston	4	10	0	.286	298	429	Denver	4	10	0	.286	303	392

AFL Championship: Buffalo 23, SAN DIEGO 0

1966

A voice came from the heavens. "Tell Nobis to sign with the Oilers," said orbiting astronaut Frank Borman. It was Borman's way of rooting for the AFL team in its bid to sign 1966's hottest college prospect, linebacker Tommy Nobis of Texas.

The Oilers almost pulled it off. But after putting Houston management on hold with the old "give us a day to think it over" routine, Nobis's agent put the last commas and zeroes on the linebacker's contract with the newly formed Atlanta Falcons of the NFL.

Score another for the senior circuit, and watch the temperature rise.

Meanwhile, voices closer to the ground than Borman's were beginning to ask more and more seriously: Why fight? Why not join?

"After the 1965 season I was convinced the structure of pro football was in trouble," said Dallas Cowboys president-general manager Tex Schramm in a 1984 interview, "because teams in both leagues were no longer drafting the best players. The draft became predicated on which players you could sign. In our league two or three teams were signing all their players—the Rams, the Cowboys, and the Packers. There were a few in the AFL—the Chiefs, the Jets, and the Raiders. Many of the other teams couldn't compete. Boston was drafting players who should have been third- or fourth-round picks in the first round because they thought they could sign them. And there was a lot of switching around of draft choices. It was just getting to be insane." (In fact, so certain were the AFL teams that Heisman Trophy winner Mike Garrett of USC would sign with the Rams, that none even bothered to draft him until the Chiefs did in the twentieth round. Garrett signed with Kansas City.)

On April 6, 1966, Schramm met Kansas City owner Lamar Hunt near the Texas Ranger statue at Love Field Airport in Dallas. The topics: detente and a possible merger.

The two sat in Schramm's car in the airport parking lot. "I told him that this was not just conversation," Schramm said, "that Pete Rozelle knew about it and approved. But I explained that only a few of our owners were aware of it and suggested that he keep it as confidential as possible for a while. Pro football owners are individualists and competitors who like to compete in public. At this stage, twenty-four owners would have made the discussions too unwieldy, so I suggested to Lamar that I be his only direct contact in the NFL, and he would be mine in the AFL."

Two days later, at an AFL meeting in Houston, Al Davis was elected to replace Joe Foss as commissioner of the AFL. Foss had been criticized by some of the owners for being an absentee commissioner. Davis, persuaded by Hunt, San Diego's Sid Gillman, and other AFL leaders to take the job, would say later, "I guess they thought I'd be a catalyst. It was a situation that called for some constant pressure to be put on the other side."

So went the odd scenario, with Hunt and Schramm quietly plotting an armistice and Davis polishing his brass knuckles. The situation exploded when New York Giants owner Wellington Mara signed Pete Gogolak, a Hungarian-born placekicker (pro football's first "soccer" stylist) who had played out his option with Buffalo of the AFL.

Until that point, the two leagues, despite their dueling for college talent, had refrained from signing each other's veteran players. All attention had been directed to the pursuit of college talent, as evidenced by the league's combined $7 million outlay for 1966 draft choices (Green Bay alone spent $1 million for running backs Donny Anderson and Jim Grabowski,

neither of whom immediately would be a regular starter). Now, by signing Gogolak, Mara had broken into the demilitarized zone, as it were.

Davis came out swinging. He recruited Houston general manager Don Klosterman and Oakland general manager Scotty Stirling. Their mission: Go after the NFL's star players—especially the quarterbacks—and spare no expense.

Klosterman and Oilers owner Bud Adams offered San Francisco 49ers quarterback John Brodie $750,000 over 10 years. Chicago Bears tight end Mike Ditka signed with the Oilers for

Left: Ready for battle, newly elected AFL commissioner Al Davis (right) sat with the league's director of public relations, Jack Horrigan. Below: A key figure in the AFL-NFL merger, San Francisco quarterback John Brodie was offered a $750,000 10-year contract with the Houston Oilers.

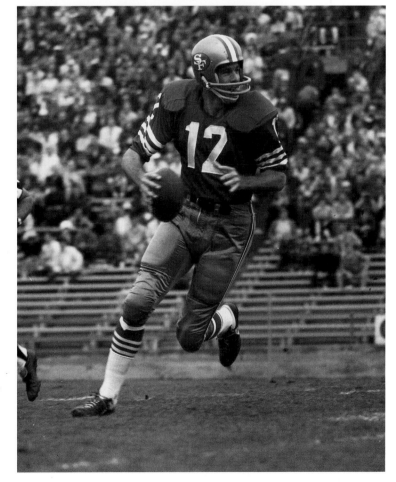

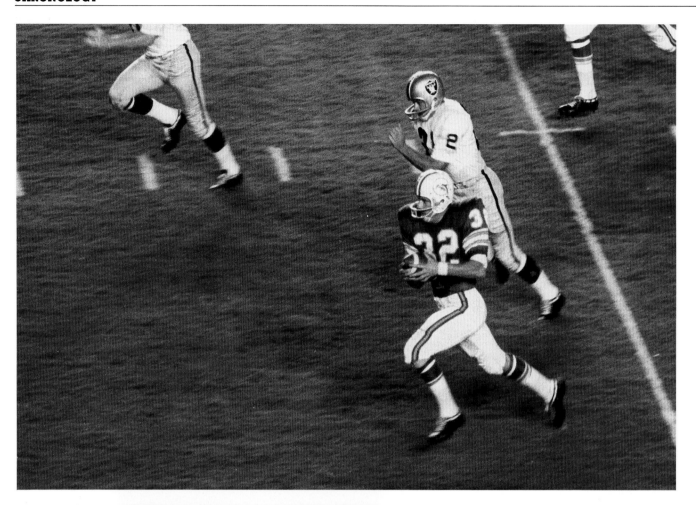

Above: Joe Auer of Miami took the opening kickoff of the first game in Dolphins history and returned it 95 yards for a touchdown against Oakland.

Right: Former Chicago Bears defensive assistant George Allen took over as head coach of the Los Angeles Rams in 1966.

a $50,000 bonus. Stirling signed Los Angeles Rams quarterback Roman Gabriel with a reported $100,000 down payment. All this six-figure activity aroused interest among other NFL stars, including quarterbacks Sonny Jurgensen of Washington, Fran Tarkenton of Minnesota, and Milt Plum of Detroit. Davis admitted contacting Green Bay defensive backs Willie Wood and Herb Adderley and steering them toward Jets owner Sonny Werblin. George Wilson, head coach of the AFL's new Miami franchise, was rumored to be talking contract with Detroit tackle Alex Karras.

Whether these player-contract talks served as a stimulus or hindrance to a possible merger is debatable. But Schramm and Hunt quickened the pace of their merger discussions. On May 31, Hunt went to Schramm's home in Dallas and went over the formal merger proposal. Hunt took down all of Schramm's provisions on a legal-sized yellow notepad. Schramm said, "There it is. If you accept, this deal has been approved by every NFL club. If you have to alter it too much, it will blow up."

A week later, after Hunt had had time to run the details past AFL owners and Rozelle had been rounding up pro-merger votes (especially from skeptics such as Mara and San Francisco 49ers president Lou Spadia), all was in readiness. The merger was announced June 8 at a press conference at the Warwick Hotel in New York.

Highlights of the announced agreement included:

—a world championship game between the two leagues, beginning at the end of the 1966 season;

—a common draft, with the first scheduled for January, 1967;

—preseason interleague play beginning in 1967;

—a single NFL regular-season schedule beginning in 1970;

—an $18-million indemnity to be paid by the AFL to the NFL over 20 years;

—two expansion franchises to be added by 1968, one in each league;

—no relocation of existing clubs.

Pete Rozelle would be the commissioner.

John Brodie would be rich.

San Francisco retained rights to Brodie as specified by the merger agreement, but he still had a valuable napkin. On it was written the agreement he had reached with Klosterman and the Oilers.

"Somebody owes me $750,000," Brodie said. A month later, a deal was struck guaranteeing him a minimum of $921,000 over 12 years, plus legal fees. The 49ers agreed to pay more than half the figure, and the other 23 teams (from both leagues) contributed equal shares to settle

the difference. Gabriel and Ditka got their money too, but the main news was an end to the big bonus outlays.

On October 21, Congress passed special legislation exempting the merger agreement from United States antitrust laws.

Atlanta, the NFL's fifteenth team, was placed in the Eastern Conference and finished 3-11, avoiding last place thanks to the New York Giants' 1-12-1 showing.

This also was the inaugural year for the Miami Dolphins of the AFL. In their first game, running back Joe Auer returned the opening kickoff 95 yards for a touchdown, but Oakland spoiled the party 23-14.

Two teams headed for no particular distinction in the year's Eastern Conference standings, Washington and the New York Giants, gained special distinction November 27 by playing the highest-scoring game in NFL history at D.C. Stadium. The Redskins won 72-41.

The Dallas Cowboys "arrived" in the seventh year of their existence, becoming the first expansion team in history to win a division or conference title. They took their 10-3-1 record against Green Bay (12-2) in the NFL Championship Game and gave the Packers a good scare.

Left: A neighbor of St. Louis's famed Gateway Arch, Busch Memorial Stadium opened in 1966 as the home of the football (and baseball) Cardinals.
Right: Draft prize Tommy Nobis (60), shown here stopping Baltimore's Lenny Moore, was an immediate hit with the newborn Atlanta Falcons.

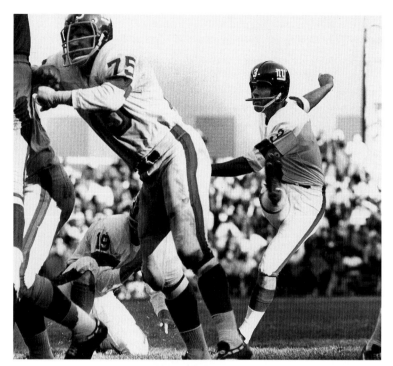

up a touchdown by halfback Elijah Pitts. Quarterback Bart Starr threw two touchdown passes to Max McGee and was voted the game's most valuable player.

With the presence of teams from both leagues on the same field, pro football had entered a new era.

1966 NFL

	W	L	T	Pct.	Pts.	OP		W	L	T	Pct.	Pts.	OP
EASTERN CONFERENCE							**WESTERN CONFERENCE**						
Dallas	10	3	1	.769	445	239	Green Bay	12	2	0	.857	335	163
Cleveland	9	5	0	.643	403	259	Baltimore	9	5	0	.643	314	226
Philadelphia	9	5	0	.643	326	340	Los Angeles	8	6	0	.571	289	212
St. Louis	8	5	1	.615	264	265	San Francisco	6	6	2	.500	320	325
Washington	7	7	0	.500	351	355	Chicago	5	7	2	.417	234	272
Pittsburgh	5	8	1	.385	316	347	Detroit	4	9	1	.308	206	317
Atlanta	3	11	0	.214	204	437	Minnesota	4	9	1	.308	292	304
N.Y. Giants	1	12	1	.077	263	501							

NFL Championship: Green Bay 34, DALLAS 27
Super Bowl I: Green Bay (NFL) 35, Kansas City (AFL) 10, at Memorial Coliseum, Los Angeles, California

1966 AFL

	W	L	T	Pct.	Pts.	OP		W	L	T	Pct.	Pts.	OP
EASTERN DIVISION							**WESTERN DIVISION**						
Buffalo	9	4	1	.692	358	255	Kansas City	11	2	1	.846	448	276
Boston Patriots	8	4	2	.677	315	283	Oakland	8	5	1	.615	315	288
N.Y. Jets	6	6	2	.500	322	312	San Diego	7	6	1	.538	335	284
Houston	3	11	0	.214	355	396	Denver	4	10	0	.286	196	381
Miami	3	11	0	.214	213	362							

AFL Championship: Kansas City 31, BUFFALO 7

1967

How many NFL fans still can name the four "C's"? The Capitol and Century divisions of the Eastern Conference and the Central and Coastal divisions of the Western Conference would be the league's competitive framework for the years 1967-69.

In the first common draft combining teams from the AFL and NFL, Baltimore used the first choice to take Michigan State defensive end Bubba Smith. The Colts had traded with newcomer New Orleans, whose debut at Tulane Stadium under head coach Tom Fears began Dolphins-style. Echoing the feat of Joe Auer, Saints rookie John Gilliam took the opening kickoff 94 yards for a touchdown. The opponent was Fears's former team, the Los Angeles Rams, who came back to win 27-13. The Saints won only 3 of 14 that year.

Another "first" had entered the record books when an NFL team, Detroit, met an AFL team, Denver, in a preseason game at Denver's Bears Stadium. The Broncos became the first AFL team to defeat an NFL team. The date was August 5. The score was 13-7.

Placekickers everywhere joined fans of the St. Louis Cardinals in a standing ovation when the team defeated Pittsburgh 28-14. Why this unique union of supporters? Jim Bakken accounted for all the points the Cardinals would need, kicking a record seven field goals.

Above: Pete Gogolak, pro football's first soccer-style placekicker, became the first player to leave the AFL and sign with an NFL club. He played out his option with Buffalo, became a free agent, and was picked up by the New York Giants.

Left: David A. (Sonny) Werblin, co-owner and president of the New York Jets, brought a much-needed flair for public relations when he arrived in 1963. He stayed until 1968, when his partners purchased his share of the club.

The Cowboys reached the Green Bay 2-yard line late in the game, when Don Meredith, hit hard by linebacker Dave Robinson, managed to get a pass away, only to have it intercepted by Tom Brown in the end zone. Green Bay held on 34-27.

The Kansas City Chiefs—coached by Hank Stram, quarterbacked by Len Dawson and fortified on defense by tackle Buck Buchanan and linebacker Bobby Bell—defeated the Buffalo Bills 31-7 for the AFL title, earning the right to meet Vince Lombardi's Packers in the first AFL-NFL World Championship Game.

The contest was telecast by both CBS and NBC and was blacked out in Los Angeles. It was not a sellout, drawing 63,035 to the Los Angeles Memorial Coliseum, which could hold 98,000. The Packers took a 14-10 halftime lead and drew away early in the second half when Willie Wood's 50-yard interception return set

Above: In his team's first game, New Orleans's John Gilliam returned the opening kickoff 94 yards for a touchdown, duplicating the feat of Miami's Joe Auer in 1966. The Saints lost 27-13 to Los Angeles. Left: The New York Giants traded two first-round and two second-round draft choices to Minnesota for quarterback Fran Tarkenton (10), shown here with owner Wellington Mara and flanker Homer Jones. Right: The Vikings hired Bud Grant to replace Norm Van Brocklin, who resigned in February, 1967.

Above left: In 1967, Green Bay's Travis Williams leaped to daylight, becoming the first player to return four kickoffs for touchdowns in a season.
Above right: Fullback Jim Taylor, having played out his option with the Packers, signed with his home state's new NFL team, the New Orleans Saints, and was the club's leading rusher with 390 yards.
Right: The Jets' Joe Namath became the first quarterback to surpass 4,000 yards passing with 4,007.
Below: Jim Bakken's seven field goals in St. Louis's 28-14 victory over Pittsburgh set an NFL record.

For the fourth and last time, George Halas removed himself from the head-coaching job of the team he owned, the Chicago Bears, finishing the season with a 7-6-1 record, second-best in the Central Division behind Green Bay. The Packers, who seemed to have reached their competitive apogee in early November with a 55-7 trouncing of Cleveland in what was billed as the matchup of the year, went on to knock over the red-hot Los Angeles Rams 28-7 in the first round of the playoffs, then defeated Dallas 21-17 for the NFL title, in a game that has become known as the Ice Bowl (see page 108).

In the AFL, the individual accomplishment of 1967 belonged to New York Jets quarterback Joe Namath, whose record 4,007 yards passing and 26 touchdowns still did not translate to a league, or even a division, championship. The Jets (8-5-1) lost out to Houston (9-4-1), and the Oilers went on to play doormat to Oakland, losing to the Raiders 40-7 in the AFL Championship Game.

The Oilers had released 39-year-old George

1967 NFL

EASTERN CONFERENCE
Capitol Division

	W	L	T	Pct.	Pts.	OP
Dallas	9	5	0	.643	342	268
Philadelphia	6	7	1	.462	351	409
Washington	5	6	3	.455	347	353
New Orleans	3	11	0	.214	233	379

Century Division

	W	L	T	Pct.	Pts.	OP
Cleveland	9	5	0	.643	334	297
N.Y. Giants	7	7	0	.500	369	379
St. Louis	6	7	1	.462	333	356
Pittsburgh	4	9	1	.308	281	320

WESTERN CONFERENCE
Coastal Division

	W	L	T	Pct.	Pts.	OP
Los Angeles	11	1	2	.917	398	196
Baltimore	11	1	2	.917	394	198
San Francisco	7	7	0	.500	273	337
Atlanta	1	12	1	.077	175	422

Central Division

	W	L	T	Pct.	Pts.	OP
Green Bay	9	4	1	.692	332	209
Chicago	7	6	1	.538	239	218
Detroit	5	7	2	.417	260	259
Minnesota	3	8	3	.273	233	294

Los Angeles won division title on the basis of advantage in points (58-34) in two games vs. Baltimore.
Conference championships: DALLAS 52, Cleveland 14; GREEN BAY 28, Los Angeles 7
NFL Championship: GREEN BAY 21, Dallas 17
Super Bowl II: Green Bay (NFL) 33, Oakland (AFL) 14, at Orange Bowl, Miami, Florida

1967 AFL

EASTERN DIVISION

	W	L	T	Pct.	Pts.	OP
Houston	9	4	1	.692	258	199
N.Y. Jets	8	5	1	.615	371	329
Buffalo	4	10	0	.286	237	285
Miami	4	10	0	.286	219	407
Boston Patriots	3	10	1	.231	280	389

WESTERN DIVISION

	W	L	T	Pct.	Pts.	OP
Oakland	13	1	0	.929	468	233
Kansas City	9	5	0	.643	408	254
San Diego	8	5	1	.615	360	352
Denver	3	11	0	.214	256	409

AFL Championship: OAKLAND 40, Houston 7

Blanda, and the Raiders had signed him as a free agent. Blanda spent the year as Oakland's kicker and a back-up to quarterback Daryle Lamonica, who also was a find for Oakland. After spending four years in Buffalo, in 1967 Lamonica joined the Raiders, led the AFL in passing, and was named the league's most valuable player.

In the second AFL-NFL World Championship Game, played at Miami's Orange Bowl, the Packers got four field goals from Don Chandler and easily defeated the Raiders 33-14. Two weeks later, it was announced that Vince Lombardi had resigned as Green Bay's head coach. Lombardi would take over as the Packers' general manager, and assistant Phil Bengtson would take his place. "Take his place" was a figure of speech.

1968

If social change in America reached its full 50-state boiling point in 1968, pro football shared part of the front burner. One labor agreement—between the AFL and its players association—was reached, while similar talks in the NFL screeched to a halt, then lunged to settlement a few days before training camps opened. The football world was sure to change, too, with the return of Paul Brown as part-owner and head coach of this year's expansion team, the Cincinnati Bengals of the AFL.

This was the year of the "Heidi Game," the Raiders' 43-32 victory over the New York Jets at Oakland (see page 110). Denied the final minutes of the telecast when it was pre-empted by the movie "Heidi," fans went crazy.

This also was the year the Houston Oilers moved from Rice Stadium to the Astrodome, a.k.a. the Great Indoors, a.k.a. the Eighth Wonder of the World. Also the home of baseball's Astros, it was America's first domed stadium, the first to use AstroTurf (what else?), the first to have luxury suites, and the first to have an animated scoreboard. Houston's Bud Adams, now the owner of the NFL's first team to air-condition its home games (the thermostat was set at 72 degrees), would say years later, "If the Astrodome is the Eighth Wonder of the World, the rent is the Ninth."

Meanwhile, there was a new order in New York, as Sonny Werblin sold the Jets to four partners. One of them, Don Lillis, became head of the corporation. When Lillis died two

months later, Phil Iselin was named president of the club. The Jets finished the season 11-3, champions of the AFL's Eastern Division by a four-game margin over Houston. When the Jets avenged their "Heidi Game" loss with a 27-23 victory over Oakland in the AFL Championship Game at Shea Stadium (see page 112), Weeb Ewbank became the first coach ever to win titles in both the NFL and the AFL.

Ewbank had coached the Baltimore Colts to the NFL championship in 1958, the storied sudden-death overtime victory with its final drive steered by Johnny Unitas in the early winter darkness at Yankee Stadium. Unitas to Raymond Berry. Unitas to Jim Mutscheller. Unitas giving to Alan Ameche, through a hole opened by Mutscheller, George Preas, and Lenny Moore . . . and into an empty end zone. Ewbank was there.

Now he was headed for Miami and Super

Green Bay guard Jerry Kramer helped carry Vince Lombardi on his last victory ride as the Packers' head coach, following a 33-14 triumph over Oakland in Super Bowl II. Two weeks later, Lombardi resigned and became Green Bay's general manager.

In 1968, the Chargers moved from antiquated Balboa Stadium to San Diego Stadium (left), later to be named after local sports editor Jack Murphy, who campaigned most vigorously for the new facility.

Above: Purple People Eaters and their prey: Minnesota's Carl Eller (81) put the clamps on Green Bay quarterback Bart Starr, and Alan Page (88) did the rest.
Top right: The Houston Astrodome was the state of the art among 1960s indoor arenas.
Bottom right: New Cincinnati Bengals head coach Paul Brown inspected a variety of helmet designs for the just-born AFL team, two of which looked a lot like the headgear the team eventually adopted in 1981.

Bowl III, the first of the series to take the name. The heavily favored NFL champion Colts no sooner had arrived in town when they began hearing their supremacy challenged by the upstart pretenders from the "other league." The high point came at a banquet during Super Bowl week, when quarterback Joe Namath gave his "guarantee" that the Jets would win on Sunday. They did, 16-7 (see page 114).

The Colts team that lost to the Jets that day was coached by Don Shula, who had the use of an older and more brittle Unitas—to open the season, that is. When Unitas went out with an elbow injury, Shula replaced him with Earl Morrall. The former Michigan State star threw 26 touchdown passes, and the Colts went 13-1 before beating Minnesota (which had won its first Central Division title) 24-14 for the championship of the Western Conference. The Browns, winners of the Century Division after a quarterback switch of their own (Bill Nelsen replacing Frank Ryan), beat Capitol Division winner Dallas but were no match for the Colts in the NFL Championship Game. The Colts won 34-0, as Tom Matte scored three touchdowns.

Even before the season had begun, a record of sorts fell to a team that had been doing its share for a number of years in the talent department—the University of Southern California Trojans. Since 1968, no school has been as highly represented in the first round of the draft. Five USC players were among the first 24 chosen: tackle Ron Yary (first to Minnesota), tackle Mike Taylor (tenth to Pittsburgh), defensive end Tim Rossovich (fourteenth to Philadelphia), running back Mike Hull (sixteenth to Chicago), and wide receiver Earl McCullouch (twenty-fourth to Detroit).

1968 NFL

EASTERN CONFERENCE

Capitol Division

	W	L	T	Pct.	Pts.	OP
Dallas	12	2	0	.857	431	186
N.Y. Giants	7	7	0	.500	294	325
Washington	5	9	0	.357	249	358
Philadelphia	2	12	0	.143	202	351

Century Division

	W	L	T	Pct.	Pts.	OP
Cleveland	10	4	0	.714	394	273
St. Louis	9	4	1	.692	325	289
New Orleans	4	9	1	.308	246	327
Pittsburgh	2	11	1	.154	244	397

WESTERN CONFERENCE

Coastal Division

	W	L	T	Pct.	Pts.	OP
Baltimore	13	1	0	.929	402	144
Los Angeles	10	3	1	.769	312	200
San Francisco	7	6	1	.538	303	310
Atlanta	2	12	0	.143	170	389

Central Division

	W	L	T	Pct.	Pts.	OP
Minnesota	8	6	0	.571	282	242
Chicago	7	7	0	.500	250	333
Green Bay	6	7	1	.462	281	227
Detroit	4	8	2	.333	207	241

Conference championships: CLEVELAND 31, Dallas 20; BALTIMORE 24, Minnesota 14
NFL Championship: Baltimore 34, CLEVELAND 0
Super Bowl III: N.Y. Jets (AFL) 16, Baltimore (NFL) 7, at Orange Bowl, Miami, Florida

1968 AFL

EASTERN DIVISION

	W	L	T	Pct.	Pts.	OP
N.Y. Jets	11	3	0	.786	419	280
Houston	7	7	0	.500	303	248
Miami	5	8	1	.385	276	355
Boston Patriots	4	10	0	.286	229	406
Buffalo	1	12	1	.077	199	367

WESTERN DIVISION

	W	L	T	Pct.	Pts.	OP
Oakland	12	2	0	.857	453	233
Kansas City	12	2	0	.857	371	170
San Diego	9	5	0	.643	382	310
Denver	5	9	0	.357	255	404
Cincinnati	3	11	0	.214	215	329

Western Division playoff: OAKLAND 41, Kansas City 6
AFL Championship: N.Y. JETS 27, Oakland 23

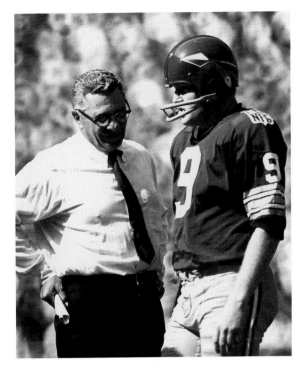

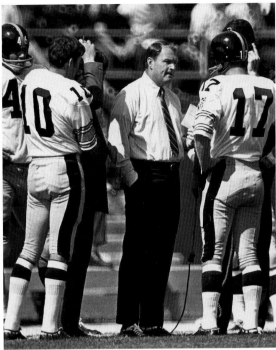

Left: Pittsburgh also made a coaching change in 1969, hiring Chuck Noll, who would lead the team to dynasty status in the 1970s.

1969

A meeting of NFL and AFL owners took almost 36 consecutive hours to come up with it, but the restructured NFL arrived on the scene May 17. Two 13-team conferences were formed by joining three teams from the previous NFL—Baltimore, Cleveland, and Pittsburgh—with the 10 teams from the AFL. The new amalgam was called the American Football Conference (AFC), and the remaining 13 teams made up the new National Football Conference (NFC). Each Conference would inlcude three divisions—East, Central, and West.

The common draft among all 26 teams was a common occurrence by now, but what made it uncommon in 1969 was the presence of O.J. Simpson, USC's Heisman Trophy running back, who was drafted by Buffalo. Two more players whose careers would unfold to Hall-of-Fame dimensions, linebacker Ted Hendricks of Miami and defensive tackle Joe Greene of North Texas State, were taken by Baltimore and Pittsburgh, respectively.

Greene was the first draft choice of new head coach Chuck Noll, a former guard and linebacker with the Cleveland Browns (1953-59) and later an AFL and NFL assistant. Noll served as Don Shula's defensive backfield coach at Baltimore before accepting the Steelers' offer. In Noll's first season as head coach, the Steelers won their first game, then lost their last 13. By the time the 1979 season was over,

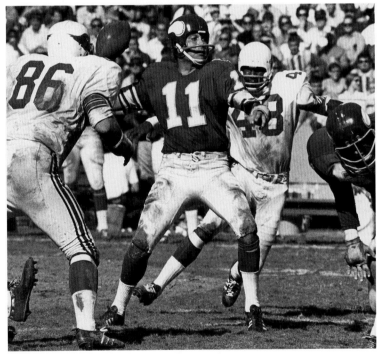

they would be four-time Super Bowl champions.

For some NFL teams, getting ready for the 1969 season, let alone a dynasty, was enough of a production in itself.

The Oakland Raiders, like Pittsburgh, got a new head coach, former assistant John Madden. Unlike Noll, Madden was expected to maintain a winning tradition. He would respond with 112 victories in a 10-year career, including a 32-14 triumph over Minnesota in Super Bowl XI. Madden left coaching after the 1978 season and eventually became CBS's most popular football analyst, combining his knowledge of the

Above: Joe Kapp, the macho Minnesota quarterback, led the Vikings to Super Bowl IV with limited grace and unlimited gusto.

Above: Buffalo rookie O.J. Simpson, the Heisman Trophy winner and the first player taken in the NFL draft, was used partly as a kick returner in 1969. Right: Quarterback Daryle Lamonica of the Oakland Raiders threw 34 touchdown passes en route to the AFL Western Division title. In this game with San Diego, the team won its fifteenth consecutive game, equalling a pro football record.

game with a folksy, let's-get-acquainted repartee that was fine-tuned in the Amtrak club cars he chose over jetliners. Madden also became a familiar figure in television commercials, syndicated a radio broadcast, and wrote numerous articles on the game for the NFL's *PRO!* magazine. His 1984 collaboration with Dave Anderson, *Hey, Wait a Minute! I Wrote a Book,* was a mainstay on the best-seller lists throughout the football season.

This was the year the Washington Redskins got the services of an NFL legend and lost a legendary former owner. Vince Lombardi became part-owner, executive vice president, and head coach of the Redskins in February, and in August, George Preston Marshall died at age 72.

Marshall, who owned the team since its infancy in Boston, never was known for his mild demeanor...or for making himself obscure. One of the game's master pitchmen, he fielded pro football's first marching band (complete with its team's own fight song) and set up a radio network that carried the Redskins' games throughout the South. Marshall was responsible for major competitive changes in the 1930s, including a set schedule, divisional playoffs, moving the goal posts to the goal lines, and redesigning the ball in a narrower shape to encourage more forward passing. He also was the last owner to integrate his team when, in 1962, he traded for Cleveland halfback Bobby Mitchell. (With the draft choice they received in exchange for Mitchell, the Browns selected Syracuse's Ernie Davis, planning to team him with Jim Brown in a dream backfield. Davis never played professional football. He died of leukemia in 1963.)

In Los Angeles, owner Dan Reeves reluctantly recanted when his players protested the firing of head coach George Allen, and the Rams' troubled ship rocked to an 11-3 record, comfortably ahead of Coastal Division runner-up Baltimore, mortal again (8-5-1) in its post-Super Bowl slide.

Teams of the NFL wore a patch in the shape and design of the league's trademark shield, with the numeral "50" stitched prominently to commemorate the fiftieth anniversary of the league's founding in a Canton, Ohio, automobile showroom in 1920.

The New Orleans Saints, who had won three games in their initial season of 1967 and four in 1968, stuck to their pattern by winning five in 1969. One of those victories, a 51-42 offensive field day against St. Louis, put Saints quarterback Billy Kilmer and Cardinals quarterback Charley Johnson in the record book for the highest total of touchdown passes in one game, 12. Saints wide receiver Danny Abramowicz led the NFL with 73 catches. The highlight film ended about there, as the Saints, like the Cardinals, finished third in their division.

The AFL's leading receiver for the second straight year, Lance Alworth of San Diego, completed a string of 96 consecutive games with at least one reception—a record Abramowicz would break five years later after being traded to San Francisco. Alworth, eventually inducted into the Pro Football Hall of Fame in 1978 (and the first AFL player to be so honored), teamed with John Hadl in coach Sid Gillman's pass-oriented system. They nicknamed Alworth "Bambi," after Walt Disney's fawn, for his youthful features and the leaping grace of his receiving style.

San Diego's Gillman was forced to resign after nine games. Assistant Charlie Waller took over, and the Chargers finished off the pace, third in the AFL's Western Division at 8-6.

The 1969 AFL playoff structure took a new turn. Instead of playing within their divisions in the opening round, teams crisscrossed, with the Eastern Division champion Jets (10-4) playing Western Division runner-up Kansas City (11-3), and Oakland (12-1-1) meeting Houston (6-6-2) in the other postseason opener.

The latter game proved to be the mismatch the experts expected. Raiders quarterback Daryle Lamonica, who had thrown 34 touchdown passes during the regular season, got six more against the Oilers, and Oakland breezed 56-7. In cold, windy Shea Stadium, Kansas City defeated the Jets 13-6 in their playoff game, moving 80 yards in two plays to score the only touchdown of the day, a 19-yard pass from Len Dawson to Gloster Richardson.

The last AFL Championship Game was tied 7-7 midway through the third quarter at Oakland when Dawson, on third-and-14, scrambled out of trouble in his end zone and completed a 35-yard pass to Otis Taylor. That began a 98-yard drive to a go-ahead touchdown. The Chiefs eventually won 17-7, turning the ball over three times inside their own 30 in the fourth quarter but intercepting Lamonica (who had returned to the game with a jammed throwing hand) three times during that span, as well.

The NFL playoff picture was dominated by a purple haze, as the Minnesota Vikings became the first expansion team to win the league championship. They did it behind the macho-gritty leadership of quarterback Joe Kapp, down from eight seasons in the Canadian Football League and given to lumbering rollouts and a just-get-it-there passing style. Kapp led a come-from-behind drive that defeated Los Angeles in the first round of the playoffs on an icy field in Minnesota; the former University of California Bear banged in from two yards out for the go-ahead touchdown.

The Cleveland Browns came to the title game via a mud-soaked 38-14 playoff victory over Dallas. Kapp welcomed them to sunny, but freezing, Metropolitan Stadium in Bloomington with a 14-point first quarter: his 7-yard touchdown run and a 75-yard scoring pass to Gene Washington. It was 24-0 Vikings at the half and 27-7 at the end.

Kansas City never trailed the heavily favored Vikings in Super Bowl IV in New Orleans. The Chiefs drove to field goals of 48, 32, and 25 yards by Jan Stenerud on their first three possessions, then took a 16-0 lead at intermission when Mike Garrett ran five yards for a touchdown with 5:34 remaining in the half. The Vikings' comeback attempt drew them to 16-7 when Dave Osborn scored on a four-yard run with 4:32 left in the third quarter. Then, starting from his own 18, Dawson led a drive that ended when, from the Vikings' 46, he hit wide receiver Taylor with a short pass. Taylor ran through cornerback Earsell Mackbee, then effectively faked safety Karl Kassulke at the 10

Top: Jan Stenerud kicked three field goals, opening the door to Kansas City's 23-7 upset of Minnesota in Super Bowl IV. Bottom: Quarterback Len Dawson led the Chiefs to Super Bowl IV. Kansas City reached the showdown with the Vikings by way of a 13-6 playoff victory over the New York Jets at chilly Shea Stadium and a Dawson-inspired 17-7 triumph over Oakland in the AFC Championship Game.

Above: John Madden's coaching career, a 10-year span with the Oakland Raiders from 1969-1978, produced 112 victories and easily that many heated exchanges with NFL officials. Right: Though his team lost to New Orleans 51-42, St. Louis quarterback Charley Johnson joined Saints quarterback Billy Kilmer for a combined 12 touchdown passes, an NFL record. Note the shoulder patch commemorating the NFL's fiftieth year.

before scoring the clincher. The Chiefs evened the score between the AFL and NFL at two Super Bowls apiece, winning 23-7.

During the game, NFL Films had put a microphone on Chiefs head coach Hank Stram, and the results were as enjoyable as his team's artistry against the Vikings. "Let's put out that fire, Leonard," the highlight film records Stram telling Dawson as Kansas City begins its insurance drive. "Let's matriculate that ball down the field," Stram shouts to his players as the drive continues.

Stram's showmanship and knack for concise explanations of the game's finer points, like John Madden's, later paid off in his radio and television commentary for CBS. NFL Films, meanwhile, had been functioning as a subsidiary of the league since 1964. The relationship had begun in 1962 when Blair Productions in Philadelphia, under the direction of Ed Sabol (soon to be joined by his son Steve) had contracted to film the Green Bay-New York Giants NFL Championship Game.

Since 1964, NFL Films has become the largest 16-millimeter film company in the world, winning 33 Emmy Awards for cinematography, editing, writing, producing, directing, and music. "We came at a time when there was a crest at both ends—football and television," said Steve Sabol, who became the company's executive vice president in 1972. "We straddled the wave."

Television waves would reach network viewers in the early 1970s via all three major networks. After being turned down by CBS and NBC because their evening prime-time schedules already were set (and successful), the NFL turned to ABC, which was lagging in the ratings race, for a Monday-night package of 13 games. On Sundays, CBS would carry the NFC and NBC the AFC, with Super Bowl coverage alternating between those two networks (a pattern that eventually would be broken by ABC's coverage of Super Bowl XIX).

The rivalry between the two competing leagues during the 1960s helped stir interest in pro football. Under one flag, the clubs would discover even greater prosperity in the 1970s.

More than anything else, it was Pete Rozelle's Midas touch with television that sent the NFL's popularity soaring. Rozelle's artistry with the law of supply and demand, and his proficiency in the mazes of network politics and Madison Avenue advertising agencies, continually got results.

"He's always known how to operate in that jungle," said Cleveland owner Art Modell, once a television and advertising executive. "I know the jungle. I came out of it."

Noting that more than 60 million viewers had watched Super Bowl IV, Rozelle shed a little perspective on the NFL-television relationship. "When you realize that more people can watch a game on television in one afternoon than see the sport in person over a five-year period," he said, "you begin to understand the impact of television in creating widespread interest."

1969 NFL

EASTERN CONFERENCE
Capitol Division

	W	L	T	Pct.	Pts.	OP
Dallas	11	2	1	.846	369	223
Washington	7	5	2	.583	307	319
New Orleans	5	9	0	.357	311	393
Philadelphia	4	9	1	.308	279	377

Century Division

	W	L	T	Pct.	Pts.	OP
Cleveland	10	3	1	.769	351	300
N.Y. Giants	6	8	0	.429	264	298
St. Louis	4	9	1	.308	314	389
Pittsburgh	1	13	0	.071	218	404

WESTERN CONFERENCE
Coastal Division

	W	L	T	Pct.	Pts.	OP
Los Angeles	11	3	0	.786	320	243
Baltimore	8	5	1	.615	279	268
Atlanta	6	8	0	.429	276	268
San Francisco	4	8	2	.333	277	319

Central Division

	W	L	T	Pct.	Pts.	OP
Minnesota	12	2	0	.857	379	133
Detroit	9	4	1	.692	259	188
Green Bay	8	6	0	.571	269	221
Chicago	1	13	0	.071	210	339

Conference championships: Cleveland 38, DALLAS 14; MINNESOTA 23, Los Angeles 20
NFL Championship: MINNESOTA 27, Cleveland 7
Super Bowl IV: Kansas City (AFL) 23, Minnesota (NFL) 7, at Tulane Stadium, New Orleans, Louisiana

1969 AFL

EASTERN DIVISION

	W	L	T	Pct.	Pts.	OP
N.Y. Jets	10	4	0	.714	353	269
Houston	6	6	2	.500	278	279
Boston Patriots	4	10	0	.286	266	316
Buffalo	4	10	0	.286	230	359
Miami	3	10	1	.231	233	332

WESTERN DIVISION

	W	L	T	Pct.	Pts.	OP
Oakland	12	1	1	.923	377	242
Kansas City	11	3	0	.786	359	177
San Diego	8	6	0	.571	288	276
Denver	5	8	1	.385	297	344
Cincinnati	4	9	1	.308	280	367

Divisional Playoffs: Kansas City 13, N.Y. JETS 6; OAKLAND 56, Houston 7
AFL Championship: Kansas City 17, OAKLAND 7

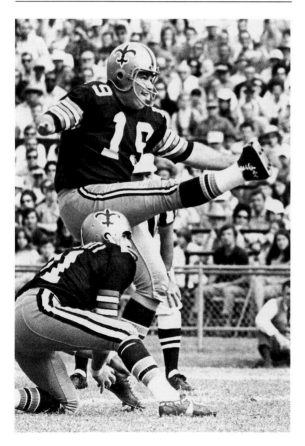

1970

Joe Scarpati didn't receive any special awards at the end of the 1970 NFL season, but he did play a vital role in the first year of the new, fully merged NFL.

Kneeling 63 yards away from a goal post at Tulane Stadium, Scarpati took a snap from center, gingerly holding the football as if it were 1970's own italicized exclamation point. Then New Orleans kicker Tom Dempsey came through with that ferocious hammer of a shoe he wore—a prosthetic device on a foot deformed at birth—and sent the NFL's longest field goal flying.

It came on the last play of a November 8 game to beat Detroit 19-17. It was the high point of Dempsey's career, which would end in 1978 with the Buffalo Bills, after a round of short stops in Philadelphia, Los Angeles, and Houston. Dempsey was traveling the road of the conventional, i.e., straight-on, placekicker, a species endangered by a steady influx of soccer-style sidewinders.

Lest 1970 be thought of as Dempsey's year, there was another conventional-style kicker,

Right: On the banks of the Ohio River in downtown Cincinnati, Riverfront Stadium, home of the Bengals opened for business in 1970. Left: New Orleans Saints placekicker Tom Dempsey made NFL history with a record 63-yard field goal to beat Detroit in the closing seconds, from the hold of Joe Scarpati.

Riverfront Stadium's up-river neighbor and look-alike, Three Rivers Stadium, welcomed the Steelers in 1970.

Above: Veteran commentator Howard Cosell (left) and former Cowboys quarterback Don Meredith joined play-by-play man Keith Jackson on ABC-TV's first Monday Night Football announcing crew. Meredith received an Emmy Award for his work.
Right: Kansas City owner and AFL founder Lamar Hunt (right) posed for a pregame photo with NFL Commissioner Pete Rozelle, prior to the Chiefs' 23-7 victory over Minnesota in Super Bowl IV.
Far right: In the long-awaited first meeting between New York's two pro football teams, Jets quarterback Al Woodall threw this 8-yard scoring pass to George Nock. The Giants won at Shea Stadium, 22-10.

one who doubled as a back-up quarterback, one whose *succession* of miracle endings has no special category in the record book, just an indelible mark in football's memory bank. Oakland's George Blanda, coming on for injured Daryle Lamonica at age 43, rescued the Raiders from apparent defeat five straight times. Two touchdown passes in a victory against Pittsburgh started the chain. The second project, a 48-yard field goal with three seconds to play, gave the Raiders a 17-17 tie with Kansas City. Next came a 52-yard field goal to beat Cleveland 23-20 with three seconds to play (see page 116), followed by a winning touchdown drive to beat Denver 24-19 and another field goal, this one with four seconds left, to beat San Diego 20-17.

The Browns had played the part of victors in another historical sidebar to the merger year by defeating the New York Jets 31-21 in the first episode of "ABC Monday Night Football." The new series featured the play-by-play of Keith Jackson, lighthearted banter from former Cowboys quarterback Don Meredith, and the high-sounding, pedantic verbiage of Howard Cosell. (In 1971, Jackson would be replaced by former New York Giants halfback-receiver Frank Gif-

ford; later color commentators would include Alex Karras, Fran Tarkenton, and O.J. Simpson.)

Getting things in place for the 1970 season took some doing. With the makeup of the AFC already decided, the structure of the NFC's three divisions went through months of discussions. Five plans were submitted. The version drawn, lottery-style, by Commissioner Pete Rozelle, is the one in use today (with Tampa Bay added to the NFC's Central Division and Seattle to the AFC's Western Division).

Two remarkably similar stadiums located 260 miles from each other on the Ohio River—Riverfront in Cincinnati and Three Rivers in Pittsburgh—opened as homes of the Bengals and Steelers, as well as baseball's Reds and Pirates. Both circular, they had almost identical seating capacities (59,754 at Riverfront, 59,000 at Three Rivers) and had their playing surfaces covered with artificial turf in the new tradition of attempting to defy the elements.

Quarterback Terry Bradshaw of Louisiana Tech, the first pick of the NFL draft, joined the Steelers, another step toward the team's impending dominance of pro football in the 1970s.

Another power center was taking shape in Miami, as Dolphins owner Joe Robbie hired head coach Don Shula away from Baltimore. It took some intervention by Commissioner Rozelle to settle charges of tampering voiced by Baltimore owner Carroll Rosenbloom. Rozelle found that Robbie had indeed fouled the process by communicating with Shula through Rosenbloom's son Steve (a Colts administrative aide) while the owner was on an Asian vacation. Rozelle compensated the Colts for their loss with a first-round draft choice in 1971 (North Carolina running back Don McCauley). Baltimore's new head coach was Don McCafferty, one of Shula's assistants from 1963-69.

Shula would take the Dolphins to Super Bowl VI the following season, but this year McCafferty took the Colts to Super Bowl V. Baltimore's NFC opponent was the Dallas Cowboys, better-known at this point in NFL history as "The Team That Couldn't Win the Big One" than as "America's Team" (a label they eventually received from NFL Films when it came time to title their 1977 highlight film).

Dallas's losses to Green Bay in the 1966 and 1967 NFL Championship Games and to Cleveland in the 1968 and 1969 Eastern Conference Championship Games—despite being heavily favored in the latter two—earned them another sobriquet: "Next Year's Champions."

In 1970, "Next Year" looked as if it had come when Dallas (10-4) won the NFC's Eastern Division, defeated Detroit 5-0 in a divisional playoff game, and beat San Francisco 17-10 in the NFC Championship Game at Kezar Stadium to earn its first Super Bowl appearance.

Super Bowl V is remembered as the Blooper Bowl because of its 11 turnovers (7 by the Colts) and 14 penalties (9 by Dallas).

With less than two minutes to play and the score tied 13-13, the Cowboys began a drive for what could have been the winning score. But quarterback Craig Morton's high pass to halfback Dan Reeves bounced out of Reeves's hands at the Dallas 41 and into the grasp of Colts linebacker Mike Curtis, who returned it to the 28.

Then, with just five seconds left, rookie Jim O'Brien kicked a 32-yard field goal to give the Colts a 16-13 victory. The Cowboys had been denied again.

In keeping with the realignment, the new AFC-NFC Pro Bowl picked up where a varied tradition of postseason all-star games had left off. The series had begun in 1939 when the New York Giants defeated a team called the "Pro All-Stars," 13-10, at the Los Angeles Coli-

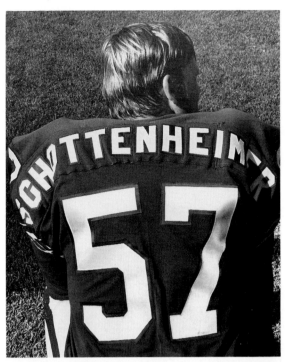

Although players such as Buffalo linebacker Marty Schottenheimer presented a real challenge, all NFL jerseys bore players' names as of 1970. Fourteen years later, Schottenheimer became head coach of the Cleveland Browns, to the chagrin of headline writers, typesetters, and proofreaders everywhere.

Right: Pallbearers carried the coffin of Vince Lombardi into St. Patrick's Cathedral in New York City. The former Packers and Redskins head coach died of cancer September 3, 1970.

Above: At San Francisco's Kezar Stadium, Dallas quarterback Craig Morton embraced coach Tom Landry in celebration of the Cowboys' first NFC championship. Also pictured, following the 17-10 victory over the 49ers, were running back Dan Reeves (left), flanker Bob Hayes (22), and fullback Calvin Hill.

End of an era: Kezar Stadium, home of the San Francisco 49ers since 1946 and in 1960 the home of the Oakland Raiders, closed its gates to pro football when the 49ers moved to Candlestick Park.

Above left: The old —George Blanda still was going strong as the Raiders' back-up quarterback and kicker. Above right: The new—Heisman Trophy-winning quarterback Jim Plunkett of Stanford was New England's first pick in the 1971 draft. Right: Denver's Floyd Little led NFL rushers in 1971 with 1,133 yards.

seum. The game evolved into an East-West event played annually in Los Angeles. The new AFC-NFC version would travel to various NFL cities during the 1970s, then move to Honolulu in 1980 for an extended run at Aloha Stadium.

1970

AMERICAN CONFERENCE EASTERN DIVISION							NATIONAL CONFERENCE EASTERN DIVISION						
	W	L	T	Pct.	Pts.	OP		W	L	T	Pct.	Pts.	OP
Baltimore	11	2	1	.846	321	234	Dallas	10	4	0	.714	299	221
Miami*	10	4	0	.714	297	228	N.Y. Giants	9	5	0	.643	301	270
N.Y. Jets	4	10	0	.286	255	286	St. Louis	8	5	1	.615	325	228
Buffalo	3	10	1	.231	204	337	Washington	6	8	0	.429	297	314
Boston Patriots	2	12	0	.143	149	361	Philadelphia	3	10	1	.231	241	332
CENTRAL DIVISION							**CENTRAL DIVISION**						
	W	L	T	Pct.	Pts.	OP		W	L	T	Pct.	Pts.	OP
Cincinnati	8	6	0	.571	312	255	Minnesota	12	2	0	.857	335	143
Cleveland	7	7	0	.500	286	265	Detroit*	10	4	0	.714	347	202
Pittsburgh	5	9	0	.357	210	272	Chicago	6	8	0	.429	256	261
Houston	3	10	1	.231	217	352	Green Bay	6	8	0	.429	196	293
WESTERN DIVISION							**WESTERN DIVISION**						
	W	L	T	Pct.	Pts.	OP		W	L	T	Pct.	Pts.	OP
Oakland	8	4	2	.667	300	293	San Francisco	10	3	1	.769	352	267
Kansas City	7	5	2	.583	272	244	Los Angeles	9	4	1	.692	325	202
San Diego	5	6	3	.455	282	278	Atlanta	4	8	2	.333	206	261
Denver	5	8	1	.385	253	264	New Orleans	2	11	1	.154	172	347

Wild-Card qualifier for playoffs
AFC divisional playoffs: BALTIMORE 17, Cincinnati 0; OAKLAND 21, Miami 14
AFC Championship: BALTIMORE 27, Oakland 17
NFC divisional playoffs: DALLAS 5, Detroit 0; San Francisco 17, MINNESOTA 14
NFC Championship: Dallas 17, SAN FRANCISCO 10
Super Bowl V: Baltimore (AFC) 16, Dallas (NFC) 13, at Orange Bowl, Miami, Florida

1971

Time and tide wait for no man, says the cliche, so George Allen decided to go the other way. "The future is now," he said, taking over as head coach of the Washington Redskins and immediately trading for veteran defensive players such as tackle Diron Talbert and linebackers Myron Pottios, Maxie Baughan, and Jack Pardee of the Rams. In doing so, he mortgaged the future of the franchise, giving up draft choices scheduled well into the 1970s.

Led by aging quarterback Billy Kilmer and running back Larry Brown, the Redskins finished second to Dallas in the NFL's Eastern Division, earning the wild-card playoff berth (the team's first playoff appearance since 1945), then proved that the future still was the future by losing to Western Division champion San Francisco 24-20 in the playoff opener. The 49ers, finishing their first season in Candlestick Park, lost the NFC Championship Game to Dallas, and the Cowboys prepared to meet AFC champion Miami.

The Dolphins' Super Bowl VI appearance was a first for the young franchise. After 10 victories in the regular season, Miami opened the playoffs with a 27-24 double-overtime win over Kansas City in the longest NFL game ever played (see page 118), then beat wild-card entry Baltimore 21-0 in the AFC Championship Game.

President Richard Nixon, a Dolphins constituent by virtue of his vacation residence in Key Biscayne, Florida, felt obligated to help coach Don Shula prepare for the game. "I think you can hit [wide receiver Paul] Warfield on that down-and-in pattern," the nation's chief executive told the coach. Warfield caught four passes; Dallas won 24-3.

The year had begun with an influx of new quarterbacks and new venues around the league. The Patriots expanded their territory, changing from "Boston" to "New England" and moving into brand-new 61,275-seat Schaefer Stadium in Foxboro, Massachusetts. Their housewarming introduced Jim Plunkett, the 1970 Heisman Trophy-winning quarterback from Stanford. In the NFL draft, New Orleans had picked up the theme by taking Mississippi's Archie Manning, and Houston had doubled the ante by drafting Santa Clara's Dan Pastorini in

the first round and Kansas State's Lynn Dickey in the third. (Plunkett, Manning, and Pastorini were the first three draft choices overall.)

Two games from the regular season would live on, not only in the memories of those who saw them, but under the "variety show" category in NFL Films's rich archives. In October, Detroit defeated Atlanta 41-38. Ten touchdowns were scored in the game, in five different ways: rushing, passing, a fumble recovery, a kickoff return, and the return of a blocked punt. Six weeks later, Washington led Chicago 15-9 until the Bears' Cyril Pinder scored on a 40-yard run in the fourth quarter. Chicago got its winning point when holder Bobby Douglass recovered an errant snap on the point-after attempt and threw a 30-yard pass to Dick Butkus, normally a linebacker, who was an eligible receiver on the play.

Four more teams changed home stadiums:

Above: The Dallas Cowboys moved into their new home, Texas Stadium.
Top left: Running back Willie Ellison of the Los Angeles Rams rushed for 247 yards, a single-game record, in a 45-28 victory over New Orleans.
Bottom left: In 1971, his rookie season, Green Bay running back John Brockington led the NFC with 1,105 yards and was named the league's rookie of the year.

Dallas, from the Cotton Bowl to Texas Stadium in suburban Irving; Philadelphia, from Franklin Field to Veterans Stadium; San Francisco, from Kezar Stadium to Candlestick Park; and Chicago, from Wrigley Field to Soldier Field. All but the last could be called "modernizing." The Bears had been denizens of Wrigley (nee Cubs Park) since changing their identity from the Decatur Staleys in 1921. They now occupied the league's oldest structure, built in 1924.

1971

AMERICAN CONFERENCE EASTERN DIVISION							NATIONAL CONFERENCE EASTERN DIVISION						
	W	L	T	Pct.	Pts.	OP		W	L	T	Pct.	Pts.	OP
Miami	10	3	1	.769	315	174	Dallas	11	3	0	.786	406	222
Baltimore*	10	4	0	.714	313	140	Washington*	9	4	1	.692	276	190
New England	6	8	0	.429	238	325	Philadelphia	6	7	1	.462	221	302
N.Y. Jets	6	8	0	.429	212	299	St. Louis	4	9	1	.308	231	279
Buffalo	1	13	0	.071	184	394	N.Y. Giants	4	10	0	.286	228	362
CENTRAL DIVISION							**CENTRAL DIVISION**						
	W	L	T	Pct.	Pts.	OP		W	L	T	Pct.	Pts.	OP
Cleveland	9	5	0	.643	285	273	Minnesota	11	3	0	.786	245	139
Pittsburgh	6	8	0	.429	246	292	Detroit	7	6	1	.538	341	286
Houston	4	9	1	.308	251	330	Chicago	6	8	0	.429	185	276
Cincinnati	4	10	0	.286	284	265	Green Bay	4	8	2	.333	274	298
WESTERN DIVISION							**WESTERN DIVISION**						
	W	L	T	Pct.	Pts.	OP		W	L	T	Pct.	Pts.	OP
Kansas City	10	3	1	.769	302	208	San Francisco	9	5	0	.643	300	216
Oakland	8	4	2	.667	344	278	Los Angeles	8	5	1	.615	313	260
San Diego	6	8	0	.429	311	341	Atlanta	7	6	1	.538	274	277
Denver	4	9	1	.308	203	275	New Orleans	4	8	2	.333	266	347

*Wild-Card qualifier for playoffs
AFC divisional playoffs: Miami 27, KANSAS CITY 24, sudden death overtime; Baltimore 20, CLEVELAND 3
AFC Championship: MIAMI 21, Baltimore 0
NFC divisional playoffs: Dallas 20, MINNESOTA 12; SAN FRANCISCO 24, Washington 20
NFC Championship: DALLAS 14, San Francisco 3
Super Bowl VI: Dallas (NFC) 24, Miami (AFC) 3, at Tulane Stadium, New Orleans, Louisiana

In a September, 1972 game, Oakland's Jack Tatum picked up a fumble by Green Bay's MacArthur Lane and raced 104 yards for a touchdown, breaking George Halas's 49-year-old NFL record, in the Raiders' 20-14 victory over the Packers.

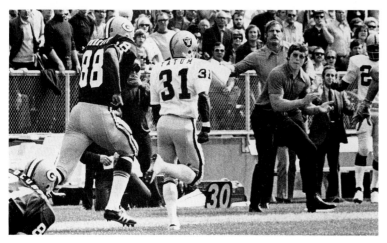

Right: En route to his team's 17-0 record, Miami head coach Don Shula became the first NFL coach to reach 100 victories in his first 10 seasons, as the Dolphins defeated New England 52-0.

1972

A year of oddities got started when two men agreed to trade their NFL franchises. Illinois businessman Robert Irsay, who had purchased the Los Angeles Rams from the estate of the late Dan Reeves, swapped with Carroll Rosenbloom, owner of the Baltimore Colts. Neither team's performance on the field matched the excitement of the trade; each finished third in its division.

No, the thrills were in Miami, where the Dolphins fashioned the NFL's first and only perfect season (17-0). En route to their 14-7 victory over Washington in Super Bowl VII, they nearly were derailed by Pittsburgh in the AFC Championship Game, surviving 21-17.

The Steelers had reached the AFC's final round by virtue of Franco Harris's "Immaculate Reception" a week earlier against Oakland (see page 120). Pittsburgh's 13-7 triumph at Three Rivers Stadium was the front end of a cross-country "Black Saturday" for both San Francisco Bay Area teams. The 49ers suffered a last-minute catastrophe of their own, as Dallas's Roger Staubach threw two touchdown passes in 38 seconds to give the Cowboys, the NFC wild-card entry, a 30-28 victory (see page 122).

Statistically, the New York Jets' Don Maynard took a measure of consolation, despite his team's 7-7 second-place division finish behind Miami. Maynard caught pass number 632 to eclipse Baltimore great Raymond Berry as the NFL's all-time reception leader.

If creature comfort could soothe the sting of second place, fans in Kansas City didn't have it so bad. The Chiefs (8-6) were runners-up to Oakland (10-3-1) for the AFL's Western Division title, but their new Arrowhead Stadium had room for 78,067 spectators, 50,000 of whom sat between the end lines. Arrowhead became the new prototype for non-domed, football-only stadiums.

At the beginning of the year, when the rules makers moved the hashmarks, or "inbound lines," three yards toward the middle of the field from either sideline, their aim was to open up the passing game by blunting the effect of the increasingly popular zone defense. The move may have had a residual, or even direct, effect on the running game's success, as a record 10 backs ran for at least 1,000 yards. The winner of this derby was Buffalo's O.J. Simpson with 1,251 yards. The list extended to Miami's

Eugene (Mercury) Morris, who, the league noticed, had been erroneously charged with a nine-yard loss that should have been marked as a fumble by quarterback Earl Morrall. Morris finished with 1,000 yards even and joined Larry Csonka (1,117 yards) as the first teammates to gain 1,000 yards each in the same season. Atlanta running back Dave Hampton made it to 1,001, but carried the ball once too often, losing 6 yards on his final carry and dropping to 995.

1972

AMERICAN CONFERENCE EASTERN DIVISION							NATIONAL CONFERENCE EASTERN DIVISION						
	W	L	T	Pct.	Pts.	OP		W	L	T	Pct.	Pts.	OP
Miami	14	0	0	1.000	385	171	Washington	11	3	0	.786	336	218
N.Y. Jets	7	7	0	.500	367	324	Dallas*	10	4	0	.714	319	240
Baltimore	5	9	0	.357	235	252	N.Y. Giants	8	6	0	.571	331	247
Buffalo	4	9	1	.321	257	377	St. Louis	4	9	1	.321	193	303
New England	3	11	0	.214	192	446	Philadelphia	2	11	1	.179	145	352
CENTRAL DIVISION							**CENTRAL DIVISION**						
	W	L	T	Pct.	Pts.	OP		W	L	T	Pct.	Pts.	OP
Pittsburgh	11	3	0	.786	343	175	Green Bay	10	4	0	.714	304	226
Cleveland*	10	4	0	.714	268	249	Detroit	8	5	1	.607	339	290
Cincinnati	8	6	0	.571	299	229	Minnesota	7	7	0	.500	301	252
Houston	1	13	0	.071	164	380	Chicago	4	9	1	.321	225	275
WESTERN DIVISION							**WESTERN DIVISION**						
	W	L	T	Pct.	Pts.	OP		W	L	T	Pct.	Pts.	OP
Oakland	10	3	1	.750	365	248	San Francisco	8	5	1	.607	353	249
Kansas City	8	6	0	.571	287	254	Atlanta	7	7	0	.500	269	274
Denver	5	9	0	.357	325	350	Los Angeles	6	7	1	.464	291	286
San Diego	4	9	1	.321	264	344	New Orleans	2	11	1	.179	215	361

*Wild-Card qualifier for playoffs

AFC divisional playoffs: PITTSBURGH 13, Oakland 7; MIAMI 20, Cleveland 14
AFC Championship: Miami 21, PITTSBURGH 17
NFC divisional playoffs: Dallas 30, SAN FRANCISCO 28; WASHINGTON 16, Green Bay 3
NFC Championship: WASHINGTON 26, Dallas 3
Super Bowl VII: Miami (AFC) 14, Washington (NFC) 7, at Memorial Coliseum, Los Angeles, California

1973

No sooner had the 1,000-yard plateau been mocked by a slew of running backs than their leader went ahead and doubled the standard. Having set a single-game record with 250 yards against New England on opening day, O.J. Simpson finished the year with a total of 2,003, rushing for 200 yards against the New York Jets in a snowstorm at Shea Stadium. (He entered the game needing 61 yards to pass Jim Brown's one-season record of 1,863.)

Give credit to Simpson's offensive line, the vaunted Electric Company (O.J. had become "Juice," hence the need for a power source): center Mike Montler, guards Joe DeLamielleure and Reggie McKenzie, tackles Steve Foley and Donnie Green, and tight end Paul Seymour.

But 1,000 yards was linked to another name in 1973, as Green Bay's John Brockington became the first man in NFL history to reach that total in each of his first three seasons.

Congress passed a bill that lifted the hometown blackout on any game sold out 72 hours before kickoff. The new law prompted the addi-

Hired in January, 1973, after a successful college coaching career, new St. Louis head coach Don Coryell (left) pulled off a 34-27 upset of George Allen's Washington Redskins. Joining the celebration were assistants Ray Willsey (center) and Jim Hanifan.

Late in Super Bowl VII, Miami place-kicker Garo Yepremian's ill-advised passing attempt led to a fumble recovery by Washington's Mike Bass (41), who took it 49 yards for a touchdown as the Redskins lost to the Dolphins 14-7. Yepremian wound up on his back, head over heels beneath an official (right).

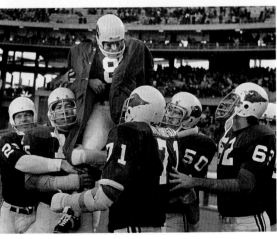

St. Louis safety Larry Wilson was carried off the field by his teammates after the final game of his 13-year career. Wilson, an eventual Hall of Fame enshrinee, retired with 32 interceptions.

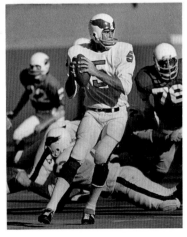

Philadelphia quarterback Roman Gabriel, acquired in June of 1973 in a major trade with Los Angeles, was named the NFL's comeback player of the year, leading the league in four passing categories, including his total of 23 touchdowns.

Top: This was the carry that put O.J. Simpson over the 2,000-yard rushing plateau. He reached 2,003 in Buffalo's final game of 1973, a 34-14 victory over the New York Jets at Shea Stadium.
Above left: In his eighteenth season, Johnny Unitas, traded from Baltimore to San Diego, opened for the Chargers at quarterback.
Above right: Backing up Unitas was Dan Fouts, a rookie third-round draft choice from Oregon.
Right: New Rams head coach Chuck Knox (left) and offensive assistant Ray Prochaska.

tion of "no-shows" to the NFL glossary, to describe those who bought tickets but chose television on game day.

The up-and-down Cincinnati Bengals won the AFC Central with a 10-4 record, edging Pittsburgh, also 10-4, on the basis of a better record in intraconference games. Quarterback Ken Anderson, wide receiver Isaac Curtis, and running backs Essex Johnson and Boobie Clark were the offensive leaders for the Bengals, who lost 34-16 to Miami in a divisional playoff game. The Dolphins rumbled to their second straight Super Bowl victory, 24-7 over Minnesota. Miami fullback Larry Csonka set a Super Bowl record, rushing for 145 yards at Rice Stadium in Houston. The Dolphins' "No-Name" (read "No Stars, Just A Well-Coordinated Unit Under Assistant Bill Arnsparger") defense unscrambled quarterback Fran Tarkenton.

As the NFL appointed a committee, headed by Pittsburgh Steelers president Dan Rooney, to explore the possibilities of future expansion, others outside the league were starting from scratch. An October meeting in Los Angeles ended with the announcement that the World Football League would begin play in 1974.

1973

AMERICAN CONFERENCE EASTERN DIVISION							NATIONAL CONFERENCE EASTERN DIVISION						
	W	L	T	Pct.	Pts.	OP		W	L	T	Pct.	Pts.	OP
Miami	12	2	0	.857	343	150	Dallas	10	4	0	.714	382	203
Buffalo	9	5	0	.643	259	230	Washington*	10	4	0	.714	325	198
New England	5	9	0	.357	258	300	Philadelphia	5	8	1	.393	310	393
Baltimore	4	10	0	.286	226	341	St. Louis	4	9	1	.321	286	365
N.Y. Jets	4	10	0	.286	240	306	N.Y. Giants	2	11	1	.179	226	362
CENTRAL DIVISION							**CENTRAL DIVISION**						
	W	L	T	Pct.	Pts.	OP		W	L	T	Pct.	Pts.	OP
Cincinnati	10	4	0	.714	286	231	Minnesota	12	2	0	.857	296	168
Pittsburgh*	10	4	0	.714	347	210	Detroit	6	7	1	.464	271	247
Cleveland	7	5	2	.571	234	255	Green Bay	5	7	2	.429	202	259
Houston	1	13	0	.071	199	447	Chicago	3	11	0	.214	195	334
WESTERN DIVISION							**WESTERN DIVISION**						
	W	L	T	Pct.	Pts.	OP		W	L	T	Pct.	Pts.	OP
Oakland	9	4	1	.679	292	175	Los Angeles	12	2	0	.857	388	178
Denver	7	5	2	.571	354	296	Atlanta	9	5	0	.643	318	224
Kansas City	7	5	2	.571	231	192	New Orleans	5	9	0	.357	163	312
San Diego	2	11	1	.179	188	386	San Francisco	5	9	0	.357	262	319

*Wild-Card qualifier for playoffs
Cincinnati won division title on the basis of a better conference record than Pittsburgh (8-3 to 7-4). Dallas won division title on the basis of a better point differential vs. Washington (net 13 points).
AFC divisional playoffs: OAKLAND 33, Pittsburgh 14; MIAMI 34, Cincinnati 16
AFC Championship: MIAMI 27, Oakland 10
NFC divisional playoffs: MINNESOTA 27, Washington 20; DALLAS 27, Los Angeles 16
NFC Championship: Minnesota 27, DALLAS 10
Super Bowl VIII: Miami (AFC) 24, Minnesota (NFC) 7, at Rice Stadium, Houston, Texas

1974

When the season opened, new rules took effect: Defensive players were allowed only one "bump" or "chuck," a reaction to the evolving "bump-and-run" style of pass coverage. On punts, only two outside men from the kicking team were allowed downfield before the ball was kicked. The penalty for offensive holding

moved down from Chicago. The highlight of the postseason tournament, however, was Oakland's last-minute 28-26 victory over Miami in the first round of the AFC divisional playoffs (see page 126).

The Raiders' magic vanished a week later when Pittsburgh won the AFC championship 24-13 in Oakland. The Steelers made their first Super Bowl trip a successful one, giving owner Art Rooney his first championship in 42 years.

Far left: Pittsburgh's draft bonanza of 1974 included linebacker Jack Lambert of Kent State. The Steelers' first five choices were wide receiver Lynn Swann, Lambert, defensive back Jimmy Allen, wide receiver John Stallworth, and center Mike Webster.

1974

AMERICAN CONFERENCE EASTERN DIVISION						NATIONAL CONFERENCE EASTERN DIVISION					
	W	L	T	Pct.	Pts.	OP		W	L	T	Pct.	Pts.	OP
Miami	11	3	0	.786	327	216	St. Louis	10	4	0	.714	285	218
Buffalo*	9	5	0	.643	264	244	Washington*	10	4	0	.714	320	196
New England	7	7	0	.500	348	289	Dallas	8	6	0	.571	297	235
N.Y. Jets	7	7	0	.500	279	300	Philadelphia	7	7	0	.500	242	217
Baltimore	2	12	0	.143	190	329	N.Y. Giants	2	12	0	.143	195	299

CENTRAL DIVISION							CENTRAL DIVISION					
	W	L	T	Pct.	Pts.	OP		W	L	T	Pct.	Pts.	OP
Pittsburgh	10	3	1	.750	305	189	Minnesota	10	4	0	.714	310	195
Cincinnati	7	7	0	.500	283	259	Detroit	7	7	0	.500	256	270
Houston	7	7	0	.500	236	282	Green Bay	6	8	0	.429	210	206
Cleveland	4	10	0	.286	251	344	Chicago	4	10	0	.286	152	279

WESTERN DIVISION							WESTERN DIVISION					
	W	L	T	Pct.	Pts.	OP		W	L	T	Pct.	Pts.	OP
Oakland	12	2	0	.857	355	228	Los Angeles	10	4	0	.714	263	181
Denver	7	6	1	.536	302	294	San Francisco	6	8	0	.429	226	236
Kansas City	5	9	0	.357	233	293	New Orleans	5	9	0	.357	166	263
San Diego	5	9	0	.357	212	285	Atlanta	3	11	0	.214	111	271

*Wild-Card qualifier for playoffs
St. Louis won division title because of a two-game sweep over Washington.
AFC divisional playoffs: OAKLAND 28, Miami 26; PITTSBURGH 32, Buffalo 14
AFC Championship: Pittsburgh 24, OAKLAND 13
NFC divisional playoffs: MINNESOTA 30, St. Louis 14; LOS ANGELES 19, Washington 10
NFC Championship: MINNESOTA 14, Los Angeles 10
Super Bowl IX: Pittsburgh (AFC) 16, Minnesota (NFC) 6, at Tulane Stadium, New Orleans, Louisiana

was reduced to 10 yards. Receivers no longer could make "crack-back" blocks below the waist.

Goal posts were moved to the end lines. Teams kicked off from the 35-yard line instead of the 40. Miss a field goal from outside the 20, and your opponent got to start from the original line of scrimmage.

The results were predictable: more touchdowns, fewer field goals. The revised punting rules led to fewer fair catches and longer runbacks.

But even before the season began, owners and players had found themselves deadlocked over a new collective-bargaining agreement. The old four-year contract had expired, and it wasn't until August 28 that an interim agreement could be reached.

Cincinnati quarterback Ken Anderson and Baltimore quarterback Bert Jones played a game of "Can You Top This?" Anderson completed 16 consecutive passes against the Colts, an NFL record. Jones must have studied Anderson well, because a month later, he broke the record with 17 in a row against the New York Jets.

St. Louis, under coach Don Coryell, was in the playoffs for the first time since the club had

Baltimore's Lydell Mitchell led the NFL in receptions in 1974 with 72, the most ever for a running back. The total put Mitchell nine catches ahead of the season's runner-up, tight end Charle Young of Philadelphia.

The NFL's sudden-death overtime rule went into effect in 1974, and its first use resulted in a 35-35 tie between Pittsburgh and Denver at Mile High Stadium. Broncos running back Otis Armstrong (24) was the game's leading rusher (131 yards) and scored on passes of 45 and 23 yards.

Top left: Franco Harris (32) and Joe Greene (75) carried coach Chuck Noll off the field after the Steelers' 16-6 victory over Minnesota in Super Bowl IX. Top right: Washington's Charley Taylor became the NFL's all-time leading receiver with this catch, number 634, en route to 649 when he retired in 1977.

Above: Fran Tarkenton broke four of Johnny Unitas's all-time career passing records in 1975. Above, right: The latest addition to the New Orleans cityscape was the Louisiana Superdome.

A 16-6 victory over three-time Super Bowl loser Minnesota at Tulane Stadium in New Orleans included a record 158-yard rushing performance by Franco Harris and the defensive dominance of a line nicknamed the Steel Curtain—ends Dwight White and L.C. Greenwood and tackles Joe Greene and Ernie Holmes.

1975

"The Packers have a long road back to the top," said Bart Starr, taking over as head coach of the team he had quarterbacked to five NFL titles. It was a remark anyone could have made, witness Green Bay's 45-49-5 record since its last title under Vince Lombardi in 1967.

Starr would go 4-10 in 1975 and 53-77-3 in a nine-year period before being replaced in 1983.

The league abolished the "taxi squad," a kind of designated reserve tank that had picked up its name when former Cleveland owner Mickey McBride, who also had a taxi company, employed his leftover players as cabbies during the 1940s, the better to keep them on hand in case roster players were injured.

The Detroit Lions became the first NFL team to play its home games under a Teflon roof, moving into the Pontiac Silverdome (capacity: 80,638). Meanwhile, the New Orleans Saints relocated to the Louisiana Superdome (capacity: 71,647), with its 273-foot ceiling and five giant television screens, all mounted on a single carousel that hung above midfield.

One quarterback, Minnesota's Fran Tarkenton, had a banner year, while another, Oakland's George Blanda, bade a hero's farewell. Tarkenton set all-time records for career touchdown passes (291), completions (2,931), and attempts (5,225), all formerly held by Johnny Unitas, who had retired in 1974. Blanda left the game at age 49, with records for active seasons (26), games played (340), consecutive games played (224), points (2,002), field goals (335), and points after touchdown (959).

The Raiders went 11-3 to win the AFC West but finished their season on the Pittsburgh Steelers' 15-yard line at icy Three Rivers Stadium. Linebacker Jack Lambert recovered three fumbles in the Steelers' 16-10 victory for the AFC championship.

For the Houston Oilers, 10-4 under new head coach Oail ("Cain't nobody spell it or pronounce it or anything") A. Phillips, affectionately nicknamed "Bum," this was the first winning season since 1967.

You could get technical about it and remind everyone that the Kansas City Chiefs had advanced from a second-place finish to a Super Bowl victory in 1969, but theirs was *de facto* wild-card status. This time around, the Dallas Cowboys became the first wild-card team to reach the NFL's ultimate game since that designation became official. It was academic. The Cowboys fell to dynasty-bound Pittsburgh in Miami's Orange Bowl, 21-17 (see page 130).

The World Football League went out of business in October.

Turn out the lights . . . . With 1:22 left to play in the third quarter of the 1976 College All-Star Game and a torrential downpour inundating Soldier Field, Commissioner Pete Rozelle called off the game. Pittsburgh won 24-0 in what was to be the end of a 42-year Chicago tradition.

1975

AMERICAN CONFERENCE EASTERN DIVISION							NATIONAL CONFERENCE EASTERN DIVISION						
	W	L	T	Pct.	Pts.	OP		W	L	T	Pct.	Pts.	OP
Baltimore	10	4	0	.714	395	269	St. Louis	11	3	0	.786	356	276
Miami	10	4	0	.714	357	222	Dallas*	10	4	0	.714	350	268
Buffalo	8	6	0	.571	420	355	Washington	8	6	0	.571	325	276
New England	3	11	0	.214	258	358	N.Y. Giants	5	9	0	.357	216	306
N.Y. Jets	3	11	0	.214	258	433	Philadelphia	4	10	0	.286	225	302
CENTRAL DIVISION							**CENTRAL DIVISION**						
	W	L	T	Pct.	Pts.	OP		W	L	T	Pct.	Pts.	OP
Pittsburgh	12	2	0	.857	373	162	Minnesota	12	2	0	.857	377	180
Cincinnati*	11	3	0	.786	340	246	Detroit	7	7	0	.500	245	262
Houston	10	4	0	.714	293	226	Chicago	4	10	0	.286	191	379
Cleveland	3	11	0	.214	218	372	Green Bay	4	10	0	.286	226	285
WESTERN DIVISION							**WESTERN DIVISION**						
	W	L	T	Pct.	Pts.	OP		W	L	T	Pct.	Pts.	OP
Oakland	11	3	0	.786	375	255	Los Angeles	12	2	0	.857	312	135
Denver	6	8	0	.429	254	307	San Francisco	5	9	0	.357	255	286
Kansas City	5	9	0	.357	282	341	Atlanta	4	10	0	.286	240	289
San Diego	2	12	0	.143	189	345	New Orleans	2	12	0	.143	165	360

*Wild-Card qualifier for playoffs
Baltimore won division title on the basis of a two-game sweep over Miami.
AFC divisional playoffs: PITTSBURGH 28, Baltimore 10; OAKLAND 31, Cincinnati 28
AFC Championship: PITTSBURGH 16, Oakland 10
NFC divisional playoffs: LOS ANGELES 35, St. Louis 23; Dallas 17, MINNESOTA 14
NFC Championship: Dallas 37, LOS ANGELES 7
Super Bowl X: Pittsburgh (AFC) 21, Dallas (NFC) 17, at Orange Bowl, Miami, Florida

1976

Seattle and Tampa Bay housed their new teams, the Seahawks and Buccaneers, in the Kingdome and Tampa Stadium. The latter was expanded to seat 71,400, while the former boasted the world's largest free-standing roof.

The NFL draft was delayed until the second week of April, and the Buccaneers made Oklahoma's Lee Roy Selmon, a defensive lineman, their first pick. They got to go first by winning a coin flip, which turned out to be their only victory of the year. On the field, they went 0-14. The Seahawks fared better at 2-12, building their offense around the passing combination of Jim Zorn, who set a record for passing yardage by a rookie (2,571), and rookie wide receiver Steve Largent, who caught 54 passes to rank third in the NFC. The Buccaneers spent their first year in the AFC, then permanently swapped conferences with the Seahawks.

The rest of the NFL went about revising the

Above: Under construction, Giants Stadium rose out of the New Jersey Meadowlands, looming large against the Manhattan skyline in 1976. Left: Oakland quarterback Ken Stabler dived into New England's end zone with 10 seconds left for the one-yard touchdown that gave the Raiders a 24-21 victory over the Patriots in the 1976 AFC playoffs.

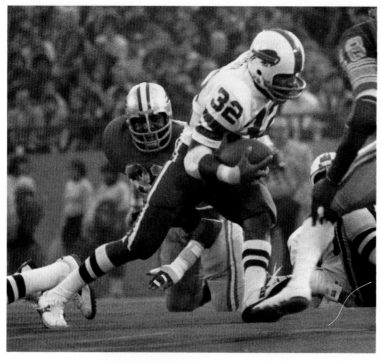

Top: Minnesota's Nate Allen blocked Tom Dempsey's field-goal attempt, and Bobby Bryant (20) took it 90 yards to begin the Vikings' 24-13 victory over Los Angeles in the 1976 NFC Championship Game. Above: O.J. Simpson celebrated Thanksgiving with an NFL record 273-yard rushing performance in Buffalo's 27-27 tie with Detroit. Right: Seattle defeated Tampa Bay 13-10 in the battle of 1976 expansion teams. Thirty-five penalties were assessed in the game.

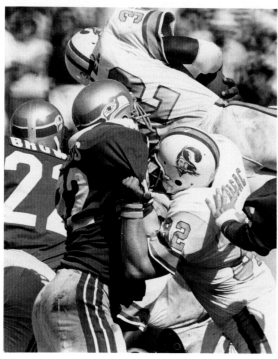

record book some more. The 10-man 1,000-yard extravaganza of 1972 was surpassed when O.J. Simpson led 12 backs beyond the mark. Part of Simpson's 1,503-yard total was a single-game-record 273-yard performance against Detroit on Thanksgiving Day.

Other milestones included Fran Tarkenton's finishing the season with 41,801 yards passing, an all-time record that moved Johnny Unitas into second place. Tarkenton's Minnesota teammate Jim Marshall, of wrong-way fame, moved past George Blanda to lead the all-time consecutive games list at 236. Oakland's Ken Stabler completed passes for a 66.7 percentage, the NFL's best since Sammy Baugh of Washington connected for 70.3 in 1945.

In an AFC Divisional Playoff Game against New England, a controversial roughing-the-passer call set up Stabler's scrambling, diving touchdown run, and the Raiders advanced to the AFC Championship Game. There, they met a Pittsburgh team that had lost running backs Franco Harris and Rocky Bleier to injuries, and the Steelers' dynasty went on hold, 24-7. Conversely, the AFC title gave the Raiders their first trip to the Super Bowl in 10 years, after having lost six AFC Championship Games in the interim.

One Super Bowl tradition lived on. Minnesota lost its fourth Super Bowl in as many attempts. In game XI at Pasadena's Rose Bowl, Stabler and wide receiver Fred Biletnikoff shredded the Vikings' secondary and running back Clarence Davis rushed for 137 yards, part of the Raiders' record 429 yards of total offense en route to a 32-14 victory.

1976

AMERICAN CONFERENCE EASTERN DIVISION							NATIONAL CONFERENCE EASTERN DIVISION						
	W	L	T	Pct.	Pts.	OP		W	L	T	Pct.	Pts.	OP
Baltimore	11	3	0	.786	417	246	Dallas	11	3	0	.786	296	194
New England*	11	3	0	.786	376	236	Washington*	10	4	0	.714	291	217
Miami	6	8	0	.429	263	264	St. Louis	10	4	0	.714	309	267
N.Y. Jets	3	11	0	.214	169	383	Philadelphia	4	10	0	.286	165	286
Buffalo	2	12	0	.143	245	363	N.Y. Giants	3	11	0	.214	170	250
CENTRAL DIVISION							**CENTRAL DIVISION**						
	W	L	T	Pct.	Pts.	OP		W	L	T	Pct.	Pts.	OP
Pittsburgh	10	4	0	.714	342	138	Minnesota	11	2	1	.821	305	176
Cincinnati	10	4	0	.714	335	210	Chicago	7	7	0	.500	253	216
Cleveland	9	5	0	.643	267	287	Detroit	6	8	0	.429	262	220
Houston	5	9	0	.357	222	273	Green Bay	5	9	0	.357	218	299
WESTERN DIVISION							**WESTERN DIVISION**						
	W	L	T	Pct.	Pts.	OP		W	L	T	Pct.	Pts.	OP
Oakland	13	1	0	.929	350	237	Los Angeles	10	3	1	.750	351	190
Denver	9	5	0	.643	315	206	San Francisco	8	6	0	.571	270	190
San Diego	6	8	0	.429	248	285	Atlanta	4	10	0	.286	172	312
Kansas City	5	9	0	.357	290	376	New Orleans	4	10	0	.286	253	346
Tampa Bay	0	14	0	.000	125	412	Seattle	2	12	0	.143	229	429

Wild-Card qualifier for playoffs

Baltimore won division title on the basis of a better division record than New England (7-1 to 6-2). Pittsburgh won division title because of a two-game sweep over Cincinnati. Washington won wild-card berth over St. Louis because of a two-game sweep over Cardinals.
AFC divisional playoffs: OAKLAND 24, New England 21; Pittsburgh 40, BALTIMORE 14
AFC Championship: OAKLAND 24, Pittsburgh 7
NFC divisional playoffs: MINNESOTA 35, Washington 20; Los Angeles 14, DALLAS 12
NFC Championship: MINNESOTA 24, Los Angeles 13
Super Bowl XI: Oakland (AFC) 32, Minnesota (NFC) 14, at Rose Bowl, Pasadena, California

1977

The spoils of Tampa Bay's winless maiden season, such as they were, began (and probably ended) with the first pick in the draft, and the Buccaneers drew mild surprise around the league by taking USC running back Ricky Bell. Mild, because in bypassing Heisman Trophy winner Tony Dorsett of Pittsburgh, Buccaneers coach John McKay was opting for a man he'd known two years earlier while coaching him with the Trojans.

Seattle, meanwhile, had traded its first pick to Dallas, which grabbed Dorsett. Winning the Heisman and being the focal point of the first round, it turned out, were only two-thirds of a pre-NFL triple play for the little speedster, who announced that from then on, when his last name was pronounced, the emphasis would be placed on the second syllable, not the first.

The trend toward a higher-scoring, safer game continued, as rules changes emphasized more freedom for the passing attack and protection from two techniques—the head slap by defensive linemen and clipping by wide receivers, even in the "legal clipping zone." Pass defenders were limited to only one contact with a receiver, bringing bump-and-run coverage a step closer to its knees.

From safety to serenity: The National Football League Players Association and the NFL Management Council ratified a collective bargaining agreement that would extend until mid-1982. Highlights of the agreement: Contributions to the pension plan for the next five years—plus the years 1974, 1975, and 1976— would come to more than $55 million. A player would be vested in the pension plan after four years, down from the previous five. The player limit was set at 43 per club. Minimum salaries were increased, as were paychecks for preseason and postseason play.

Never mind the rules changes designed to open up the passing game, seemed to be the message of running backs O.J. Simpson and Walter Payton. The latter erased the former's single-game rushing record when he went 275 yards against Minnesota on his way to a league-leading 1,852-yard season, third-highest in NFL history. For his part, Simpson, despite a knee injury, became only the second back to gain 10,000 yards in his career, joining Jim Brown.

Minnesota kicker Fred Cox reached a similar

Above: In the twilight at Pasadena's Rose Bowl, Oakland coach John Madden took a victory ride after his team's 32-14 devastation of Minnesota in Super Bowl XI.

Right: Quarterback Jim Plunkett, forced from San Francisco's 7-0 loss to Atlanta with a rib injury, mirrored the day and the 49ers' 1977 season (5-9).

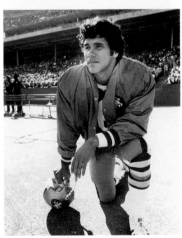

Below: Chicago's Walter Payton broke O.J. Simpson's one-year-old single-game rushing record with 275 yards in the Bears' 10-7 victory over Minnesota.

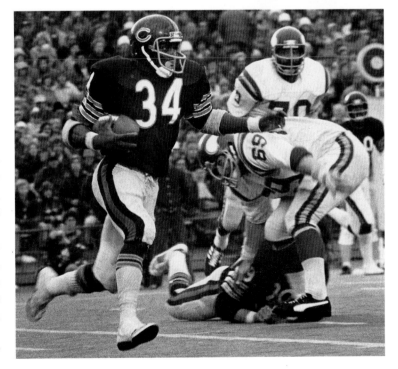

In 1977, Minnesota's Fred Cox kicked his way into second place on the all-time NFL scoring list.

Above: Los Angeles linebacker Jim Youngblood (53) struggled to contain Minnesota's Chuck Foreman during the Mud Bowl playoff game. Right: Tampa Bay made the late Ricky Bell the first choice of the 1977 NFL draft. Bell died in 1984 of a rare muscle disease. Far right: Denver defenders Bernard Jackson and Lyle Alzado (77) combined to stop Oakland's Clarence Davis in the Broncos' 20-17 AFC Championship Game victory over the Raiders.

height, passing Lou Groza to take over second place behind George Blanda on the all-time scoring list. Cox's Vikings won the NFC Central, and, in the first round of the playoffs, improvised in the muddy bottom of the Los Angeles Coliseum. With a December rainstorm inundating southern California, the Vikings—with Bob Lee substituting at quarterback for injured Fran Tarkenton—took advantage of what footing there was in the first quarter and took a 7-0 lead over the Rams. The two teams spun their wheels in the slop for the next 45 minutes, and Minnesota won the Mud Bowl 14-7.

Dallas, having easily dispensed with wild card Chicago, easily dispensed with the Vikings the following week, then went on to easily dispense with Denver in Super Bowl XII, 27-10. The Broncos had arrived at the Superdome in New Orleans on the strength of a defense nicknamed the Orange Crush, led by linebacker Randy Gradishar and defensive end Lyle Alzado. However, the day belonged to Dallas's Flex defense, well-publicized for its complexity and befitting the team that had pioneered and perfected the use of computerized scouting. Defenders Harvey Martin and Randy White represented the unit as they picked up the Super Bowl's first (and still its only) co-most valuable player award.

The Broncos and first-year head coach Robert (Red) Miller had become a regional phenomenon. When the Oakland Raiders came to town, the fans dressed for "Orange Sunday" at Mile High Stadium, where no-shows dare not show their faces after their first offense. The Broncos had entered a new age of competence, just by reaching New Orleans. Their route was littered with conference giants such as Pittsburgh and Oakland, the latter "fresh" from a dramatic double-sudden-death overtime victory

over the Baltimore Colts (see page 132).

No account of the 1977 season, however brief, should end without filling in the fate of Tampa Bay. After extending their 0-14 of 1976 to 0-26, the longest losing streak in NFL history, the Buccaneers met New Orleans at the Superdome on December 11. Scoring three touchdowns on interceptions, they earned the first victory in the history of the franchise, 33-14. After returning to an airport crowd of 8,000, the Buccaneers proved they could win at home, finishing the season with a 17-7 victory over St. Louis.

1977

AMERICAN CONFERENCE EASTERN DIVISION						
	W	L	T	Pct.	Pts.	OP
Baltimore	10	4	0	.714	295	221
Miami	10	4	0	.714	313	197
New England	9	5	0	.643	278	217
N.Y. Jets	3	11	0	.214	191	300
Buffalo	3	11	0	.214	160	313

CENTRAL DIVISION						
	W	L	T	Pct.	Pts.	OP
Pittsburgh	9	5	0	.643	283	243
Houston	8	6	0	.571	299	230
Cincinnati	8	6	0	.571	238	235
Cleveland	6	8	0	.429	269	267

WESTERN DIVISION						
	W	L	T	Pct.	Pts.	OP
Denver	12	2	0	.857	274	148
Oakland*	11	3	0	.786	351	230
San Diego	7	7	0	.500	222	205
Seattle	5	9	0	.357	282	373
Kansas City	2	12	0	.143	225	349

NATIONAL CONFERENCE EASTERN DIVISION						
	W	L	T	Pct.	Pts.	OP
Dallas	12	2	0	.857	345	212
Washington	9	5	0	.643	196	189
St. Louis	7	7	0	.500	272	287
Philadelphia	5	9	0	.357	220	207
N.Y. Giants	5	9	0	.357	181	265

CENTRAL DIVISION						
	W	L	T	Pct.	Pts.	OP
Minnesota	9	5	0	.643	231	227
Chicago*	9	5	0	.643	255	253
Detroit	6	8	0	.429	183	252
Green Bay	4	10	0	.286	134	219
Tampa Bay	2	12	0	.143	103	223

WESTERN DIVISION						
	W	L	T	Pct.	Pts.	OP
Los Angeles	10	4	0	.714	302	146
Atlanta	7	7	0	.500	179	129
San Francisco	5	9	0	.357	220	260
New Orleans	3	11	0	.214	232	336

*Wild-Card qualifier for playoffs

Baltimore won division title on the basis of a better conference record than Miami (9-3 to 8-4). Chicago won a wild-card berth over Washington on the basis of best net points in conference games (plus 48 net points to plus 4).

AFC divisional playoffs: DENVER 34, Pittsburgh 21; Oakland 37, BALTIMORE 31 (sudden-death overtime)
AFC Championship: DENVER 20, Oakland 17
NFC divisional playoffs: DALLAS 37, Chicago 7; Minnesota 14, LOS ANGELES 7
NFC Championship: DALLAS 23, Minnesota 6.
Super Bowl XII: Dallas (NFC) 27, Denver (AFC) 10, at Louisiana Superdome, New Orleans, Louisiana

1978

More bad news for pass defenders: A "bump" zone inhibited them from making contact with receivers beyond a point five yards from the line of scrimmage. For offenses, the green light got greener.

The league added a seventh official, the side judge, to keep an eye on technicalities in the vicinity of scrimmage, such as the new bump rule and liberalized pass-blocking that allowed an offensive lineman to extend his arms. The number of regular-season games was increased from 14 to 16, while preseason games were cut from 6 to 4. A new television contract was worth over $5 million to each club. Another wild-card team was added to the playoff structure, setting up an extra weekend for games between the two wild-card teams in each conference.

Another familiar sight was the revolving door, as nine teams changed head coaches before the season began—one of them twice. The new men: Jack Pardee in Washington, Neill Armstrong in Chicago replacing Pardee, Bud Wilkinson in St. Louis, Sam Rutigliano in

New St. Louis head coach Bud Wilkinson waited until week 9 of the 1978 season for his first victory, 16-10 over Philadelphia. He received the game ball from kicker Jim Bakken.

Left: The 1978 season was a romp for Houston's rookie running back Earl Campbell, as the Heisman Trophy winner from Texas led NFL rushers with 1,450 yards and the Oilers made it to the AFC Championship Game.

Left: George Allen accepted the Los Angeles Rams' head coaching job in 1978, replacing Chuck Knox, then was fired before the season began.

Cleveland, Marv Levy in Kansas City, Dick Nolan in New Orleans, Monte Clark in Detroit, Chuck Knox in Buffalo, and George Allen from Washington to replace Knox in Los Angeles. Allen was fired even before the season began, and Ray Malavasi was named to the position.

Four more teams had new coaches before the end of the season. After four games, Tommy Prothro resigned in San Diego and was replaced by Don Coryell. The next week, Cincinnati replaced Bill Johnson with Homer Rice. A 1-8 record in San Francisco preceded the firing of Pete McCulley, who was followed by Fred O'Connor. And before the season finale, New England's Chuck Fairbanks announced he was resigning to become head coach at Colorado. Although the legal complications continued for several months, Fairbanks was succeeded in the last game by assistants Ron Erhardt and Hank Bullough.

Minnesota's Fran Tarkenton and Rickey Young revised a few passing and receiving categories of the NFL record book. Tarkenton increased his own marks for number of completions and attempts, going 345 for 572. Young set a record for receptions by a running back,

and also led the league with his 88 catches.

Houston had used the first pick in the 1978 draft to take Heisman Trophy-winning halfback Earl Campbell of Texas, and the early dividends included Campbell's leading the Oilers to the AFC Championship Game with the best-ever rookie season for a ball carrier, 1,450 yards.

Oilers quarterback Dan Pastorini, when asked what it felt like to hand off to Campbell, replied, "Comfortable." The feeling must have been in full force on November 20, as Campbell rushed for 199 yards and four touchdowns in a seesaw 35-30 victory over Miami (see page 134). Comfort had its limits, however, as Pastorini suffered rib injuries during the course of the season and had to be fitted with a special device for the playoffs. Wearing the flak jacket of inventor Byron Donzis (whose quality-control tests included swinging a baseball bat into the rib cage of his guinea pig—often Donzis himself), Pastorini completed 20 of 29 passing attempts in a 17-9 AFC wild-card game victory over Miami. The following week, again protected by the vest, he bombed the New England Patriots (12 of 20 for 200 yards and three touchdowns) in a 31-14 victory.

In Dallas's 28-0 NFC Championship Game victory over Los Angeles, Tony Dorsett rushed for 101 yards and put the Cowboys ahead to stay with this five-yard touchdown run in the third quarter.

Right: Minnesota's Rickey Young caught six passes in this game with Detroit, part of his league-leading total of 88, a record for a running back.

Right: Philadelphia kicker Mike Michel's body language said it all, as he missed a 34-yard field-goal attempt with 13 seconds left in the Eagles' 14-13 NFC wild-card loss to Atlanta.

The Oilers were thrashed 34-5 by Pittsburgh in the AFC Championship Game, and that set up the first rematch in Super Bowl history, the Steelers versus the Dallas Cowboys (see page 136). The Cowboys beat Atlanta, a wild-card winner over Philadelphia, then shut out Los Angeles in the opening two rounds. Their rendezvous with the Steelers at Miami's Orange Bowl was enough to engage thousands in "best Super Bowl of all" debates (X versus XIII) well into the next decade, and maybe another.

1978

AMERICAN CONFERENCE EASTERN DIVISION	W	L	T	Pct.	Pts.	OP
New England	11	5	0	.688	358	286
Miami*	11	5	0	.688	372	254
N.Y. Jets	8	8	0	.500	359	364
Buffalo	5	11	0	.313	302	354
Baltimore	5	11	0	.313	239	421
CENTRAL DIVISION	W	L	T	Pct.	Pts.	OP
Pittsburgh	14	2	0	.875	356	195
Houston*	10	6	0	.625	283	298
Cleveland	8	8	0	.500	334	356
Cincinnati	4	12	0	.250	252	284
WESTERN DIVISION	W	L	T	Pct.	Pts.	OP
Denver	10	6	0	.625	282	198
Oakland	9	7	0	.563	311	283
Seattle	9	7	0	.563	345	358
San Diego	9	7	0	.563	355	309
Kansas City	4	12	0	.250	243	327

NATIONAL CONFERENCE EASTERN DIVISION	W	L	T	Pct.	Pts.	OP
Dallas	12	4	0	.750	384	208
Philadelphia*	9	7	0	.563	270	250
Washington	8	8	0	.500	273	283
St. Louis	6	10	0	.375	248	296
N.Y. Giants	6	10	0	.375	264	298
CENTRAL DIVISION	W	L	T	Pct.	Pts.	OP
Minnesota	8	7	1	.531	294	306
Green Bay	8	7	1	.531	249	269
Detroit	7	9	0	.438	290	300
Chicago	7	9	0	.438	253	274
Tampa Bay	5	11	0	.313	241	259
WESTERN DIVISION	W	L	T	Pct.	Pts.	OP
Los Angeles	12	4	0	.750	316	245
Atlanta*	9	7	0	.563	240	290
New Orleans	7	9	0	.438	281	298
San Francisco	2	14	0	.125	219	350

*Wild-Card qualifiers for playoffs
New England won division title on the basis of a better division record than Miami (6-2 to 5-3). Minnesota won division title because of a better head-to-head record against Green Bay (1-0-1).
AFC first-round playoff: Houston 17, MIAMI 9
AFC divisional playoffs: Houston 31, NEW ENGLAND 14; PITTSBURGH 33, Denver 10
AFC Championship: PITTSBURGH 34, Houston 5
NFC first-round playoff: ATLANTA 14, Philadelphia 13
NFC divisional playoffs: DALLAS 27, Atlanta 20; LOS ANGELES 34, Minnesota 10
NFC Championship: Dallas 28, LOS ANGELES 0
Super Bowl XIII: Pittsburgh (AFC) 35, Dallas (NFC) 31, at Orange Bowl, Miami, Florida

1979

Air raid! As an appropriate commemorative of the NFL's sixtieth year, San Diego's Dan Fouts broke Joe Namath's single-season passing yardage record with 4,082 yards. It was the infancy of "Air Coryell," named for head coach Don Coryell, a proponent of Sid Gillman's upfield, or "vertical," passing attitude. Among Fouts's receivers was rookie tight end Kellen Winslow, essentially a wide receiver in San Diego's system before breaking his leg. The Chargers, not incidentally, were on their way to the championship of the AFC West.

If Fouts was telling his people to "go long," San Francisco's Steve DeBerg had people going everywhere. New 49ers coach Bill Walsh, up from a successful term at Stanford, installed a multiple-choice passing scheme that took full advantage of running backs as receivers. DeBerg's 347 completions in 1979 established a single-season record.

Philadelphia wide receiver Harold Carmi-chael set an NFL record for consecutive games with at least one reception, 112.

The retirement of Fran Tarkenton, after 16 years at quarterback for Minnesota and the New York Giants, froze the major career passing records for a while. Tarkenton left the game with lifetime marks for attempts (6,467), completions (3,686), yards (47,003), and touchdown passes (342).

Player safety was the guidepost for rules changes, which prohibited blocking below the waist on kickoffs, punts, and field-goal attempts. The no-crackback zone was extended. Torn or altered equipment was prohibited, as were exposed pads—all hazards. And chalk up another for the passing game: Officials were instructed to whistle a play dead if the quarterback clearly was in the grasp of a defender. (Interpretation of this tricky concept would give officials, players, coaches, announcers,

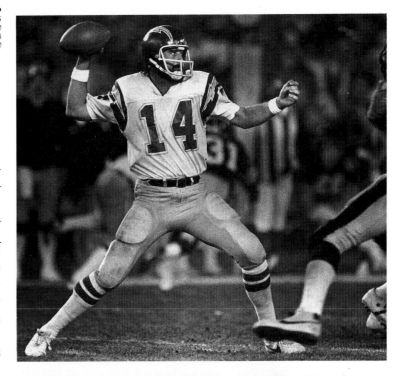

San Diego's Dan Fouts took aim and fired 4,082 yards worth of passes in 1979, setting an NFL single-season record.

His team lost to Cleveland 24-19, but Eagles wide receiver Harold Carmichael (left) caught this pass to set an NFL record for consecutive games with at least one reception, 106.

Bradshaw won his second automobile as the recipient of the game's most valuable player award.

1979

	W	L	T	Pct.	Pts.	OP		W	L	T	Pct.	Pts.	OP
AMERICAN CONFERENCE							**NATIONAL CONFERENCE**						
EASTERN DIVISION							**EASTERN DIVISION**						
Miami	10	6	0	.625	341	257	Dallas	11	5	0	.688	371	313
New England	9	7	0	.563	411	326	Philadelphia*	11	5	0	.688	339	282
N.Y. Jets	8	8	0	.500	337	383	Washington	10	6	0	.625	348	295
Buffalo	7	9	0	.438	268	279	N.Y. Giants	6	10	0	.375	237	323
Baltimore	5	11	0	.313	271	351	St. Louis	5	11	0	.313	307	358
CENTRAL DIVISION							**CENTRAL DIVISION**						
Pittsburgh	12	4	0	.750	416	262	Tampa Bay	10	6	0	.625	273	237
Houston*	11	5	0	.688	362	331	Chicago*	10	6	0	.625	306	249
Cleveland	9	7	0	.563	359	352	Minnesota	7	9	0	.438	259	337
Cincinnati	4	12	0	.250	337	421	Green Bay	5	11	0	.313	246	316
							Detroit	2	14	0	.125	219	365
WESTERN DIVISION							**WESTERN DIVISION**						
San Diego	12	4	0	.750	411	246							
Denver*	10	6	0	.625	289	262	Los Angeles	9	7	0	.563	323	309
Seattle	9	7	0	.563	378	372	New Orleans	8	8	0	.500	370	360
Oakland	9	7	0	.563	365	337	Atlanta	6	10	0	.375*	300	388
Kansas City	7	9	0	.438	238	262	San Francisco	2	14	0	.125	308	416

*Wild-Card qualifier for playoffs

Dallas won division title because of a better conference record than Philadelphia (10-2 to 9-3). Tampa Bay won division title because of a better division record than Chicago (6-2 to 5-3). Chicago won a wild-card berth over Washington on the basis of best net points in all games (plus 57 net points to plus 53).
AFC first-round playoff: HOUSTON 13, Denver 7
AFC divisional playoffs: Houston 17, SAN DIEGO 14; PITTSBURGH 34, Miami 14
AFC Championship: PITTSBURGH 27, Houston 13
NFC first-round playoff: PHILADELPHIA 27, Chicago 17
NFC divisional playoffs: TAMPA BAY 24, Philadelphia 17; Los Angeles 21, DALLAS 19
NFC Championship: Los Angeles 9, TAMPA BAY 0
Super Bowl XIV: Pittsburgh (AFC) 31, Los Angeles (NFC) 19, at Rose Bowl, Pasadena, California

1980

In leading the Cleveland Browns to the AFC Central championship, Brian Sipe set club records for passing yardage and touchdown passes. But it wasn't Sipe's statistical feats that made the Browns the NFL's top entertainers in 1980. There was nothing ordinary, mind you, about Sipe's 30 touchdowns or his 4,132 yards, better than Dan Fouts's all-time single-season record of a year earlier and an NFL record if Fouts himself had not thrown for a staggering 4,715 this time around. (Sipe thus became the third quarterback in NFL history to throw for more than 4,000 yards, joining Joe Namath and Fouts. He finished the season with a league-leading 91.4 passer rating and was named NFL player of the year.)

No, it wasn't Sipe's numbers. It was the way he and the Browns continually chose to wrest victory from their opponents in the closing seconds. For this, coach Sam Rutigliano's club earned the title of Kardiac Kids. Of their 16 games, 13 were decided by seven points or fewer.

Their next-to-last outing of the regular season, however, found the Browns in a role reversal with the Minnesota Vikings. Both clubs needed to win the game to clinch a division championship, and the Vikings did it Browns-style. They scored three times in the

Top: Pittsburgh's Terry Bradshaw (12), the game's most valuable player, performed this midfield pas de deux with running back Franco Harris in the Steelers' 31-19 Super Bowl XIV victory over Los Angeles. Above left: New San Francisco head coach Bill Walsh (right) received post-game congratulations from assistant Mike White after his first NFL victory, 20-15 over Atlanta in week 8 of 1979. Above right: Los Angeles Rams owner Carroll Rosenbloom posed with his wife Georgia. In the spring of 1979, he drowned while swimming at Miami Beach; she became the new owner.

Opposite page: O.J. Simpson ended his 11-year career with a quiet walk to the locker room after the 49ers' season finale at Atlanta.

fans—everybody—their moments in the coming years. "Was he in the grasp or wasn't he? You make the call.")

The Los Angeles Rams, in their final season at the Los Angeles Memorial Coliseum before moving 32 miles south to Anaheim Stadium, won their seventh consecutive NFC West title despite a number of key injuries. Two minutes remained in a divisional playoff game when Vince Ferragamo hit Billy Waddy with a touchdown pass for a 21-19 victory over Dallas. By the time the Rams had defeated Tampa Bay 9-0 for the NFC championship (the Buccaneers had shed their doormat status, going 10-6 to win the NFC Central title), the Pittsburgh Steelers had rolled through the AFC, handily defeating Miami 31-14 and Houston 27-13. The Steelers were in the Super Bowl for the fourth time.

Playing before 103,985 at the Rose Bowl in Pasadena and a record television audience of 35,330,000 homes, Pittsburgh won its fourth Lombardi Trophy, overcoming the Rams' third-quarter 19-17 lead. The go-ahead touchdown was a 73-yard pass from Terry Bradshaw to wide receiver John Stallworth. The Steelers added a grace touchdown for a final count of 31-19.

Above: Chicago's Walter Payton and Houston's Earl Campbell shared a laugh after the Oilers' 10-6 victory over the Bears, the first time the two running backs appeared in the same game. Campbell gained 206 yards rushing; Payton had 60 and caught six passes for 63 more.

last five minutes to win 28-23. As time expired, Minnesota quarterback Tommy Kramer lofted a long pass toward a gathering of Vikings and Browns near the goal line and not far from the sideline. The ball was tipped, then cradled by Vikings wide receiver Ahmad Rashad, who backed into the end zone.

A week later, the Browns became AFC Central champions, defeating Cincinnati 27-24. It was Cleveland's first division championship in nine years. Celebrations were short-lived, however, as the Browns were eliminated in the first round of the AFC playoffs.

Trailing the Oakland Raiders 14-12 on a frozen field in Cleveland, the Browns appeared to be rehearsing for the Super Bowl from their familiar script when Raiders safety Mike Davis stepped in front of Ozzie Newsome in the end zone and intercepted Sipe's third-down pass, thrown with enough time for another play and

the ball on the Oakland 13. "I should have thrown it into Lake Erie," Sipe said.

The Raiders won a 34-27 roller coaster of a game against San Diego a week later to take the AFC title, becoming the second wild-card team to reach the Super Bowl. They became the first wild-card team to win it, defeating head coach Dick Vermeil's rejuvenated Philadelphia Eagles 27-10 at the Louisiana Superdome, mostly due to the passing of Jim Plunkett. The former Heisman Trophy winner, written off by New England and later San Francisco in the 1970s, was named the game's most valuable player. Raiders linebacker Rod Martin intercepted three passes from Eagles quarterback Ron Jaworski, providing counterpoint to Plunkett's three touchdown passes.

Vermeil was a minor media phenomenon, having gained a certain measure of notoriety for a work ethic that included spending the night in his office and one time falling asleep at the wheel of his car in the early morning after having pulled into his driveway.

The Eagles got to New Orleans by taking advantage of eight Minnesota turnovers ("We had twenty-six in the regular season," said Vikings head coach Bud Grant, "so the law of averages had to catch up with us.") for a 31-16 first-round victory, then grinding out 263 rushing yards to defeat Dallas 20-7 in the NFC Championship Game.

Of the 224 NFL games played during the 1980 season, one deserves mention for its special place in league history. On December 12, the San Francisco 49ers staged the greatest second-half comeback ever. After trailing the New Orleans Saints 35-7 at intermission, the 49ers came back with four touchdowns and a field goal to win 38-35. By season's end, San Francisco rookie running back Earl Cooper led the NFC in receptions with 83, and behind him was San Francisco wide receiver Dwight Clark with 82. Were the 49ers sending the league a message?

Pittsburgh defensive tackle Joe Greene scored an off-the-field hit in 1981 with his memorable commercial for Coca-Cola.

1980

AMERICAN CONFERENCE
EASTERN DIVISION

	W	L	T	Pct.	Pts.	OP
Buffalo	11	5	0	.688	320	260
New England	10	6	0	.625	441	325
Miami	8	8	0	.500	266	305
Baltimore	7	9	0	.438	355	387
N.Y. Jets	4	12	0	.250	302	395

CENTRAL DIVISION

	W	L	T	Pct.	Pts.	OP
Cleveland	11	5	0	.688	357	310
Houston*	11	5	0	.688	295	251
Pittsburgh	9	7	0	.563	352	313
Cincinnati	6	10	0	.375	244	312

WESTERN DIVISION

	W	L	T	Pct.	Pts.	OP
San Diego	11	5	0	.688	418	327
Oakland*	11	5	0	.688	364	306
Kansas City	8	8	0	.500	319	336
Denver	8	8	0	.500	310	323
Seattle	4	12	0	.250	291	408

NATIONAL CONFERENCE
EASTERN DIVISION

	W	L	T	Pct.	Pts.	OP
Philadelphia	12	4	0	.750	384	222
Dallas*	12	4	0	.750	454	311
Washington	6	10	0	.375	261	293
St. Louis	5	11	0	.313	299	350
N.Y. Giants	4	12	0	.250	249	425

CENTRAL DIVISION

	W	L	T	Pct.	Pts.	OP
Minnesota	9	7	0	.563	317	308
Detroit	9	7	0	.563	334	272
Chicago	7	9	0	.438	304	264
Tampa Bay	5	10	1	.344	271	341
Green Bay	5	10	1	.344	231	371

WESTERN DIVISION

	W	L	T	Pct.	Pts.	OP
Atlanta	12	4	0	.750	405	272
Los Angeles*	11	5	0	.688	424	289
San Francisco	6	10	0	.375	320	415
New Orleans	1	15	0	.063	291	487

Wild-Card qualifiers for playoffs

Philadelphia won division title over Dallas on the basis of best net points in division games (plus 84 net points to plus 50). Minnesota won division title because of a better conference record than Detroit (8-4 to 9-5). Cleveland won division title because of a better conference record than Houston (8-4 to 7-5). San Diego won division title over Oakland on the basis of best net points in division games (plus 60 net points to plus 37).
AFC first-round playoff: OAKLAND 27, Houston 7
AFC divisional playoffs: SAN DIEGO 20, Buffalo 14; Oakland 14, CLEVELAND 12
AFC Championship: Oakland 34, SAN DIEGO 27
NFC first-round playoff: DALLAS 34, Los Angeles 13
NFC divisional playoffs: PHILADELPHIA 31, Minnesota 16; Dallas 30, ATLANTA 27
NFC Championship: PHILADELPHIA 20, Dallas 7
Super Bowl XV: Oakland (AFC) 27, Philadelphia (NFC) 10, at Louisiana Superdome, New Orleans, Louisiana

1981

Want to take a stab at naming the play of the year? Was it Jack (Hacksaw) Reynolds's tackling Cincinnati fullback Pete Johnson at the 1-foot line on fourth down, the finale of San Francisco's storied goal-line stand in its Super Bowl XVI victory? Or maybe Dan Bunz's tackling running back Charles Alexander at the 1-yard line on the previous down? Or maybe

the flea-flicker from Don Strock to Duriel Harris to Tony Nathan that brought Miami to within reach 24-17 after trailing 24-0 earlier in its classic overtime struggle against San Diego in an AFC Divisional Playoff Game (see page 140)?

Keep nominating. . . but don't leave out Joe Greene's pass completion to a small boy in a dimly lit tunnel. The image of Greene tossing his number 75 Pittsburgh Steelers jersey to the near-speechless kid, which served as the visual tag line to a commercial for Coca-Cola, impressed viewers so strongly that three years later, when a company called Video Storyboard Tests published the results of its annual survey of outstanding TV commercials in *Adweek* magazine, it turned out that viewers identified the spot as the best commercial they had seen in the past *four weeks*.

It wasn't as if the NFL needed a survey to know that its star players had reached a high level of identifiability. When Joe Namath modeled his legs in a pantyhose commercial during the early 1970s, the advertisers had a hit on their hands. Ditto Lite Beer from Miller, "everything you ever wanted in a beer. . . and less," the ideal vehicle for such NFL notables as Dick Butkus, Bubba Smith, John Madden, Bert Jones, and L.C. Greenwood.

Now, what about the 49ers? In a year noted for competitive oddities—such as Oakland's 7-9 fourth-place showing in the AFC West, a mark that included three straight shutout losses—coach Bill Walsh's San Francisco club went 13-3. After brushing aside the New York Giants in the opening round of the playoffs, the 49ers met Dallas at Candlestick Park for the NFC championship. Nine years after "Black Saturday" (see pages 120 and 122), the 49ers repaid the Cowboys in kind (see page 142). Add Joe Montana's six-yard touchdown pass to

Right: John Jefferson, traded by San Diego to Green Bay after a contract dispute, made his first appearance as a Packer and caught seven passes for 121 yards in a 30-13 loss to Minnesota.

Left: Cincinnati's Ken Anderson kept the Bengals warm in the record-cold 1981 AFC Championship Game, completing 14 of 22 passes for 161 yards and two touchdowns as the Bengals beat San Diego.

Dwight Clark with 51 seconds remaining to the list of 1981's most memorable plays.

In Super Bowl XVI, the 49ers met Cincinnati, whose "home-field advantage" in the AFC Championship Game had been a record-setting (for both the city of Cincinnati and the NFL) wind-chill factor of minus-59 degrees. It's a good bet no team ever will approach the one-week 130-degree turnaround San Diego experienced between Miami and Cincinnati. On the Chargers' team bus traveling to Riverfront Stadium on game day, head coach Don Coryell jumped up and, pointing to ominous clouds of steam rising from the Ohio River, exhorted his players. "See? See?" he said. "It's not that cold out there." At the time, nobody had the courage to explain the phenomenon: The air temperature was well below the water temperature. The Chargers froze and lost 27-7.

Sometime during the aftermath, it must have

Below left: Washington general manager Bobby Beathard (left) congratulates Redskins coach Joe Gibbs after Gibbs's first victory, 24-7 over Chicago in week 6 of 1981. Below right: Fans in Cleveland offered "Ain'ts" headgear to their New Orleans counterparts, who had initiated the gimmick.

been mentioned, as weak consolation, that Chargers quarterback Dan Fouts had broken his own passing records for a second straight year. Fouts's totals: 609 attempts, 360 completions, and 4,802 yards.

Super Bowl XVI took place indoors, in comfortable Pontiac Silverdome. The salient statistics of the day were Cincinnati quarterback Ken Anderson's Super Bowl-record 25 completions and his teammate Dan Ross's record 11 receptions. But the winning numbers belonged to San Francisco quarterback Montana, honored as the game's most valuable player (14 completions in 22 attempts for 157 yards and one touchdown), and Ray Wersching (a record-tying four field goals and effective squib kickoffs). Numbers aside, major credit for the 49ers' 26-21 victory went to the San Francisco defense.

Just as the 49ers had prefaced their championship year with a proliferation of passing in 1980, the Washington Redskins used 1981 as a stepping stone to something greater. Under new head coach Joe Gibbs, the team began the 1981 season by dropping its first five games. During the week prior to the sixth game, quarterback Joe Theismann, who had drawn criticism for paying too much attention to his restaurant, radio program, and other off-the-field interests, paid an impromptu late-evening visit to a nearby neighbor—Gibbs.

"I just walked up to his house at eleven o'clock at night and knocked on his door," Theismann told Michael Madden in an interview for *PRO!* magazine. "I told him, 'Coach, I think it's time you and I sat down and talked because something's not right, and I'd like to talk to you about it.' I wanted to clarify for him that football was the most important thing in my life."

The following Sunday, the Redskins beat Chicago 24-7. Washington won seven of its re-

maining 10 games, finishing the season at 8-8. Theismann had the second-highest single-season passing yardage total (3,568) in Washington history. He and the Redskins were ready for 1982.

1981

AMERICAN CONFERENCE							**NATIONAL CONFERENCE**					
EASTERN DIVISION							**EASTERN DIVISION**					
	W	L	T	Pct.	Pts.	OP		W	L	T	Pct.	Pts.	OP

	W	L	T	Pct.	Pts.	OP		W	L	T	Pct.	Pts.	OP
Miami	11	4	1	.719	345	275	Dallas	12	4	0	.750	367	277
N.Y. Jets*	10	5	1	.656	355	287	Philadelphia*	10	6	0	.625	368	221
Buffalo*	10	6	0	.625	311	276	N.Y. Giants*	9	7	0	.563	295	257
Baltimore	2	14	0	.125	259	533	Washington	8	8	0	.500	347	349
New England	2	14	0	.125	322	370	St. Louis	7	9	0	.438	315	408
CENTRAL DIVISION							**CENTRAL DIVISION**					
Cincinnati	12	4	0	.750	421	304	Tampa Bay	9	7	0	.563	315	268
Pittsburgh	8	8	0	.500	356	297	Detroit	8	8	0	.500	397	322
Houston	7	9	0	.438	281	355	Green Bay	8	8	0	.500	324	361
Cleveland	5	11	0	.313	276	375	Minnesota	7	9	0	.438	325	369
							Chicago	6	10	0	.375	253	324
WESTERN DIVISION							**WESTERN DIVISION**					
San Diego	10	6	0	.625	478	390	San Francisco	13	3	0	.813	357	250
Denver	10	6	0	.625	321	289	Atlanta	7	9	0	.438	426	355
Kansas City	9	7	0	.563	343	290	Los Angeles	6	10	0	.375	303	351
Oakland	7	9	0	.438	273	343	New Orleans	4	12	0	.250	207	378
Seattle	6	10	0	.375	322	388							

*Wild-Card qualifiers for playoffs
San Diego won AFC Western title over Denver on the basis of a better division record (6-2 to 5-3). Buffalo won a Wild-Card playoff berth over Denver as the result of a 9-7 victory in head-to-head competition.
AFC first-round playoff: Buffalo 31, NEW YORK JETS 27
AFC divisional playoffs: San Diego 41, MIAMI 38 (sudden-death overtime); CINCINNATI 28, Buffalo 21
AFC Championship: CINCINNATI 27, San Diego 7
NFC first-round playoff: New York Giants 27, PHILADELPHIA 21
NFC divisional playoffs: DALLAS 38, Tampa Bay 0; SAN FRANCISCO 38, New York Giants 24
NFC Championship: SAN FRANCISCO 28, Dallas 27
Super Bowl XVI: San Francisco (NFC) 26, Cincinnati (AFC) 21, at Silverdome, Pontiac, Michigan

1982

My *Favorite Year* was the title of a 1982 movie. The movie was not about anyone connected with the NFL.

On May 11, a new pro football league—the United States Football League—was formed and announced it would play in the springtime starting in 1983.

After two games of the NFL's regular season had been played, a 57-day players strike began on September 22, gouging the schedule with a seven-week void whose impact would reverberate in the coming years. Suddenly, television

viewers no longer had the Oilers versus the Saints on Sunday afternoon.

The expiration, on July 15, of the NFL Players Association's contract with the league, came amid well-publicized but little-understood NFLPA demands that the players as a group receive 55 percent of the 28 clubs' gross revenues. By the time the strike was settled, that figure virtually had disappeared from all discussions and had dissolved into agreements on such items as higher salaries and a first-ever severance pay plan for professional sports.

The strike interrupted the first year in Los Angeles for the Raiders, who had defied an NFL rule that forbids moving a franchise without the approval of three-fourths of the clubs.

When post-strike play resumed on November 21, the idea of divisions was temporarily suspended. Instead, playoff bids for a special post-season tournament would go to the top eight teams in the two 14-team conferences. It was agreed that an extra week would be added to the remaining schedule, so that each team would total nine games.

Even with the hiatus, the short season presented pro football with a fair supply of exciting new talent. Kenneth Sims, a 270-pound All-America defensive end from the University of Texas, was the number-one choice in the draft and went to the New England Patriots. Further into the first round, and further than the Los Angeles Raiders expected, USC's Heisman Trophy-winning tailback Marcus Allen still was available. They took him as the tenth pick overall in the draft, and he led the league in touchdowns (14) and points scored (84), finishing fourth in the overall rushing statistics with 697 yards. Versatility, however, was his main value. He also caught 38 passes for 401 yards and three touchdowns. The Raiders' 8-1 record was the American Football Conference's best,

San Francisco linebacker Dan Bunz (57) stops Cincinnati's Charles Alexander at the 49ers' 1-yard line, part of a brilliant goal-line stand that arrested the Bengals' comeback attempt in the third quarter of Super Bowl XVI.

A lonely father and son sat out a post-strike NFL game in 1982, silent testimony to fans' disenchantment with the players' strike that interrupted the season for 57 days, the longest labor dispute in American professional sports. The sign in the foreground alluded to NFL Players Association director Ed Garvey.

and the rookie got his share of the credit.

The Raiders played their first two games on the road, so Los Angeles fans, impatient by nature, were forced to wait more than two months for a look at what they were getting. When it arrived, it looked the same as it had in Oakland. It was Raiders football, all right, Raiders versus Chargers, packaged expressly for a Monday night football presentation from a half-full Los Angeles Memorial Coliseum. San Diego broke on top 24-0, but the Raiders managed a fumble recovery and a quick touchdown just before halftime. Two short touchdown runs by Allen and a clincher by running back Frank Hawkins from one yard out gave the Raiders a 28-24 victory, credibility in L.A., and incredibility in the all-time Monday night standings, which they now led by a mile at 19-2-1.

All San Diego could dredge from the loss was a fact for its 1983 press guide: By passing for 357 yards, Fouts drew even with Johnny Unitas for the all-time career leadership in 300-yard games.

Any strike year worth its anguish is going to need some high-quality comic relief. So turn the calendar to December 12. The scene was snow-covered Schaefer (now known as Sulli-

van) Stadium, home of the Patriots, hosts that afternoon to Miami. In attendance, waiting on the sideline at the wheel of a John Deere 314 tractor, was Mark Henderson, on a one-day work-release leave from Norfolk State Prison. Before the game began, Henderson had helped clear away a layer of snow to make the field halfway playable.

With 4:45 left in a scoreless tie, Patriots placekicker John Smith lined up to try a 33-yard field goal. As New England coach Ron Meyer watched Smith and holder Matt Cavanaugh clearing snow from the kicking area, inspiration struck.

"I looked out on the field," Meyer said, "and I saw John chipping away at the ground, and I thought, 'Let's get the sweeper out there. There's a guy on the sideline who can help us.' "

Henderson did help. Smith hit the field goal. The Patriots won 3-0.

"We told the officials, 'Hey, what's this guy doing?' said Dolphins nose tackle Bob Baumhower. "They said it was perfectly legal."

A month later, it was perfectly academic, as the Dolphins welcomed the Patriots to round one of the AFC playoffs at the Orange Bowl.

Along the sideline, in one corner of the field, someone had piled man-made snow. Next to it was parked a John Deere 314 tractor. The Dolphins, behind a 16-for-19, 246-yard passing performance by David Woodley, eliminated the Patriots 28-13.

A game the day before the snow-plow incident, a continent away and maybe in another galaxy, matched San Diego with San Francisco at Candlestick Park. The Chargers defeated the 49ers 41-37, but if ever a game's drama outweighed its final score, here was that game. San Francisco quarterback Joe Montana dueled with Dan Fouts, and the volley produced an NFL-record 65 complete passes (Montana was 32 for 47 for 366 yards with three touchdowns, Fouts 33 for 48 for 444 yards, the third 400-yard performance of his career, with five touchdowns).

The game was tied twice and had four lead changes, the last coming when Fouts fired the three-yard game-winner to running back Chuck Muncie with 3:22 remaining.

The statistical banquet went on. The combined total yardage came to 1,009. The Chargers' three starting receivers—Wes Chandler, Charlie Joiner, and Kellen Winslow—each had at least 100 yards.

The 16-team postseason festival got underway, and the first great drama came in the second round of the AFC playoffs. A crowd of 90,688 packed the Los Angeles Coliseum for what was billed as a "matchup" between Marcus Allen and New York Jets running back Freeman McNeil, the former UCLA star and the league's leading rusher with 786 yards. McNeil won that "battle," outgaining Allen 105-36, but two interceptions by Jets linebacker Lance Mehl in the final two minutes were the game's focal plays, and the Jets won 17-14.

A week later, interceptions knocked the Jets out of the Super Bowl XVII picture, as Miami's "Killer B's" defense, so-called for its abundance of "B" surnames, got a lift from a "D," linebacker A.J. Duhe. In the mud at the Orange Bowl, Duhe intercepted three passes by Richard Todd, returning the third 35 yards for a touchdown, as the Dolphins won 14-0.

Meanwhile, the Washington Redskins—replete with a catalog of group nicknames of their own, such as the Hogs (their enormous offensive line), the Fun Bunch, and a group of receivers so small they were called Smurfs, after the popular kids' toy miniatures—laid waste to NFC postseason foes Detroit (31-7), Minnesota

Above left: Former Bears tight end Mike Ditka took over the Chicago head coaching job in 1982. Above right: Coveted linebacker Tom Cousineau joined the Browns after three years in the Canadian League. Left: San Diego's Wes Chandler beat San Francisco's Eric Wright for one of his two touchdowns in the Chargers' wild 41-37 victory at Candlestick Park.

New England's Matt Cavanaugh (12) warmed his hands and waited for a snowplow to clear the artificial turf at Schaefer Stadium, in preparation for John Smith's game-winning field goal against Miami in 1982.

(21-7), and longtime rival Dallas (31-17).

At the end of January, the Redskins defeated the Dolphins 27-17 at the Rose Bowl in Pasadena, California. Redskins fullback John Riggins, whose four-game postseason rushing yardage, 610, looked odd next to his 553 for the regular season, rushed for a Super Bowl-record 166 yards, including a 43-yard touchdown run, and was named the game's most valuable player. "On game days," said Gibbs, "John tells us, 'Hey, just get the wagon out, hitch it up, and I'll pull it. Everybody get on.' "

Had there been an award for most valuable

Near right: Washington's John Riggins began his 1982 post-season tear with a 119-yard performance in the Redskins' 31-7 first-round playoff victory over Detroit.

Far right: A crowd of 90,688 jammed the Los Angeles Memorial Coliseum for the Raiders' second-round playoff game with the Jets. New York won 17-14.

The Redskins kept their locomotive, Riggins, running all the way to a 27-17 victory over Miami in Super Bowl XVII, topped off by the fullback's record 43-yard touchdown run, part of another record: 166 yards rushing for the day.

1982

AMERICAN CONFERENCE	W	L	T	Pct.	Pts.	OP		NATIONAL CONFERENCE	W	L	T	Pct.	Pts.	OP
L.A. Raiders	8	1	0	.889	260	200		Washington	8	1	0	.889	190	128
Miami	7	2	0	.778	198	131		Dallas	6	3	0	.667	226	145
Cincinnati	7	2	0	.778	232	177		Green Bay	5	3	1	.611	226	169
Pittsburgh	6	3	0	.667	204	146		Minnesota	5	4	0	.556	187	198
San Diego	6	3	0	.667	288	221		Atlanta	5	4	0	.556	183	199
N.Y. Jets	6	3	0	.667	245	166		St. Louis	5	4	0	.556	135	170
New England	5	4	0	.556	143	157		Tampa Bay	5	4	0	.556	158	178
Cleveland	4	5	0	.444	140	182		Detroit	4	5	0	.444	181	176
Buffalo	4	5	0	.444	150	154		New Orleans	4	5	0	.444	129	160
Seattle	4	5	0	.444	127	147		N.Y. Giants	4	5	0	.444	164	160
Kansas City	3	6	0	.333	176	184		San Francisco	3	6	0	.333	209	206
Denver	2	7	0	.222	148	226		Chicago	3	6	0	.333	141	174
Houston	1	8	0	.111	136	245		Philadelphia	3	6	0	.333	191	195
Baltimore	0	8	1	.056	113	236		L.A. Rams	2	7	0	.222	200	250

As the result of a 57-day players' strike, the 1982 NFL regular-season schedule was reduced from 16 weeks to 9. At the conclusion of the regular season, the NFL conducted a 16-team postseason Super Bowl Tournament. Eight teams from each conference were seeded 1-8 based on their records during the season.

Miami finished ahead of Cincinnati based on better conference record (6-1 to 6-2). Pittsburgh won common games tie-breaker with San Diego (3-1 to 2-1) after Jets were eliminated from three-way tie based on conference record (Pittsburgh and San Diego 5-3 vs. Jets 2-3). Cleveland finished ahead of Buffalo and Seattle based on better conference record (4-3 to 3-5). Minnesota (4-1), Atlanta (4-3), St. Louis (5-4), Tampa Bay (3-3) seeds were determined by best won-lost record in conference games. Detroit finished ahead of New Orleans and the New York Giants based on better conference record (4-4 to 3-5 to 3-5).

AFC first round playoff:	MIAMI 28, New England 13
	LOS ANGELES RAIDERS 27, Cleveland 10
	New York Jets 44, CINCINNATI 17
	San Diego 31, PITTSBURGH 28
AFC second round playoff:	New York Jets 17, LOS ANGELES RAIDERS 14
	MIAMI 34, San Diego 13
AFC Championship:	MIAMI 14, New York Jets 0
NFC first round playoff:	WASHINGTON 31, Detroit 7
	GREEN BAY 41, St. Louis 16
	MINNESOTA 30, Atlanta 24
	DALLAS 30, Tampa Bay 17
NFC second round playoff:	WASHINGTON 21, Minnesota 7
	DALLAS 37, Green Bay 26
NFC Championship:	WASHINGTON 31, Dallas 17
Super Bowl XVII:	Washington (NFC) 27, Miami (AFC) 17 at Rose Bowl, Pasadena, California

Home teams in playoff games are indicated by capital letters.

play, Joe Theismann would have been the automatic recipient. Noted more for his passing arm, Theismann made a move late in the third quarter that at least qualified as an act of defensive ingenuity, if not valor. With the Redskins trailing 17-13, Theismann's short passing attempt from near his own end zone was batted in the air by Miami's Kim Bokamper. As Bokamper tried to control the ball for an interception that would have given him a clear touchdown, Theismann lunged, got a hand in, and knocked the ball away.

"Very few quarterbacks have the ability or the courage to make that play," Dolphins coach Don Shula said.

Theismann's recollection: "I said, 'Oh, my God.' Then I went for him. . . . I didn't think, I just went. It was the biggest play I made all day."

1983

With the prospect of a full season facing them, NFL-watchers focused on youth. They focused too much, perhaps, on one particular youth. Too much, because after the merry-go-round stopped spinning for John Elway, there was no way he'd be living up to all the expectations heaped on his rookie shoulders.

The Baltimore Colts had the first pick in the draft and made the Stanford quarterback the number-one choice. But Elway had been insisting that he would play only on the West Coast. He even went so far as to sign with the New York Yankees, and he played a season with their Oneonta, New York, farm club.

Shortly after draft day, the Colts turned Denver into a West Coast city, trading Elway to the Broncos for several draft choices and another first-rounder, offensive lineman Chris Hinton of Northwestern. Irony of the year: Elway completed 47.5 percent of his passes for a middling 1,663 yards, tasting only a playoff *hors d'oeuvre* as the Broncos got no further than a loss to Seattle in the AFC Wild Gard Game. Hinton, meanwhile, fit perfectly at left guard for the Colts and finished the season as a starter on the AFC Pro Bowl squad.

The first weekend of October, 1983, held a portent of Super Bowl XVIII. In the regular season's fifth week, the Los Angeles Raiders and Washington Redskins hammered away at each other for a full 60 minutes at RFK Stadium. The outcome, 37-35 Redskins (see page 144), merely whetted the Raiders' appetite for a rematch. There was only one way that could happen this season. . . and the time would come.

Elwaymania in Denver—local television stations set up command posts at the Broncos' training camp—may have blotted out other outstanding newcomers on the NFL landscape, but not for long. Each conference had a rookie running back to ogle. In Los Angeles of the NFC, it was the Rams' Eric Dickerson, chopping into opposing secondaries with his high knees, sprinter's acceleration, and 220 pounds on a 6-foot 3-inch frame. Dickerson led the league in rushing with 1,808 yards, an NFL rookie record.

Next in the overall NFL rushing statistics, but no less valuable to his team, was Seattle's Curt Warner, who amplified new head coach Chuck Knox's tendency to build his offense around the running game. Warner led the AFC with 1,449 yards, running with a see-you-later pivot reminiscent of Hugh McElhenny's swerving forays in the 1950s.

Knox had answered Seattle's call earlier in the year, when the Seahawks were looking to replace Mike McCormack (who replaced Jack Patera), and Knox was having contractual problems in Buffalo. His "Ground Chuck" recipe became the Seahawks' main course, supplemented by the new leadership of quarterback Dave Krieg (who replaced veteran Jim Zorn at midseason) and a defense that hit with second-year safety Kenny Easley, a Pro Bowler seemingly from birth. The payoff, in the end, was a trip to the AFC Championship Game.

Seattle gave life to another NFL phenomenon, an activity that soon reached sporting crowds everywhere: The Wave. This new way of getting excited—a vertically shaped undulation of fans standing up, section by section, around and around the stadium—had come over from the University of Washington. No

matter. The masses loved it. By 1984, there would be the Triple Wave, the Opposite-Directions Wave, the Silent Wave. . . .

Before round one of the 1983 draft ended, teams had selected no fewer than six quarterbacks. The last of these, and the twenty-seventh man chosen, was University of Pittsburgh quarterback Dan Marino. The Miami Dolphins chose him, and by the end of the 1983 season a lot of clubs wished they'd been as perceptive. Marino's 96.0 passer rating, boosted mainly by a touchdown-passes-to-interceptions ratio of 20-6, led the AFC. The AFC made the rookie quarterback its Pro Bowl starter, although Marino eventually had to forgo the all-star game on account of an ankle injury. What really mattered was that the Dolphins had an offensive mainspring.

New York Jets defensive end Mark Gastineau brought about the beginning of the end for a re-

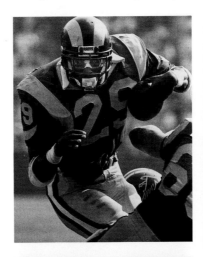
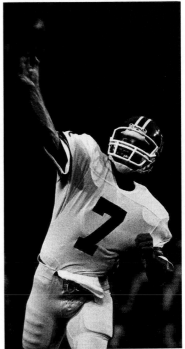

Top left: Los Angeles Rams running back Eric Dickerson set a rookie rushing record in 1983, leading the NFL with 1,808 yards. Top right: Prized rookie quarterback John Elway wound up in Denver after an East Coast-Almost-to-West-Coast shuffle. Bottom left: Miami's Dan Marino turned out to be 1983's rookie sensation. Bottom right: Seattle's Curt Warner was runner-up to Dickerson in the NFL rushing race, leading the AFC with 1,449 yards.

cent NFL trend: well-rehearsed rubbing it in. Choreographed celebrations had become fashionable among designated groups of players, e.g. the Washington Redskins' "Fun Bunch," which, after one of its members (mostly receivers) scored a touchdown, would form a circle in the end zone, count to three, leap up, and touch hands.

Mark Gastineau was a major contributor to this genre, having developed over the past couple of years something called the "Sack Dance," a frenzied me-Tarzan breast-beating, air-punching rampage that lasted a good five or

Right: Mark Moseley's 25-yard field goal with 43 seconds left gave Washington a 24-21 victory over San Francisco in the NFC Championship Game.
Below: Los Angeles Raiders linebacker Jack Squirek intercepted Joe Theismann's pass with 12 seconds left in the first half of Super Bowl XVIII and scored to give the Raiders a 21-3 lead; they won 38-9.

ten seconds after any of Gastineau's quarterback sacks. Fans at Shea Stadium got a big kick out of it. Fans elsewhere showered Gastineau with abuse.

By the time the 1984 season began, rules makers had added "excessive or premeditated celebration by individual players or groups of players" to the list of misdemeanors.

Seattle and the Los Angeles Rams won the AFC and NFC Wild Card Games, the former a 31-7 rout of Denver, the latter a mild 24-17 upset of Dallas. Seattle scored a major upset the following week, knocking over Miami 27-20. The Rams, meanwhile, faced reality in the form of a 51-7 loss at Washington.

Round one of the NFC bracket gave San Francisco fits. The 49ers survived Detroit's 14-point binge in the fourth quarter, then danced in disbelief as Lions kicker Eddie Murray barely missed a 43-yard field-goal attempt with 11 seconds remaining. San Francisco 24, Detroit 23.

The 49ers were eliminated by a field goal in the NFC Championship Game, as Washington's Mark Moseley kicked a 25-yarder with 40 seconds left to give the Redskins a 24-21 victory and a chance at a second straight Super Bowl championship. The Redskins had taken a 21-0 lead into the fourth quarter, but, in a span of slightly more than seven minutes, 49ers quarterback Joe Montana threw three touchdown passes to draw San Francisco even.

The drive toward Moseley's kick was aided by a pair of controversial plays: a pass interference call against 49ers cornerback Eric Wright

and a holding penalty against San Francisco's other cornerback, Ronnie Lott.

Meanwhile, the Los Angeles Raiders were rolling comfortably toward Tampa and Super Bowl XVIII with victories over Pittsburgh (38-10) in the first round of the playoffs and Seattle (30-14) for the AFC title. The Seahawks game, played in Los Angeles, attracted a playoff-record crowd of 92,335. Does the Raiders' 38-9 rout of the Redskins on the NFL's ultimate Sunday call for broad documentation? Some pertinent facts, and one pertinent name, will do: Marcus Allen's record 191 yards rushing, his escape from a *cul-de-sac* for a record 74-yard touchdown run, and his most-valuable-player award.

John Riggins's anticipated rushing rampage flopped as the Raiders' defensive front penned the Hogs, and Joe Theismann had a tough time locating many open Smurfs.

"We attacked the Hogs and made sure there weren't any running lanes open for Riggins," said Raiders linebacker Rod Martin.

When Raiders managing general partner Al Davis stepped to the CBS microphone to accept the Lombardi Trophy from Commissioner Pete Rozelle, Davis said his thank you, then revealed the full text of his pregame locker room talk:

"Just win, baby."

The year had a midseason epilogue, a hitch in time, a note that doesn't fit a breezy run-through of anecdotes and results. On October 31, George Halas, the last surviving founder of the NFL, died at 88. Player, coach, and owner of the Chicago Bears, "Papa Bear" was the league's patriarch. As Mickey Herskowitz wrote in *PRO!* magazine, "George Halas was chairman of the board, a millionaire, a man who earned everything he got. He was the last of the pioneers. He helped deliver pro football from the sandlots to the super stadiums. His contributions to the sport are beyond measure."

1984

The mark of any NFL season usually is an amalgam of statistics, off-the-field developments, and individual milestones. Once those have identified themselves, time goes to work on the weaker ones. NFL years wear names. Fast forward, from the Green Bay-Lombardi 1960s. . . . 1968: Namath. 1970: Merger. 1972: Dolphins. 1973: O.J. 1974: Steelers. 1975: Steelers. 1978: Steelers. 1979: Steelers. 1982: Strike.

Then came 1984.

The 61,000-seat Hoosier Dome became the new home of the Colts, who moved from Baltimore to Indianapolis in April, 1984.

Dallas opened its twenty-fifth season in the midst of a see-saw quarterback controversy. Intending to introduce Gary Hogeboom (14) as his choice over Danny White, coach Tom Landry mistakenly said the new quarterback "will be [Phil] Pozderac." Pozderac (75) did appear at left tackle in the club's opening night 20-13 victory over the Rams.

1983

AMERICAN CONFERENCE EASTERN DIVISION	W	L	T	Pct.	Pts.	OP
Miami	12	4	0	.750	389	250
New England	8	8	0	.500	274	289
Buffalo	8	8	0	.500	283	351
Baltimore	7	9	0	.438	264	354
N.Y. Jets	7	9	0	.438	313	331

CENTRAL DIVISION	W	L	T	Pct.	Pts.	OP
Pittsburgh	10	6	0	.625	355	303
Cleveland	9	7	0	.563	356	342
Cincinnati	7	9	0	.438	346	302
Houston	2	14	0	.125	288	460

WESTERN DIVISION	W	L	T	Pct.	Pts.	OP
L.A. Raiders	12	4	0	.750	442	338
Seattle*	9	7	0	.563	403	397
Denver*	9	7	0	.563	302	327
San Diego	6	10	0	.375	358	462
Kansas City	6	10	0	.375	386	367

NATIONAL CONFERENCE EASTERN DIVISION	W	L	T	Pct.	Pts.	OP
Washington	14	2	0	.875	541	332
Dallas*	12	4	0	.750	479	360
St. Louis	8	7	1	.531	374	428
Philadelphia	5	11	0	.313	233	322
N.Y. Giants	3	12	1	.219	267	347

CENTRAL DIVISION	W	L	T	Pct.	Pts.	OP
Detroit	9	7	0	.563	347	286
Green Bay	8	8	0	.500	429	439
Chicago	8	8	0	.500	311	301
Minnesota	8	8	0	.500	316	348
Tampa Bay	2	14	0	.125	241	380

WESTERN DIVISION	W	L	T	Pct.	Pts.	OP
San Francisco	10	6	0	.625	432	293
L.A. Rams*	9	7	0	.563	361	344
New Orleans	8	8	0	.500	319	337
Atlanta	7	9	0	.438	370	389

*Wild-Card qualifiers for playoffs
Seattle and Denver gained Wild-Card berths over Cleveland because of their victories over the Browns.
AFC first-round playoff: SEATTLE 31, Denver 7
AFC divisional playoffs: Seattle 27, MIAMI 20, L.A. RAIDERS 38, Pittsburgh 10
AFC Championship: L.A. RAIDERS 30, Seattle 14
NFC first-round playoff: Los Angeles Rams 24, DALLAS 17
NFC divisional playoffs: SAN FRANCISCO 24, Detroit 23, WASHINGTON 51, L.A. Rams 7
NFC Championship: WASHINGTON 24, San Francisco 21
Super Bowl XVIII: Los Angeles Raiders (AFC) 38, Washington (NFC) 9 at Tampa Stadium, Tampa, Florida.

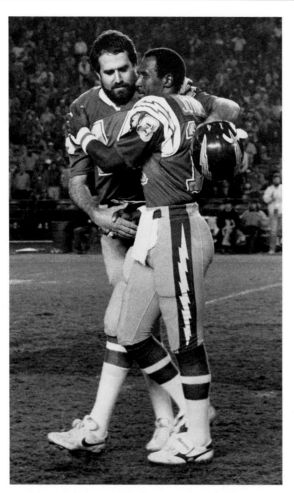

Near right: The San Diego Chargers honored wide receiver Charlie Joiner (18) with a special half-time ceremony, marking his new NFL record for career receptions. Joiner got a congratulatory hug from quarterback Dan Fouts. Far right: Eric Dickerson saluted the Anaheim Stadium crowd following his 47-yard touchdown run that put the Rams ahead of Atlanta 28-27. Los Angeles lost 30-28 on the last play of the game. Dickerson went on to power his way to a new single-season rushing record (2,105 yards), among others.

Ominous overtones and overused references to George Orwell's novel aside, this was a year of exaggeration around the NFL. No season in recent memory, in fact no season ever, had matched the epidemic of record-breaking that visited the league. The breakdown:

—Miami quarterback Dan Marino threw 48 touchdown passes, well outdistancing the former single-season record of 36 held by Y.A. Tittle and George Blanda. In the process, Marino also became the first man ever to throw for more than 5,000 yards in one NFL season, finishing with 5,084.

—Marino's wide receiver Mark Clayton caught 18 of those scoring passes, breaking a 42-year-old mark.

—Chicago running back Walter Payton set a new record for career rushing yardage, surpassing Jim Brown's previously sacrosanct standard of 12,312 in early October and extending his total to 13,309 by season's end.

—Los Angeles Rams running back Eric Dickerson broke O.J. Simpson's single-season rushing record of 2,003 yards, finishing 1984 with 2,105. (Speaking of Dickerson's pace—3,915 yards after only two years in the league—Payton said of his own career total, "I think I'd like

to stop if I get to 15,000. But that record won't be safe. The only way I could keep it away from Eric would be to play until I'm forty-three." Payton turns 43 in 1997.)

—Dickerson also broke the record for combined yardage in one season, breaking Simpson's 1975 total by a single yard with 2,244. Dickerson's 12 games with at least 100 yards rushing surpassed another of O.J.'s marks. The former Buffalo star had done it 11 times in 1973, as had Houston's Earl Campbell in 1979.

—Washington's Art Monk broke the 20-year-old record for receptions in a single season (101) set by Houston's Charley Hennigan in 1964, catching 11 passes in the Redskins' final game against St. Louis to finish with 106 for the year.

—San Diego wide receiver Charlie Joiner topped Charley Taylor's record of 649 career receptions, then extended his total to 657. The 37-year-old veteran of 16 seasons with Houston, Cincinnati, and the Chargers also became the fourth receiver to surpass 10,000 yards, finishing 1984 with 10,774 (in second place behind all-time yardage record-holder Don Maynard's 11,834).

—The Chicago Bears' defense set a single-season record with 72 quarterback sacks, 17½ of which belonged to second-year defensive end Richard Dent, the top total in the NFC.

—The San Francisco 49ers went 15-1 in the regular season, a record for total victories. The 49ers' only loss came in week seven, a 20-17 setback against Pittsburgh that nearly reached overtime when Ray Wersching's field-goal attempt sailed wide. The 49ers' 15 victories were one better than the Miami Dolphins' 14 in their perfect 1972 season and the Pittsburgh Steelers' 14 in 1978, when they went on to win Super Bowl XIII.

—Kansas City placekicker Nick Lowery qualified for consideration in the category of field-goal career accuracy by attempting his 150th three-pointer. Doing so, he became the NFL's all-time leader, with 74.7 percent.

—Tampa Bay running back James Wilder set an all-time record for rushing attempts in a single season, 407.

Wilder fell just 15 yards short of Dickerson's record of 2,244 combined rushing and pass-receiving yards.

Postseason activities in the two conferences yielded an intriguing, emotionally charged Super Bowl XIX matchup that seemed ordained from the time the clubs had sorted themselves into the tournament brackets. Miami and its "Marino Corps" strutted through the opening round and the AFC Championship Game with victories over Seattle (31-10) and Pittsburgh (45-

Above: The focal point of the Year of Records was Chicago's Walter Payton, who broke Jim Brown's career rushing mark and extended his own total to 13,309 yards.
Left: Tampa Bay's James Wilder set an NFL record for rushing attempts in a season, 407.
Far left: In Chicago's 1984 playoff victory over Washington, defensive end Richard Dent (95) had three of the Bears' seven sacks against Redskins quarterback Joe Theismann (7).

Miami quarterback Dan Marino (13) exchanged congratulations with running back Tony Nathan after Nathan's two-yard touchdown run in the first half of the Dolphins' 45-28 AFC Championship Game victory over Pittsburgh.

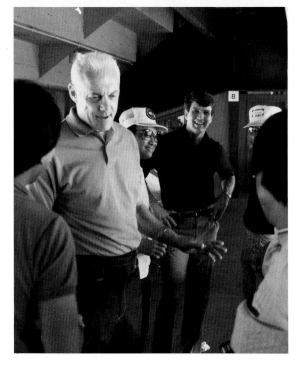

Above: Washington wide receiver Art Monk ran to the sideline with a souvenir, the ball he caught for reception number 102, breaking Charley Hennigan's single-season record on the way to an 11-catch performance against St. Louis. Monk finished 1984 with 106 receptions. Right: At the 1984 AFC-NFC Pro Bowl in Honolulu, retired Minnesota coach Bud Grant chatted with fans. A year later, his replacement Les Steckel (background) was fired by the Vikings after a 3-13 season, and Grant returned to the job.

28). The Dolphins' mortal moments of 1984 appeared to be well behind them—an overtime loss to San Diego in mid-November and an early-December setback against the Los Angeles Raiders that obscured Marino's best passing effort of the season, 470 yards and four touchdowns (see page 146).

San Francisco's postseason march was even less charitable than its 15-1 treatment of regular-season opponents. Neither the New York Giants, 21-10 losers in the playoff opener, nor the Chicago Bears, 23-0 losers in the NFC Championship Game, could get a touchdown from their offensive unit. Reporters, electronic and print, came out of the deal with egg on their collective face, having predicted tough times for the 49ers' offense against the league-leading Bears' defense, the alleged heir to the old "Monsters of the Midway" monicker.

If predicting the Super Bowl contestants had been a ho-hum proposition, the pregame discussions and analyses generated an almost pre-thermonuclear climate.

Topic A was Marino. How would the 49ers contain this human cannon, with his stable of speed merchants—Clayton, Mark Duper, *et al*—poised to run the San Francisco secondary out of Stanford Stadium? From there, the conversation might turn, within five minutes, to whether Marino was the greatest of all time.

San Francisco quarterback Joe Montana, second-rated in the NFL behind Marino and a good 1,400 yards shorter in the 1984 passing statistics, said, "I think our offense is sort of being overlooked. We may have something to prove."

The 49ers beat the Dolphins 38-16, as Montana threw for three touchdowns, rushed for one, and totaled 390 offensive yards for the day, winning Super Bowl most-valuable-player honors for the second time in his six-year career. The game also marked a high point in the two-year career of 49ers running back Roger Craig, an all-purpose running and pass-receiving back with skills perfectly matched to Bill Walsh's offensive variety show. Craig scored three of the 49ers' touchdowns.

But in the end, it was a defensive gambit that deserved the highest praise. In the face of San Francisco's four-man front, Marino's vision was colored red throughout the afternoon. He was sacked four times for a total of 29 yards. Meanwhile, upfield, San Francisco's five defensive backs, four of them Pro Bowlers, allowed Clayton and Duper a combined total of seven receptions, no touchdowns, and 103 yards.

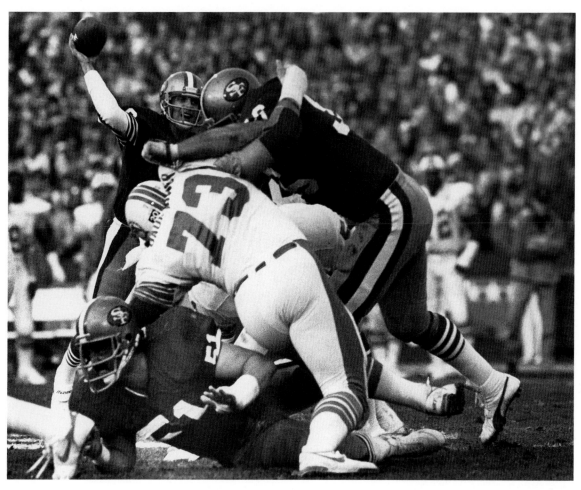

It was this way all day in Super Bowl XIX at Stanford Stadium. Miami nose tackle Bob Baumhower (73) couldn't penetrate the blocking of San Francisco guard Randy Cross (51) and center Fred Quillan, and quarterback Joe Montana, the game's most valuable player, bombarded the Dolphins in a 38-16 romp.

The 1984 season had another mark, one that came quickly, raised a furor, then took its place in the changing picture of the league. Colts owner Robert Irsay loaded his team's belongings aboard a fleet of moving vans and set out for Indianapolis. The club's new home: the 61,000-seat Hoosier Dome, part of an $82-million downtown stadium and convention center.

The AFC East had reached out and touched the Midwest. What next?

In the 1990s, and beyond, the face of the league will change further, perhaps dramatically.

New expansion franchises are certain to appear in the future, perhaps even in different countries. Maybe one day, there really will be a "world" football league. The NFL already has staged preseason games in Tokyo, Mexico City, and London, and there are professional football leagues in Italy, West Germany, and Japan.

"When you think about the next several evolutionary stages in the transportation industry," Pete Rozelle says, "when you can greatly shrink the time it takes to get from one continent to another, the thought of international play becomes feasible. But the timing will have to be right."

Could international play have a sequel?

Once, during a nationally televised night game, CBS director Sandy Grossman cut to a glorious view of a full moon on the rise. Without missing a beat, color analyst John Madden quipped, "I wonder if they'll ever play a game up there?"

Everyone assumed Madden was kidding. In January, 1969, everyone thought Joe Namath was kidding, too.

1984

AMERICAN CONFERENCE EASTERN DIVISION							NATIONAL CONFERENCE EASTERN DIVISION						
	W	L	T	Pct.	Pts.	OP		W	L	T	Pct.	Pts.	OP
Miami	14	2	0	.875	513	298	Washington	11	5	0	.688	426	310
New England	9	7	0	.563	362	352	N.Y. Giants*	9	7	0	.563	299	301
N.Y. Jets	7	9	0	.438	332	364	St. Louis	9	7	0	.563	423	345
Indianapolis	4	12	0	.250	239	414	Dallas	9	7	0	.563	308	308
Buffalo	2	14	0	.125	250	454	Philadelphia	6	9	1	.407	278	320
CENTRAL DIVISION							**CENTRAL DIVISION**						
	W	L	T	Pct.	Pts.	OP		W	L	T	Pct.	Pts.	OP
Pittsburgh	9	7	0	.563	387	310	Chicago	10	6	0	.625	325	248
Cincinnati	8	8	0	.500	339	339	Green Bay	8	8	0	.500	390	309
Cleveland	5	11	0	.313	250	297	Tampa Bay	6	10	0	.375	335	380
Houston	3	13	0	.188	240	437	Detroit	4	11	1	.282	283	408
							Minnesota	3	13	0	.188	276	484
WESTERN DIVISION							**WESTERN DIVISION**						
	W	L	T	Pct.	Pts.	OP		W	L	T	Pct.	Pts.	OP
Denver	13	3	0	.813	353	241	San Francisco	15	1	0	.939	475	227
Seattle*	12	4	0	.750	418	282	L.A. Rams*	10	6	0	.625	346	316
L.A. Raiders*	11	5	0	.688	368	278	New Orleans	7	9	0	.438	298	361
Kansas City	8	8	0	.500	314	324	Atlanta	4	12	0	.250	182	382
San Diego	7	9	0	.438	394	413							

Wild-Card qualifiers for playoffs

AFC first-round playoff: SEATTLE 13, Los Angeles Raiders 7
AFC divisional playoffs: MIAMI 31, Seattle 10; Pittsburgh 24, DENVER 17
AFC Championship: MIAMI 45, Pittsburgh 28
NFC first-round playoff: New York Giants 16, LOS ANGELES RAMS 13
NFC divisional playoffs: SAN FRANCISCO 21, New York Giants 10; Chicago 23, WASHINGTON 19
NFC Championship: SAN FRANCISCO 23, Chicago 0
Super Bowl XIX: San Francisco 38, Miami 16 at Stanford Stadium, Stanford, California.

AFL-NFL 1960-1984 ALL-STAR TEAM

To commemorate pro football's last quarter-century, the Pro Football Hall of Fame Selection Committee has chosen a 1960-1984 AFL-NFL All-Star team. This team includes players and coaches who spent all or part of their pro football careers in either the American Football League, the National Football League, or both, since 1960.

PART II

First Team

OFFENSE
Lance Alworth, *wide receiver*
1962-1970 San Diego Chargers,
1971-72 Dallas Cowboys
Raymond Berry, *wide receiver*
1955-1967 Baltimore Colts
Kellen Winslow, *tight end*
1979-present San Diego Chargers
Forrest Gregg, *tackle*
1958-1970 Green Bay Packers,
1971 Dallas Cowboys
Ron Mix, *tackle*
1960-69 Los Angeles / San Diego
Chargers
1971 Oakland Raiders
Jim Parker, *guard*
1957-1967 Baltimore Colts
John Hannah, *guard*
1973-present New England Patriots
Jim Otto, *center*
1960-1974 Oakland Raiders
Johnny Unitas, *quarterback*
1956-1972 Baltimore Colts,
1973 San Diego Chargers
Jim Brown, *running back*
1957-1965 Cleveland Browns
O.J. Simpson, *running back*
1969-1977 Buffalo Bills,
1978-79 San Francisco 49ers

DEFENSE
Gino Marchetti, *defensive end*
1952 Dallas Texans,
1953-1964, 1966 Baltimore Colts
Willie Davis, *defensive end*
1958-59 Cleveland Browns,
1960-69 Green Bay Packers
Bob Lilly, *defensive tackle*
1961-1974 Dallas Cowboys
Merlin Olsen, *defensive tackle*
1962-1976 Los Angeles Rams

Dick Butkus, *linebacker*
1965-1973 Chicago Bears
Jack Lambert, *linebacker*
1974-present Pittsburgh Steelers
Ray Nitschke, *linebacker*
1958-1972 Green Bay Packers
Willie Brown, *cornerback*
1963-66 Denver Broncos,
1967-1978 Oakland Raiders
Dick (Night Train) Lane,
cornerback
1952-53 Los Angeles Rams,
1954-59 Chicago Cardinals,
1960-65 Detroit Lions
Larry Wilson, *safety*
1960-1972 St. Louis Cardinals
Yale Lary, *safety*
1952-53, 1956-1964 Detroit Lions

SPECIALISTS
Ray Guy, *punter*
1973-present Oakland / Los Angeles
Raiders
Jan Stenerud, *placekicker*
1967-1979 Kansas City Chiefs,
1980-83 Green Bay Packers,
1984-present Minnesota Vikings
Gale Sayers, *kick returner*
1965-1971 Chicago Bears
Rick Upchurch, *kick returner*
1975-1983 Denver Broncos

COACHES*
Don Shula
1963-69 Baltimore Colts,
1970-present Miami Dolphins
Vince Lombardi
1959-1967 Green Bay Packers,
1969 Washington Redskins
* Shula and Lombardi received the same number of votes.

Second Team

OFFENSE
Paul Warfield, *wide receiver*
1964-69, 1976-77 Cleveland Browns,
1970-74 Miami Dolphins
Lynn Swann, *wide receiver*
1974-1981 Pittsburgh Steelers
John Mackey, *tight end*
1963-1971 Baltimore Colts
1972 San Diego Chargers
Art Shell, *tackle*
1968-1982 Oakland / Los Angeles
Raiders
Ron Yary, *tackle*
1968-1982 Minnesota Vikings,
1982 Los Angeles Rams
Bob Kuechenberg, *guard*
1970-1984 Miami Dolphins
Gene Upshaw, *guard*
1967-1982 Oakland / Los Angeles
Raiders
Jim Ringo, *center*
1953-1963 Green Bay Packers,
1964-67 Philadelphia Eagles
Terry Bradshaw, *quarterback*
1970-1983 Pittsburgh Steelers
Gale Sayers, *running back*
1965-1971 Chicago Bears
Walter Payton, *running back*
1975-present Chicago Bears

DEFENSE
Doug Atkins, *defensive end*
1953-54 Cleveland Browns,
1955-1966 Chicago Bears,
1967-69 New Orleans Saints
David (Deacon) Jones, *defensive end*
1961-1971 Los Angeles Rams,
1972-73 San Diego Chargers,
1974 Washington Redskins
Joe Greene, *defensive tackle*
1969-1981 Pittsburgh Steelers

Alan Page, *defensive tackle*
1967-1978 Minnesota Vikings
1978-1981 Chicago Bears
Joe Schmidt, *linebacker*
1953-1965 Detroit Lions
Ted Hendricks, *linebacker*
1969-1973 Baltimore Colts,
1974 Green Bay Packers,
1975-1983 Oakland / Los Angeles
Raiders
Bobby Bell, *linebacker*
1963-1974 Kansas City Chiefs
Herb Adderley, *cornerback*
1961-69 Green Bay Packers,
1970-72 Dallas Cowboys
Mel Blount, *cornerback*
1970-1983 Pittsburgh Steelers
Willie Wood, *safety*
1960-1971 Green Bay Packers
Dick Anderson, *safety*
1968-1975, 1977 Miami Dolphins

SPECIALISTS
Don Chandler, *punter*
1956-1964 New York Giants,
1965-67 Green Bay Packers
George Blanda, *placekicker*
1950-1958 Chicago Bears,
1950 Baltimore Colts,
1960-66 Houston Oilers,
1967-1976 Oakland Raiders
Billy (White Shoes) Johnson,
kick returner
1974-1980 Houston Oilers,
1982-present Atlanta Falcons
Travis Williams, *kick returner*
1967-1970 Green Bay Packers,
1971 Los Angeles Rams

★ *Co-Head Coach*

Vince Lombardi

Green Bay Packers, 1959-1967; Washington Redskins, 1969.
Vince Lombardi spent nine seasons as head coach of the Green Bay Packers. His teams won five NFL titles, including the first two Super Bowls. Lombardi requested perfect execution and demanded total effort. He often received both.

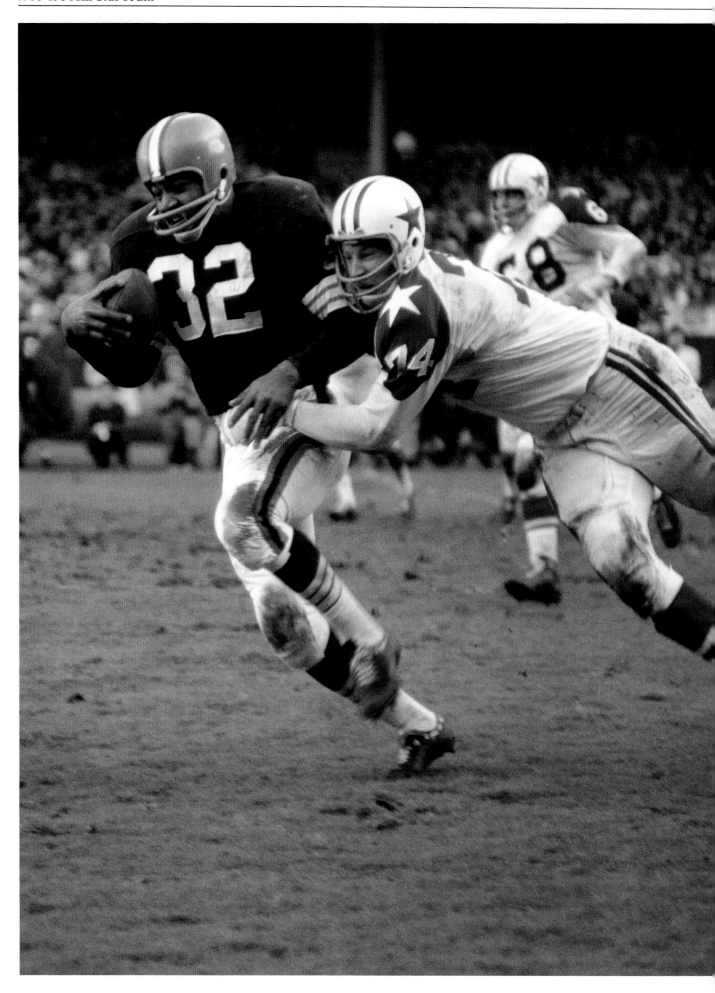

★ *Running back*

Jim Brown

(32) 6-2, 232. Cleveland Browns, 1957-1965.
Jim Brown's impact on pro football is difficult to capsulize. For nine memorable seasons with Cleveland—in eight of which he led the NFL in rushing—Brown set standards for running backs that will serve as barometers for greatness as long as the game is played.

★ *Defensive tackle*

Bob Lilly

(74) 6-5, 260. Dallas Cowboys, 1961-1974.
Bob Lilly put the doom in Dallas's Doomsday defense. The 11-time Pro Bowl tackle, shown at left tackling Jim Brown (and arrayed in the Cowboys' original Lone Star uniform), was renowned for his relentless pursuit.

★ *Placekicker*

Jan Stenerud

(3) 6-2, 190. Kansas City Chiefs, 1967-1979; Green Bay Packers, 1980-83; Minnesota Vikings, 1984-present.
Norwegian native Jan Stenerud broke an NFL record in 1983 many thought permanently belonged to George Blanda: most field goals in a career. He also set a Super Bowl record with a 48-yard field goal in Game IV.

★ *Linebacker*

Ray Nitschke

(66) 6-3, 235. Green Bay Packers, 1958-1972.

If one man were chosen to symbolize the fierce determination and aggressive fury of the 1960s Green Bay Packers, it would be linebacker Ray Nitschke. Nitschke was a withering tornado in green and gold, relentlessly sweeping up ball carriers and flattening quarterbacks.

 ★ *Punter*

Ray Guy

(8) 6-3, 195. Oakland/Los Angeles Raiders, 1973-present.

The first punter ever selected in the first round of the college draft, Ray Guy justified that honor in his rookie season by setting a Raiders single-season punting record. He had six consecutive all-pro seasons (1973-78) and has played in seven Pro Bowls.

★ *Center*

Jim Otto

(00) 6-2, 255. Oakland Raiders, 1960-1974.
Longevity distinguished by productivity is one way to describe the legacy of Jim Otto, who appeared in 210 consecutive games during his stellar 15-year career. He was the only all-star center in the AFL's 10-year history, and after that played in three AFC-NFC Pro Bowls.

★ *Kick Returner*

Rick Upchurch

(80) 5-10, 176. Denver Broncos, 1975-1983.
Rick Upchurch, also a receiver, thrilled NFL crowds as a rookie, and never slowed up. In 1976, he returned four punts for touchdowns, and later became the NFL's all-time career record-holder for both punt return average and yardage.

★ *Tackle*

Forrest Gregg

*(75) 6-4, 250. Green Bay Packers, 1958-1970;
Dallas Cowboys, 1971.*
A rock-solid tackle who also played guard during his career, Forrest Gregg made nine trips to the Pro Bowl. Vince Lombardi probably paid him the ultimate tribute when he called Gregg "the greatest player I ever coached."

★ *Cornerback*

Dick (Night Train) Lane

(81) 6-2, 210. Los Angeles Rams, 1952-53; Chicago Cardinals, 1954-59; Detroit Lions, 1960-65.

One of the greatest free-agent discoveries ever, Dick (Night Train) Lane set an NFL record with 14 interceptions as a rookie. He spent the rest of his fabulous NFL career—distinguished by six Pro Bowl appearances—harassing receivers and quarterbacks.

★ *Running back*

O.J. Simpson

(32) 6-2, 210. Buffalo Bills, 1969-1977; San Francisco 49ers, 1978-79.

If the artistry of O.J. Simpson in the open field could be committed to canvas, it surely would hang in the Louvre. Defying defenses and description with sonic speed, gliding grace, and deceptive daring, Simpson became the first running back to rush for 2,000 yards when he totaled 2,003 in 1973.

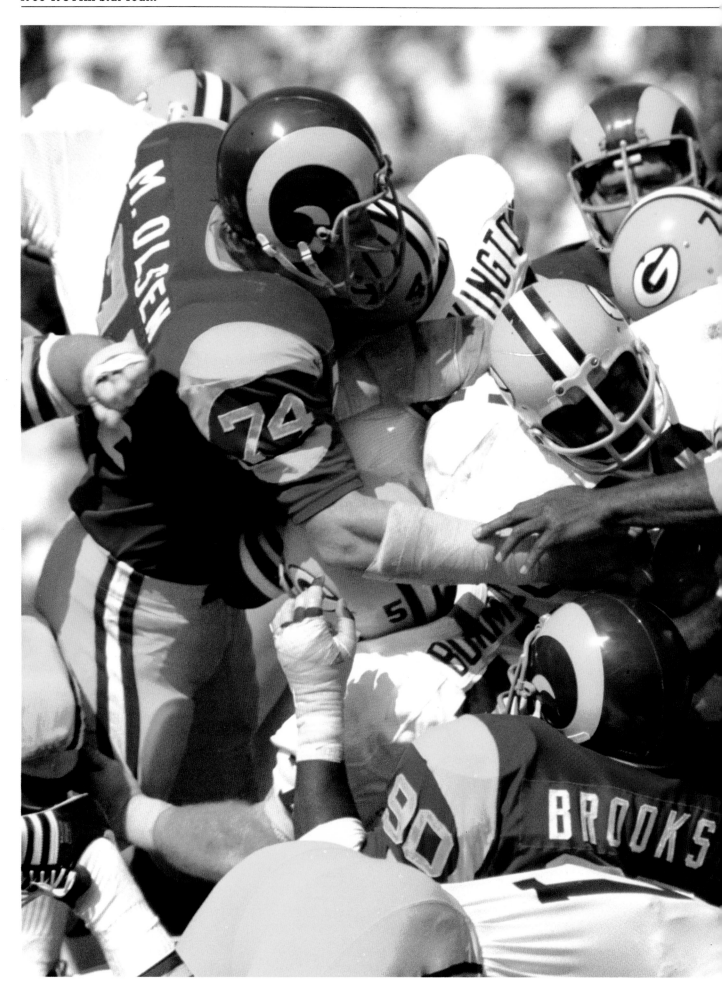

★ *Wide receiver*

Raymond Berry

(82) 6-2, 187. Baltimore Colts, 1955-1967.
Intense concentration (one fumble in 13 seasons) and hard work enabled Raymond Berry to overcome average speed and other limited physical skills. Berry teamed with Johnny Unitas to form perhaps the greatest clutch passing tandem in National Football League history.

★ *Defensive tackle*

Merlin Olsen

(74) 6-5, 270. Los Angeles Rams, 1962-1976.
No other player in the history of professional football was as consistently singled out for recognition by both his fellow players and NFL coaches as Merlin Olsen. A dominating member of the Rams' famed Fearsome Foursome defensive line, Olsen was named to the Pro Bowl team 14 times, missing only his final season.

★ *Tight end*

Kellen Winslow

(80) 6-5, 242. San Diego Chargers, 1979-present.

One of the most influential players in the 1980s, Kellen Winslow revolutionized his position. A spectacular synthesis of size, speed, grace, power, and courage, Winslow became the first tight end ever to lead the NFL in receptions two years in a row (1980-81).

★ *Guard*

Jim Parker

(77) 6-3, 273. Baltimore Colts, 1957-1967.
The first lineman ever inducted into the Pro
Football Hall of Fame exclusively as an offensive player, Jim Parker was invaluable both on
running plays and passes. His special assignment—which he executed superbly—was to
protect Colts quarterback Johnny Unitas.

★ *Defensive end*

Willie Davis

(87) 6-3, 245. Cleveland Browns, 1958-59; Green Bay Packers, 1960-69.
Willie Davis emerged from an obscure NFL beginning with Cleveland, where he was miscast as an offensive tackle, to become one of the inspirational cornerstones of the Green Bay Packers' championship dynasty. He did not miss a game in his 10-year-career with Green Bay.

★ *Linebacker*

Dick Butkus

(51) 6-3, 245. Chicago Bears, 1965-1973.
A ferocious warrior, Dick Butkus ruled the NFL as the most intimidating player of his day. Eight Pro Bowl appearances in nine years help support one popular theory that Butkus was the premier middle linebacker of all time.

★ Cornerback

Willie Brown

(24) 6-1, 210. Denver Broncos, 1963-66; Oakland Raiders, 1967-1978.

From a free agent rookie cut by the Houston Oilers in 1963, Willie Brown rose to become one of the most feared pass defenders ever. Brown's biggest moments came in crucial games. Despite the fact that his territory usually was avoided by quarterbacks, he had 54 career interceptions.

★ *Kick returner*

Gale Sayers

(40) 6-0, 200. Chicago Bears, 1965-1971.

Quicksilver Gale Sayers frustrated tacklers with escape artistry on punt and kickoff returns, and as a running back. He tied an NFL record in 1965 when he scored six touchdowns in a game against the San Francisco 49ers.

★ *Wide receiver*

Lance Alworth

(19) 6-0, 184. San Diego Chargers, 1962-1970; Dallas Cowboys, 1971-72.

Soaring high above the clutch of defenders, momentarily suspending gravity, pulling football after football out of the air, streaking downfield, eluding apprehension...these are recurrent images of Lance Alworth. Nicknamed Bambi for his uncommon grace, he was the first player from the AFL inducted into the Pro Football Hall of Fame.

★ *Safety*

Yale Lary

(28) 5-11, 189. Detroit Lions, 1956-1964.
Versatile Yale Lary was inducted into the Pro Football Hall of Fame as a punter and a safety. "If I had to pick one defensive back who had it all," says Hall of Fame quarterback Bobby Layne, "I'd take Yale Lary. He had the ability to make a quarterback think he had an open receiver, then make an inteception."

★ *Defensive end*

Gino Marchetti

(89) 6-4, 245. Dallas Texans, 1952; Baltimore Colts, 1953-1964, 1966.
In 1969, Gino Marchetti was named the top defensive end of the NFL's first 50 years, and his legend remains secure. With an irrepressible blend of speed, power, and strength, Marchetti played his position as few ever have, and was a relentless hunter of quarterbacks.

★ *Linebacker*

Jack Lambert

(58) 6-4, 220. Pittsburgh Steelers, 1974-present.
Few football fans ever had heard of Jack Lambert when he entered the NFL in 1974. He introduced himself by being named defensive rookie of the year. Four Super Bowl rings and nine Pro Bowls later, the intimidating middle linebacker no longer has an NFL identity crisis.

★ *Guard*

John Hannah

(73) 6-2, 282. New England Patriots, 1973-present.
John Hannah not only is one of the most devastating blockers ever; John Hannah is a fortress armed with tremendous pulling speed. The sight of Hannah, a six-time Pro Bowl starter, charging downfield with the throttle wide open gives pause to anyone in a different-colored jersey.

★ *Co-Head Coach*

Don Shula

Baltimore Colts, 1963-69; Miami Dolphins, 1970-present.
One of only four NFL coaches to surpass the 200-victory mark (and the first to do it in his first 20 seasons), Don Shula has taken his teams to six Super Bowls. His 1972 Dolphins, one of three consecutive Super Bowl squads, went 17-0 to become the only team in NFL history to complete an entire season undefeated.

★ *Tackle*

Ron Mix

(74) 6-4, 250. Los Angeles Chargers, 1960; San Diego Chargers, 1961-69 Oakland Raiders, 1971.
Ron Mix, a consummate technician and perfectionist, was a dynamic force in the early Chargers' explosive offense. According to San Diego records, Mix was called for holding only twice in his distinguished pro career. He was named all-AFL nine times.

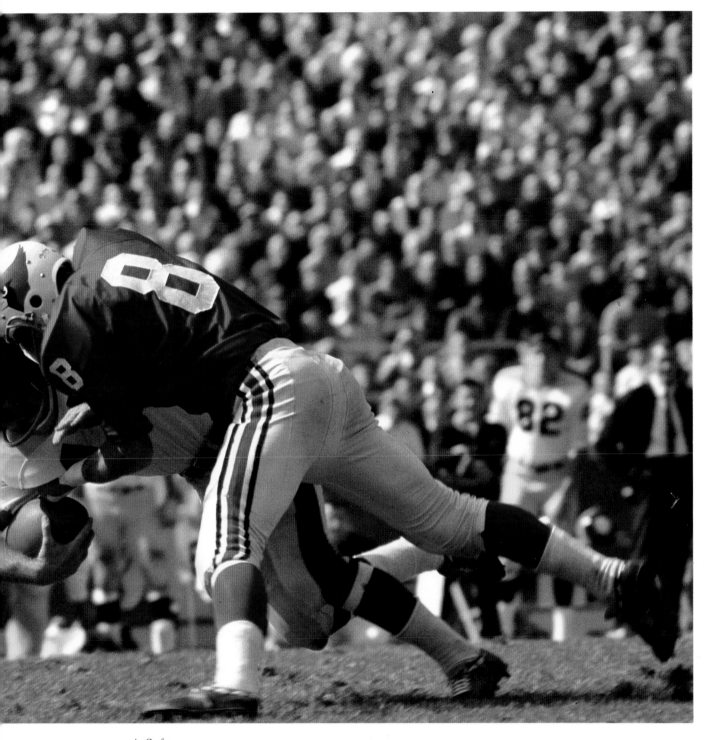

★ *Safety*

Larry Wilson

(8) 6-0, 190. St. Louis Cardinals, 1960-1972.
Pound-for-pound, one of the most rugged men
ever to play the game. Game-for-game, one of
the most consistent men to put on a jersey. Play-
for-play, one of the most frustrating obstacles
NFL quarterbacks ever have confronted. Larry
Wilson's 52 career interceptions give statistical
testimony to his ability.

★ *Quarterback*

Johnny Unitas

(19) 6-1, 195. Baltimore Colts, 1956-72; San Diego Chargers, 1973.
A quarterback for the ages, Unitas held every meaningful NFL career passing record: most attempts, most completions, most yardage, most 300-yard games, most touchdown passes. But Unitas transcended statistical analysis; his records could be—and were—broken. But no one ever can take away his gift: cool leadership under fire.

PART III

25 TO REMEMBER: INDELIBLE GAMES OF THE PAST QUARTER-CENTURY

The problem is criteria.

What qualifies a game as one of the NFL's 25 "greatest" since 1960? Excitement? Drama? Significance? An individual milestone?

Selecting the definitive list has its pitfalls. The biggest one: It's impossible.

Choose a game. Did it have dazzling, beginning-to-end action? Was there a photo finish? Were there brilliant offensive fireworks? Was it a defensive masterpiece? Did it contain a phenomenal comeback? Was it a great upset? Were there record-setting performances?

You get the idea.

Now substitute "memorable" for "greatest." Does that make things easier? There are fewer rules, fewer boundaries, fewer guidelines, fewer prerequisites. The memories simply have to endure.

There is nothing official about this compilation. Some of your favorite games may be missing. For every game that made the list, there was a painful omission.

The intent: Relive some memories. Consider how fate always has its say. See how truth usually—but not always—emerges from beneath doubt's shadow. Notice how football history sometimes turns on one improbable play.

If you like, compare our choices with your own. Just remember, the odds of any two lists of 25 memorable games being exactly the same are even longer than the odds were against the New York Jets winning Super Bowl III.

December 26, 1960

PHILADELPHIA EAGLES 17
GREEN BAY PACKERS 13

The 1960 Philadelphia Eagles had "be-yondness," a unique word coined by the team's head coach, Buck Shaw. Translation: The team was greater than the sum of its individual parts.

The Eagles had almost supernatural desire that year, which helped overcome some of their talent. Two years earlier, Philadelphia had finished last in the Eastern Division with a 2-9-1 record. By 1962, the Eagles were 3-10-1—and back in the cellar.

Things were different in 1960. On December 26, the Eagles played beyond themselves and they won a National Football League championship.

"They surfaced momentarily and mysteriously, perhaps magically, and then, like the Loch Ness monster, submerged, with no plausible explanation," wrote Larry Merchant in *The Way They Were*.

Actually, there were at least two explanations: quarterback Norm Van Brocklin and center-linebacker Chuck Bednarik.

Van Brocklin—"The Dutchman"—was a fearless competitor, a complex, driven spitfire who galvanized the Eagles with the same kind of animated spirit Bobby Layne had brought to the Detroit Lions in the 1950s.

Franklin Field, Philadelphia, Pennsylvania					
Green Bay	3	3	0	7	—13
Philadelphia	0	10	0	7	—17

HOW THEY SCORED

GB —FG Hornung 20
GB —FG Hornung 23
Phil —McDonald 35 pass from Van Brocklin (Walston kick)
Phil —FG Walston 15
GB —McGee 7 pass from Starr (Hornung kick)
Phil —Dean 5 run (Walston kick)
Attendance—67,325

Previewing the climactic confrontation that would end the game, Philadelphia's Chuck Bednarik applied a full body tackle to Green Bay running back Jim Taylor.

Bednarik was a 35-year-old anachronism, the last of the 60-minute players in an era of total two-platoon football. He was on the field for every snap of the 1960 title game.

Green Bay, coached by Vince Lombardi and on the cusp of its great dynasty, seemed to have more than enough firepower to pierce a Philadelphia defense that ranked next-to-last in the NFL in rushing. The names are familiar: Bart Starr, Jim Taylor, Paul Hornung, Boyd Dowler.

The Packers were not helped however, by the playing surface at the University of Pennsylvania's Franklin Field, which had thawed from a recent freeze into a muddy, slippery bog.

Green Bay also didn't help itself by wasting two early golden touchdown opportunities. Both times the Eagles forced the Packers to settle for field

Green Bay end Max McGee caught a seven-yard touchdown pass from quarterback Bart Starr to give the Packers a 13-10 lead.

goals of 20 and 23 yards by the versatile Hornung.

"We lost the game right there," Lombardi said. "Instead of leading 14-0, it was only 6-0."

Van Brocklin's 35-yard touchdown pass to flanker Tommy McDonald and Bobby Walston's 15-yard field goal put Philadelphia on top 10-6 at halftime.

One significant play in the scoreless third quarter was a jarring tackle by linebacker Bednarik that put Hornung out of the game with a pinched nerve.

Another was Green Bay safety John Symank's interception of a pass by Van Brocklin deep in Packers territory. Some daring by Max McGee on the ensuing drive helped put Green Bay back on top early in the fourth quarter. After dropping back to punt, McGee noticed the Eagles hadn't sent anyone in to rush him, and he raced 35 yards to the Eagles' 46. The improvisation paid off when McGee caught a seven-yard pass from Starr with 13:07 left to play, putting Green Bay in front 13-10.

The Eagles regained momentum when rookie Ted Dean escaped for a 58-yard kickoff return to the Packers' 39, then regained the lead when Dean finished a seven-play drive with a five-yard touchdown run. That put Philadelphia

ahead 17-13 with 9½ minutes remaining.

After losing a fumble (recovered by Bednarik) and stalling two other times, Green Bay began a "last hope" drive from its own 35 with 90 seconds left. Starr whisked the Packers to the Eagles' 22. Just 17 seconds remained, and Green Bay was out of time outs.

With his primary receivers blanketed, Starr dumped a swing pass to Taylor. Taylor broke several tackles, and twisted and lurched to the nine, where a lone Eagle—Bednarik—stood between him and the end zone.

It was an epic confrontation, a rampaging triceratops challenging an unflinching tyrannosaur—with a championship on the line.

"They didn't have any time outs left," Bednarik says, "and the clock was ticking away. He was coming right at me, running like hell. I knew I had to make a perfect tackle there if I ever made one. If he gets by me, he scores.

"I hit him, wrestled him to the ground, then I knelt on him. He was saying, 'Get off me, you s.o.b.' I just had my eyes on that clock. When the hands got to zero, I said, 'Okay, you can get up now. This game is over. We're the champions of the world.'

"Damn, that was a great feeling."

December 23, 1962

DALLAS TEXANS 20
HOUSTON OILERS 17

As ABC announcer Jack Buck (right, with microphone) and a national TV audience listened in, Texans captain Abner Haynes (28) fumbled the overtime coin-flip.

The 1962 American Football League Championship Game between the Dallas Texans and the Houston Oilers was a gripping, double-overtime thriller. Ironically, it is remembered most for a bizarre coin-toss decision.

At the time, the AFL was starving for attention. Aided by a national television spotlight, this game was a valuable advertisement for the "other" league.

The Oilers and Texans were the AFL's top two teams in 1962. Houston owned the league's number-one offense, and Dallas ranked second. On defense, the ranking was reversed.

An overflow crowd of 37,981 crammed into Houston's tiny Jeppesen Stadium, a remodeled high school field. It was a damp, drizzly day, with a fickle wind blowing toward the scoreboard clock behind the south end zone. The field was crabgrass choked in mud.

Houston's roster was laced with many NFL-seasoned players, including quarterback George Blanda, and the Oilers had won the AFL's first two championships (1960 and 1961). Of the Texans' 33 players, only quarterback Len Dawson had any NFL experience.

Hank Stram, the Texans' head coach, remod-eled his offense for the championship game. He positioned Jack Spikes and Curtis McClinton—both fullback types—together in the backfield, and aligned his 1,000-yard rusher, Abner Haynes, as a flanker. Stram also deployed an early version of the 3-4 defense against the Oilers, with 6-foot 7-inch rookie defensive end Bill Hull dropping back as a fourth linebacker.

Dallas "won" the first half 17-0, as Haynes caught one touchdown pass and ran for another score. The Oilers "won" the second half by exactly the same margin. Blanda, using All-AFL receiver Charley Hennigan as a decoy, began throwing instead to tight end Willard Dewveall, and connected with the former Chicago Bear for a 15-yard touchdown. A field goal by Blanda and a one-yard touchdown run by Charlie Tolar tied the score.

Dallas linebacker Sherrill Headrick's block of Blanda's 42-yard field-goal attempt with time running out forced the second sudden-death overtime in pro football history (the 1958 NFL Championship Game between the Baltimore Colts and the New York Giants was the first).

At this point, Abner Haynes joined the *faux pas* Hall of Fame.

Jeppesen Stadium, Houston, Texas

Dallas	3	14	0	0	0	3	—20
Houston	0	0	7	10	0	0	—17

HOW THEY SCORED

Dall—FG Brooker 16
Dall—Haynes 28 pass from Dawson (Brooker kick)
Dall—Haynes 2 run (Brooker kick)
Hou—Dewveall 15 pass from Blanda (Blanda kick)
Hou—FG Blanda 31
Hou—Tolar 1 run (Blanda kick)
Dall—FG Brooker 25
Attendance—37,981

Early in the second quarter, Haynes gave the Texans a 10-0 lead with a 28-yard touchdown catch of a pass from quarterback Len Dawson.

Houston quarterback George Blanda (16) connected with halfback Billy Cannon (20) for six completions and 54 yards.

Haynes was one of the AFL's best running backs for eight seasons. But he also belongs to a dubious group of sports immortals of enduring legend because of one memorable gaffe, joining men such as Mickey Owen, who dropped the famous called third strike in the 1941 World Series, and Roy (Wrong Way) Riegels, who ran 69½ yards in the wrong direction in the 1929 Rose Bowl.

Stram, mindful of Blanda's powerful leg and leery of his own kicking game—the poorest in the league—wanted to open the overtime on defense. He was afraid that if his offense got trapped deep in its own territory and had to punt into the treacherous wind, Blanda might get an easy opportunity for a game-winning field goal.

So before the overtime coin toss, Stram reviewed the options with Haynes, the Texans' captain. "If they win the toss," Stram said, "and elect to receive, we'll kick to the clock [with the wind]."

As a national television audience looked and listened (Jack Buck of ABC was holding a microphone at midfield), referee Harold (Red) Bourne flipped the coin, and told Haynes to call it.

"Heads," said Abner.

It was heads.

"Your option," Bourne told him.

"We'll kick to the clock," Haynes said.

Bourne was aghast. "Come again," he said.

"We'll kick to the clock."

Bourne then nervously explained that Haynes had to give Houston one of two choices. He could either call the kickoff or which goal to defend, but not both.

"We'll kick," Haynes said dumbfoundedly.

Al Jamieson, the astonished Houston captain, slapped his helmet and jumped up and down, not believing what he'd just heard. "We'll take

the wind," he said with more than a little glee.

Haynes had pulled an Alphonse and Gaston on himself. Given their choice of the ball or the wind, the Texans wound up with neither.

"We thought they were crazy," Blanda said.

Despite the first possession, the wind advantage, and superior field position throughout the fifth quarter, the Oilers failed to score. Blanda was intercepted twice, the second time by Hull late in the period after Houston already had reached field-goal range.

With the ball and the wind as the sixth quarter opened, Dawson moved the Texans down the field. At 2:54 of the period (17:54 of the overtime), rookie Tommy Brooker kicked a 25-yard field goal to give the Texans—soon to move to Kansas City to become the Chiefs—a 20-17 victory and a championship.

And not even Brooker was happier about it than Abner Haynes.

Postgame revelry: Dallas owner Lamar Hunt (left) was congratulated by AFL commissioner Joe Foss, as Texans head coach Hank Stram studied a champagne-soaked hat.

December 29, 1963

CHICAGO BEARS 14
NEW YORK GIANTS 10

New York Giants quarterback Y.A. Tittle was grounded by Bears linebacker Larry Morris. The second-quarter tackle strained Tittle's knee, and reduced his effectiveness.

Although he wouldn't retire for one more year, New York Giants quarterback Y.A. Tittle made the 1963 NFL Championship Game a closing verse in the bittersweet ballad of his career.

Tittle, who had spent 10 memorable seasons with the San Francisco 49ers (preceded by three years with the Baltimore Colts) before being acquired by the Giants in 1961, was an inspirational leader with a flair for the improbable—and a disregard for the impossible.

In 1963, the 37-year-old "Bald Eagle" set an NFL record with 36 touchdown passes and led the Giants to their third consecutive Eastern Conference title. But he still was looking for his first NFL title. New York had been crushed 37-0 by Green Bay in the 1961 NFL Championship Game, and had lost a bitterly fought rematch 16-7 at Yankee Stadium a year later. This time the Giants were facing the Bears on a

frigid December Sunday in Chicago.

The Bears hadn't won an NFL championship since 1946. Many fans were pulling for 68-year-old Chicago head coach George Halas, the team's owner and one of the NFL's patriarchs, to win one more title.

The game was a promoter's dream. New York had the NFL's highest-scoring team, averaging 32 points per game. Chicago's forbidding defense, directed by assistant coach George Allen, had allowed an average of only 10 points per game. The Bears led the NFL in 10 of 19 statistical categories and ranked second in eight others.

With brutally cold winds whipping through the frozen sunlight of Wrigley Field (game-time temperature: 11 degrees), many doubted Tittle would be able to pass effectively. But he staked the Giants to an early 7-0 lead with a 14-yard scoring pass to Frank Gifford.

Tittle paid a price for the touchdown; blitzing Bears linebacker Larry Morris crashed into him just as he released the pass. Tittle clutched his left knee as he limped to the sideline.

When the Giants recovered a fumble on the Chicago 31, Tittle stoically trotted onto the

Wrigley Field, Chicago, Illinois					
New York	7	3	0	0	—10
Chicago	7	0	7	0	—14

HOW THEY SCORED

NY —Gifford 14 pass from Tittle (Chandler kick)
Chi —Wade 2 run (Jencks kick)
NY —FG Chandler 13
Chi —Wade 1 run (Jencks kick)
Attendance—45,801

quarter when defensive end Ed O'Bradovich infiltrated the Giants' backfield and intercepted a short lob by Tittle at the New York 24. Wade carried into the end zone five plays later for his second touchdown and a 14-10 lead.

Thanks to two interceptions, the Bears' offense had to travel 20 yards to its 14 points.

After Chicago missed a field goal with five minutes left in the game, New York took over on its 20. Time was short, the Giants weren't moving the ball, and coach Allie Sherman considered replacing Tittle with rookie Glynn Griffing. He stuck with Tittle.

Tittle responded with a 10-play drive deep into Chicago territory. New York needed a touchdown. On third-and-five, Tittle threw to Gifford, who was open in the end zone. Bears defensive back Bennie McRae stole the pass.

All Chicago had to do was run out the clock, but the Giants' defense, which had played magnificently all day, forced a punt with a minute and a half left. Tittle had one last chance from 84 yards away. He completed three quick passes, covering 30 yards. On third down, he hit Gifford for 15 more.

The ball was on the Bears' 39, with just 15 seconds remaining. Sherman called for a bomb.

The crowd of 45,801 wondered if Tittle had any miracles left.

He didn't. His pass to Shofner was high and was intercepted by safety Richie Petitbon. The Bears were NFL champions. For the third year in a row, the Giants were bridesmaids.

"We played with half a quarterback, and they played with a full one," said Giants defensive end Andy Robustelli. "If Tittle hadn't been hurt, we'd have won."

The Bears, whose relentless five-man front kept the heat on Tittle and helped cause five interceptions, gave the game ball to Allen.

"Larry Morris got the car for being the game's most valuable player," Allen said. "But I wouldn't trade him the ball for the car."

field, trying to mask his agony. He immediately threw a bomb to split end Del Shofner, who was open in the end zone. Shofner, who routinely made inconceivable catches look easy, dropped the ball. (For one of the few times in his career, Shofner would not catch a pass.)

Then disaster struck. Morris read Tittle's intended screen pass to running back Phil King perfectly, intercepted, and lumbered 61 yards before buckling at the Giants' 5-yard line. Two plays later, Bears quarterback Bill Wade sneaked in for a touchdown. Instead of trailing 14-0 (if Shofner had caught the touchdown pass), the Bears were tied 7-7.

The Giants kicked a field goal and quickly regained possession when the Bears had to punt.

But Morris struck again. The Bears' linebacker, who was named the game's most valuable player, broke through the Giants' line and again blasted Tittle, severely aggravating the quarterback's injured knee. Tittle had to be helped to the sideline by his former San Francisco 49ers teammate Hugh McElhenny.

"It felt like someone had stuck an ice pick in it," Tittle said, "and pain was shooting up the leg as well."

Tittle had his knee treated at halftime and gamely continued in the second half. (Torn ligaments was the diagnosis.)

He was the game's captain, like Ahab continuing after his first brush with Moby Dick. The scene was familiar to hopeful Giants fans: Tittle suffering, but playing nonetheless.

Tittle's troubles intensified late in the third

December 26, 1965

GREEN BAY PACKERS 13
BALTIMORE COLTS 10

Tom Matte was a solid, productive running back for the Baltimore Colts from 1961 to 1972. He retired as the Colts' second all-time leading rusher with 4,646 yards.

Matte is honored by pro football romanticists, however, for a brief but memorable improvisation as an "instant quarterback."

The Colts were 9-3-1 going into their final game of the 1965 regular season, against the Los Angeles Rams. Quarterback Johnny Unitas had fractured a knee in the Colts' twelfth game of the year. His replacement, Gary Cuozzo, had separated a shoulder in a critical loss to Green Bay in the next-to-last regular-season game. He also was lost for the remainder of the year.

Baltimore head coach Don Shula turned to Matte, who had been a run-oriented, Split-T quarterback under coach Woody Hayes at Ohio State. Several days before the Rams game,

Shula also picked up veteran quarterback Ed Brown, who had been released by the Steelers, as a back-up to Matte. Shula rapidly redesigned the Colts' offense to emphasize more quarterback draws, pass-run option plays, and shorter pass patterns. Shula also had some of the Colts' plays typed on a small card, sealed in plastic, and taped to Matte's left wrist.

Matte completed only one of seven pass attempts for 19 yards against the Rams, but he rushed 16 times for 99 yards. The Colts' defense played heroically, and Lou Michaels kicked a decisive 23-yard field goal for a 20-17 victory.

That set up a playoff with the Packers, who also finished 10-3-1, for the Western Division championship.

The Colts and their *ad hoc* quarterback weren't given much of a chance. They previously had lost twice to the Packers, including a 42-27 drubbing on a five-touchdown day by Paul Hornung. The Packers also won the coin toss for the playoff game site; the Colts would have to brave Wisconsin refrigeration. And Brown was ineligible for the playoff, leaving cornerback Bobby Boyd, a former Oklahoma quarterback, next in line behind Matte.

But the Colts served notice on the first play that this game was not just going to be semi-tough. Green Bay tight end Bill Anderson caught a 10-yard pass from quarterback Bart Starr at the Packers' 25. Anderson was belted hard and dazed by Baltimore cornerback Lenny Lyles. The ball popped loose, and Colts linebacker Don Shinnick scooped it up and scored. In a desperate attempt to stop Shinnick, Starr got the worst of a collision with defensive back Jim Welch, and left the game with injured ribs.

Many of the Packers later

Standing beside Colts head coach Don Shula, instant quarterback Tom Matte—with his wristband in place—tried to keep his passing hand warm.

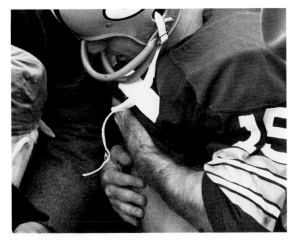

Bart Starr's rib injury on the Packers' first play from scrimmage forced him out of the game, except as a holder on kicks.

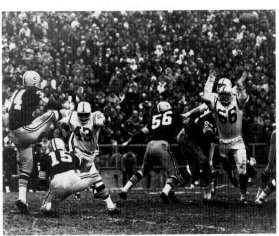

Zeke Bratkowski replaced Starr and established new playoff marks with 22 completions and 39 attempts. Don Chandler's 25-yard field goal at 13:39 of overtime won it. His 27-yard kick that forced overtime was disputed; there was no argument about the winner.

The Colts also made a strong goal-line stand in the second quarter when they stopped Hornung once and fullback Jim Taylor twice on three consecutive tries from the Colts' 1.

A botched punt by Baltimore in the third quarter set up another Green Bay scoring opportunity. This time Hornung scored from the 1 to cut the deficit to 10-7.

The Colts clung to their lead until 2:02 remained in the game. When a Green Bay drive stalled deep in Baltimore territory, Don Chandler tried a 27-yard field goal from a difficult angle. To many it appeared the ball sliced wide, higher than the uprights. Chandler himself shook his head, reacting as if the kick had missed. But field judge Jim Tunney ruled it was good.

The enraged Colts protested bitterly, but to no avail. They were further displeased when the *Baltimore News-American* later published photos that indicated the kick was no good.

(The NFL rules committee subsequently ordered the uprights extended to 20 feet above the crossbar, to reduce the need for officials to draw imaginary lines to the sky if a ball reached an altitude exceeding the upright.)

If the kick had not been ruled good, Baltimore may have held on to win. Instead it was 10-10, and the game entered sudden-death overtime. Neither team moved the ball well in the early going of the extra period. The Colts got the first scoring opportunity, but Michaels missed a 47-yard field-goal attempt.

Chandler ended the Colts' season and put the Packers into the NFL Championship Game against Cleveland with a 25-yard field goal 13 minutes and 39 seconds into overtime, making this the longest NFL game yet played.

Matte completed 5 of his 12 passes for 40 yards, and led the Colts with 57 yards rushing. The plastic crib sheet with the Colts' plays that he wore on his wrist now is on display at the Pro Football Hall of Fame in Canton, Ohio.

claimed this game was the roughest they'd ever played. Anderson provided proof of that. He caught eight passes for 78 yards, and later said he couldn't remember any of it. He was operating on automatic pilot after being knocked into the outer limits on the game's first play.

Matte wasn't much of a passing threat, but some strong running by the makeshift quarterback and running backs Lenny Moore and Jerry Hill set up a second-quarter field goal by Michaels that gave the Colts a 10-0 halftime lead.

Zeke Bratkowski, who replaced Starr at quarterback, completed 22 of his 39 passes for 248 yards. But an unfamiliar 5-1 defense by Baltimore had stifled Green Bay's rushing attack.

Lambeau Field, Green Bay, Wisconsin						
Baltimore	7	3	0	0	0	—10
Green Bay	0	0	7	3	3	—13

HOW THEY SCORED

Balt —*Shinnick 25 fumble return (Michaels kick)*
Balt —*FG Michaels 15*
GB —*Hornung 1 run (Chandler kick)*
GB —*FG Chandler 27*
GB —*FG Chandler 25*
Attendance—50,484

December 9, 1967

LOS ANGELES RAMS 27
GREEN BAY PACKERS 24

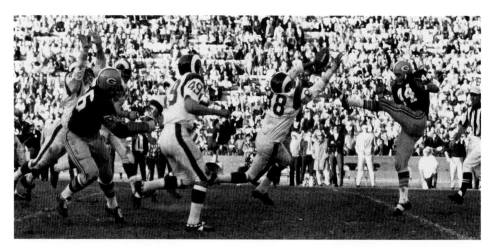

Los Angeles Rams head coach George Allen had an uneasy moment when he awoke on Sunday, December 10, 1967, the morning following an unusual late-season Saturday game against the Green Bay Packers at the Los Angeles Memorial Coliseum.

"I took a sleeping pill and retired early Saturday night," Allen said later. "When I woke up, I thought, 'Did we win or did we lose?' Honestly, when I got up, I couldn't remember whether we had won or lost."

Allen's temporary amnesia was understandable. The day after Joe Frazier decisioned Muhammad Ali in their first fight at Madison Square Garden in 1971, Frazier probably wondered the same thing.

The Rams had entered this critical game, the next-to-last outing on their schedule, with a 9-1-2 record. But a loss would have extinguished their playoff hopes, because Coastal Division leader Baltimore—Los Angeles's final regular-season opponent—was 10-0-2 and the Colts were a virtual cinch to defeat the expansion New Orleans Saints the following day (which they did).

Green Bay was playing for pride, not glory, against the Rams. The Packers already had clinched a playoff berth and the Central Division title.

Coach Vince Lombardi's team took a 7-0 lead against the Rams on a 30-yard touchdown pass from quarterback Bart Starr to wide receiver Carroll Dale late in the first quarter.

The Rams tied it early in the second quarter when quarterback Roman Gabriel hit Jack Snow with a 16-yard touchdown pass.

Don Chandler's 32-yard field goal in the

After blocking a punt by Green Bay's Donny Anderson with 34 seconds left to play (above), Rams linebacker Tony Guillory was in a state of near shock (below). Guillory's big play set up the Rams' game-winning touchdown.

final minute of the first half gave Green Bay a 10-7 lead, but another Gabriel-to-Snow touchdown pass and a 23-yard field goal by Bruce Gossett put the Rams back on top 17-10 with a minute and a half left in the third quarter.

Then the Rams made a tactical error. All game long they had squib-kicked away from Green Bay's electrifying Travis Williams, a 6-foot 1-inch, 210-pound rookie return wizard with 9.3 speed. Williams already had returned three kickoffs for touchdowns in 1967.

Following the field goal, though, Gossett boomed a kickoff to Williams, who fielded it

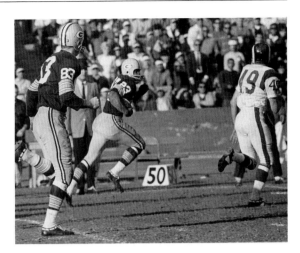

Rams quarterback Roman Gabriel (left): 20 of 36 for 227 yards, three touchdowns, and a game-winning pass to Bernie Casey.

Green Bay's Travis Williams raced 104 yards for a touchdown on this kickoff return—his fourth return for a touchdown in 1967.

four yards deep in the Packers' end zone.

Williams came rocketing out and smashed into burly Rams tackle Bob Nichols at the 15. The impact knocked the 255-pound Nichols out of one shoe. Williams bounced away from the collision, kept his balance, and sped toward the sideline. When he reached it, no one was in front of him. No one caught him. In the space of 21 seconds, the game once again was tied 17-17.

Gossett's 16-yard field goal at 4:44 of the fourth quarter gave the Rams a temporary 20-17 advantage, but Green Bay running back Chuck Mercein scored on a four-yard run with 2:19 left to put the Packers back in front 24-20.

It got more ominous for the Rams a minute later. Their offense stalled, and they had to punt the ball back to Green Bay.

But the Fearsome Foursome (Merlin Olsen, Deacon Jones, Roger Brown, and Lamar Lundy) and the rest of the Rams' defense straitjacketed the Packers for three consecutive plays, forcing Green Bay to punt from its own 27 with 54 seconds left.

Rams reserve linebacker Tony Guillory shot through the middle of the line untouched and

blocked Donny Anderson's punt—the first block in Anderson's career. The ball caromed to Los Angeles's Claude Crabbe, who rambled amid a wild pack to the Packers' 5 before being hauled down by Anderson.

On first down, Gabriel threw out of bounds, stopping the clock. Then with 37 seconds remaining, he faked a handoff to running back Tommy Mason, freezing the Green Bay secondary just long enough for end Bernie Casey to slip into the end zone, catch a game-winning pass from Gabriel, and incite delirium among the faithful who had remained in the Coliseum.

"It's the first time I ever cried at a game," Allen said.

"I wasn't worried about scoring a touchdown," said Rams defensive tackle Brown. "When we blocked the punt, I knew we would get the score. If we had to pick up a man and throw him into the end zone with the ball, we're going to get the score. The touchdown was the frosting on the cake. The blocked punt was the winner."

The following week, the Rams scored a 34-10 victory over the Colts in Los Angeles to win the Coastal Division crown.

A four-yard touchdown run by Green Bay running back Chuck Mercein (30) with 2:19 remaining gave the Packers a short-lived 24-20 lead.

Los Angeles Memorial Coliseum, Los Angeles, California

| Green Bay | 7 | 3 | 7 | 7 | —24 |
| Los Angeles | 0 | 7 | 10 | 10 | —27 |

HOW THEY SCORED

GB—Dale 30 pass from Starr (Chandler kick)
LA—Snow 16 pass from Gabriel (Gossett kick)
GB—FG Chandler 32
LA—Snow 11 pass from Gabriel (Gossett kick)
LA—FG Gossett 23
GB—Williams 104 kickoff return (Chandler kick)
LA—FG Gossett 16
GB—Mercein 4 run (Chandler kick)
LA—Casey 5 pass from Gabriel (Gossett kick)
Attendance—76,637

December 31, 1967

GREEN BAY PACKERS 21
DALLAS COWBOYS 17

"**G**ood morning," said the hotel operator. "This is your eight o'clock wakeup call. The temperature outside is minus six degrees."

That's how the Dallas Cowboys, on the morning of their 1967 NFL Championship Game against the Packers, were greeted on the coldest New Year's Eve in Green Bay history. That was the good news. By kickoff it was minus-13 degrees, and frigid northwest gusts reduced the wind-chill temperature to a cruel minus-38.

"I can't even describe how cold it was," said Dallas quarterback Don Meredith. "All I can say is, it hurt to breathe."

Dallas was stoked by the memory of its agonizing 34-27 championship game loss to Green Bay the previous year. The Cowboys, a rising NFL power, were facing Green Bay in its final hour of 1960s greatness.

A hearty but shivering crowd of 50,861, armed with thermal blankets, flasks, and thermos bottles, showed up at Lambeau Field for this intriguing title rematch. Specially erected bench shelters and liquid-gas portable heaters provided some relief for the players on the sidelines, but were no help to those on the field.

The Packers had installed an $80,000 "electric blanket" beneath the Lambeau Field turf to counteract the arctic air that knifes through Wisconsin in December. There were nearly 14 miles of heating cable juiced by 780,000 watts, six inches below the playing surface. The night before the game, the temperature plummeted so rapidly the system couldn't handle it, and the field turned into hard, glazed pavement.

Green Bay coach Vince Lombardi liked to use the cold as a psychological ploy, because the Packers were accustomed to freezing weather. But this was no ordinary cold. As the late Green Bay defensive tackle Henry Jordan put it, "Lombardi got down on his hands and knees to pray for cold, and he stayed too long."

Quarterback Bart Starr's 8-yard touchdown pass to Boyd Dowler on the opening drive of the first quarter, and another 46-yarder to Dowler early in the second, chilled the Cowboys even more, putting the Packers in front 14-0.

How cold was it in Green Bay? Cold enough for Dallas tackle Jim Boeke to try to prevent frostbitten lungs by first filtering the frigid air through a cap.

Dallas fought back, and crept ahead 17-14 early in the fourth quarter on halfback Dan Reeves's 50-yard scoring pass to flanker Lance Rentzel.

With less than five minutes to play, the Packers began a truly legendary drive.

"That last Packers drive was one of the most spine-tingling, mind-over-matter drives I've ever seen," said CBS broadcaster Ray Scott. "The field was treacherous. Impossible footing.

"I'll never forget [linebacker] Ray Nitschke screaming at the Packers' offense before the drive, his clenched fist waving in the air. 'Don't let me down. Don't let me down,' he yelled."

The Packers were 69 yards away with 4:58 left. They hadn't scored a point for nearly 38 minutes, and the inspired Dallas defense, anchored by defensive tackle Bob Lilly, hadn't yielded more than 14 yards on any of Green

---

Lambeau Field, Green Bay, Wisconsin

Dallas	0	10	0	7	—17
Green Bay	7	7	0	7	—21

HOW THEY SCORED

GB — Dowler 8 pass from Starr (Chandler kick)
GB — Dowler 46 pass from Starr (Chandler kick)
Dall — Andrie 7 fumble return (Villanueva kick)
Dall — FG Villanueva 21
Dall — Rentzel 50 pass from Reeves (Villanueva kick)
GB — Starr 1 run (Chandler kick)
Attendance—50,861

Dallas took a 17-14 lead (left) when Lance Rentzel (19) caught a 50-yard touchdown pass from halfback Dan Reeves.

Boyd Dowler clutched one of his four receptions; he caught two touchdown passes to give the Packers a 14-0 lead.

Running back Chuck Mercein (above) ran eight yards to the Dallas 3 on a "sucker play" to set up Green Bay's game winner.

The winning touchdown (right): Bart Starr plunged into the end zone over a block by guard Jerry Kramer (64).

Bay's previous 10 possessions.

But Chuck Mercein, a bargain-basement back-up acquired when the Packers' front-line backs were injured, suddenly began running like a man possessed. He gained 42 of the 68 yards on the final drive. From the Dallas 11 with 1:11 left, Mercein crashed through the left side and burrowed eight yards to the 3 as the clock ticked below the 60-second mark.

"What a gutty call that was," Mercein said. "Bart sent me in there on a sucker play. The left guard [Gale Gillingham] pulled right, hoping that Lilly would follow him. But what if Lilly slips? What if he's too tired to chase quickly?"

After giving up a first down on the 1, the Cowboys stiffened, denying the Packers twice. With 17 seconds left, and third-and-goal, Green Bay called its final time out.

Green Bay could have kicked a field goal and sent the game into overtime, but Lombardi wanted an immediate victory. "Let's run it in," he told Starr on the sideline.

Starr returned to the huddle, and asked all-pro guard Jerry Kramer if he could make the key block on Dallas's Jethro Pugh. Kramer nodded.

"All right then," Starr said, "thirty-one wedge, like a fullback dive. But I'm going to carry it. Dammit, I want it in there. Nothing short of the goal. It's up to you, Jerry."

Kramer was up to the task, and delivered one of the most famous blocks in football history.

"Jethro was on my inside shoulder, my left shoulder," Kramer described in his autobiography, *Instant Replay*. "I came off the ball as fast as I ever have in my life. I came off the ball as fast as anyone could. In fact, I wouldn't swear that I didn't beat the center's snap by a fraction of a second. I wouldn't swear that I wasn't actually offside on the play."

Kramer rammed his helmet into Pugh's chest as the big tackle fought for traction on the slippery turf and Starr lunged over Kramer's right leg into the frozen end zone. The Packers were NFL champions once again and on their way to a second consecutive victory in the AFL-NFL World Championship Game.

November 17, 1968

OAKLAND RAIDERS 43
NEW YORK JETS 32

Like millions of football fans across the country, NBC president Julian Goodman was watching his network's telecast of a wild, touchdown-crazy adventure from the West Coast between the New York Jets and the Oakland Raiders on November 17, 1968.

Both quarterbacks, New York's Broadway Joe Namath and Oakland's Daryle Lamonica, came out with six-shooters drawn and firing right at the start of the game.

Lamonica had thrown two touchdown passes and had completed a two-point conversion pass (a rule favored in the American Football League) to give the Raiders a 22-19 third-quarter lead. They were knocking on the Jets' door again as the period ended.

But New York recovered a fumble by Oakland rookie halfback Charlie Smith on its own 3-yard line on the first play of the fourth quarter. Namath immediately completed a 47-yard pass to flanker Don Maynard. On the next play, Namath hurled a 50-yard touchdown pass to Maynard, who gained a club-record 228 yards on 10 catches. Six minutes later, Jets placekicker Jim Turner kicked his third field goal of the game, and New York led 29-22.

Lamonica took the Raiders on an 88-yard scoring drive, and produced a 29-29 tie with a 22-yard scoring pass to Fred Biletnikoff.

Another field goal by Turner broke the tie with just 65 seconds left. Oakland was going to get the ball again, though. On this surreal afternoon, that meant anything could happen.

A nationwide television audience was hypnotized by the spectacle, but at NBC headquarters in New York, there was high anxiety. The network had scheduled—and heavily promoted—its television adaptation of Johanna Spyri's children's classic, "Heidi," scheduled to begin at 7 P.M. in the East. A normal football game with a 4 P.M. East Coast kickoff wouldn't have created any dilemma. But the aerial duel between Namath and Lamonica (for a combined

Daryle Lamonica (top) threw four touchdown passes. The biggest went to Charlie Smith (below) with 42 seconds left.

total of 71 passes), 19 penalties, and many time-outs had extended the game. When several minutes remained in the fourth quarter (which took 45 minutes), it became obvious to NBC executives the game was going to interfere with the start of "Heidi."

It never has been clear just who gave the order. But a decision was made to cut away from the game, and begin "Heidi" on time.

Just after Oakland had swooped into scoring territory on the Jets' 43-yard line with 50 seconds to play (on a 20-yard pass from Lamonica to Charlie Smith and the Jets' *fifth* facemask penalty of the day), the game vanished—except in areas west of Denver, where it still was only 4 P.M. The two teams were just returning to the line of scrimmage when television screens momentarily went dark.

After a commercial, incredulous millions stared as the opening credits for "Heidi" ap-

Jets tackle Winston Hill (75) had a tall order: to protect Joe Namath (12) from 6-7, 275-pound Ben Davidson (83).

A 12-yard field goal by Jim Turner (11) gave the Jets a 32-29 lead with a minute left. NBC officials decided to cut to "Heidi."

peared on the screen. What kind of lunacy was this? Where was the game? What was happening in Oakland?

The outrage was loudest in New York, where more than 10,000 mutinous callers overwhelmed and literally short-circuited the NBC switchboard at Rockefeller Center. Goodman called his office to find out who had lost their senses. He couldn't get through. Other callers, frustrated with busy signals at NBC, began calling newspapers, the telephone company, and even the New York Police Department's emergency number, demanding an explanation.

Meanwhile in Oakland, the Raiders compounded NBC's gaffe into a colossal blunder. Lamonica struck for a go-ahead touchdown with 42 seconds left on a 43-yard touchdown

pass to Smith. Then, incredibly, the Raiders scored again nine seconds later when Preston Ridlehuber recovered a Jets fumble on the following kickoff on the 2 and fell into the end zone. Final score: Oakland 43, New York 32. Meanwhile, seething football fans across the country were watching Heidi stroll up an Alpine hillside with her grandfather.

More than an hour and 20 minutes after switching to "Heidi," NBC decided to run a crawl reporting the outcome of the game. It was a scrawny olive branch. Then to redouble the evening's bad timing, NBC ran the information

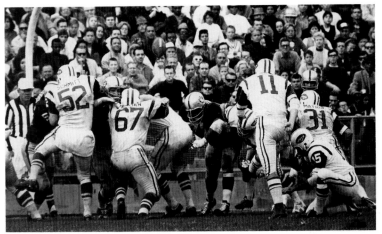

a second time—just as Heidi's paralyzed cousin Klara, in the movie's most dramatic moment, was summoning up the courage to leave her wheelchair and try to walk.

The NBC peacock should have been temporarily replaced by an ostrich.

In a statement released at 8:30 P.M., Goodman said the affair was a "forgivable error... committed by humans concerned about the children" who were expecting to see "Heidi" at 7 P.M. "I missed [watching] the end of the game as much as anyone else," he admitted.

A forgotten irony of the "Heidi" affair: Earlier in the day, NBC vice president for sports Carl Lindemann had ordered the televised Buffalo-San Diego game off the air with nearly five minutes remaining so the Jets-Raiders game could go on the air precisely at 4 P.M. in the East.

Another irony: "Heidi" was sponsored by Timex.

This cute little girl caused a lot of trouble.

Oakland-Alameda County Coliseum, Oakland, California

New York	6	6	7	13	—32
Oakland	7	7	8	21	—43

HOW THEY SCORED

NY —FG J. Turner 44
NY —FG J. Turner 18
Oak —Wells 9 pass from Lamonica (Blanda kick)
Oak —Cannon 48 pass from Lamonica (Blanda kick)
NY —Namath 1 run (pass failed)
NY —Mathis 4 run (J. Turner kick)
Oak —Smith 3 run (Lamonica pass to Dixon)
NY —Maynard 50 pass from Namath (J. Turner kick)
NY —FG J. Turner 12
Oak —Biletnikoff 22 pass from Lamonica (Blanda kick)
NY —FG J. Turner 26
Oak —Smith 43 pass from Lamonica (Blanda kick)
Oak —Ridlehuber 2 fumble return (Blanda kick)
Attendance—53,318

December 29, 1968

NEW YORK JETS 27
OAKLAND RAIDERS 23

Jets quarterback Joe Namath, scrambling to avoid two Oakland infiltrators, attempted a record 49 passes. He completed 19 for 266 yards and three touchdowns.

The 1968 season was full of thrills for the New York Jets. Yet often forgotten in the glare of their victory over the Baltimore Colts in Super Bowl III is the suspenseful afternoon two weeks earlier that delivered the Jets to Miami: the AFL Championship Game against the Raiders at Shea Stadium.

December 29, 1968, was a bitter, windswept day in New York. Jets linebacker Ralph Baker recalled the deep chill he felt when he walked onto the field at Shea to loosen up for the game and saw an unusual structure by the visiting team's bench area.

"They [the Raiders] had built a shelter over their bench to keep warm," Baker said. "It was something their players could get under, something to keep them out of the wind. I remember shaking my head and saying, 'Those guys are really smart. We play here all year and freeze to death, and they come in here and think of something like that.'"

Oakland managing general partner Al Davis had sneaked a small construction crew into Shea in the wee hours of the morning to erect the little makeshift sanctuary. But AFL president Milt Woodard ordered the Raiders to dismantle the shelter, which was blocking the line of vision for five rows in the stands.

All that was necessary to warm the crowd was its anticipation. The defending AFL champion Raiders had blistered the Kansas City Chiefs 41-6 in a Western Division playoff a week earlier for the right to meet the Eastern Division champion Jets. And, of course, the famous "Heidi" game still was fresh in everyone's memory.

This time the television audience got to see the entire contest, which turned out to be another rollicking, free-wheeling classic.

The two quarterbacks, Joe Namath and Daryle Lamonica, had trouble passing early in the game. The wind was howling and caused the dirt to blow up from the rock-hard infield in sudden, violent gusts. Namath had other problems during the game: a frightening, head-ringing sack by mammoth Raiders linemen Ben Davidson (275 pounds) and Ike Lassiter (270 pounds), a dislocated finger on his left hand, and a badly jammed thumb on his passing hand.

From the start, Namath went to work on rookie cornerback George Atkinson. Flanker Don Maynard, a survivor from the Jets' early days as the Titans, had scorched Atkinson for 228 yards on 10 catches in the "Heidi" game five weeks earlier.

"I knew they'd come at me again," Atkinson said.

Maynard caught two of the first three passes thrown his way; Atkinson was called for pass interference on the other. Then Maynard grabbed a 14-yard touchdown pass, and the Jets led 7-0. It was 10-0 before Lamonica rifled a 29-yard touchdown bullet to Fred Biletnikoff in the first minute of the second quarter. Jim Turner and George Blanda traded field goals, and the Jets led at halftime 13-10.

Another field goal by Blanda (after the Jets stopped the Raiders on three downs inside the New York 6) made it 13-13.

Then Namath, converting four third-down plays, drove the Jets 80 yards and tossed a 20-yard scoring pass to tight end Pete Lammons.

Flanker Don Maynard, being tackled by Oakland's George Atkinson, caught six passes and scored twice.

The Raiders' last chance at winning a second consecutive AFL title expired when Jets linebacker Ralph Baker (51) recovered a fumbled lateral in the closing minutes.

Shea Stadium, New York, New York

Oakland	0	10	3	10	—23
New York	10	3	7	7	—27

HOW THEY SCORED

NY —Maynard 14 pass from Namath (J. Turner kick)
NY —FG J. Turner 33
Oak —Biletnikoff 29 pass from Lamonica (Blanda kick)
NY —FG J. Turner 36
Oak —FG Blanda 26
Oak —FG Blanda 9
NY —Lammons 20 pass from Namath (J. Turner kick)
Oak —FG Blanda 20
Oak —Banaszak 5 run (Blanda kick)
NY —Maynard 6 pass from Namath (J. Turner kick)
Attendance—62,627

Early in the fourth quarter, Oakland drew to within four points on another field goal by Blanda, set up by Lamonica's 57-yard pass to Biletnikoff.

Now it was Atkinson's turn for a big moment. Reading Maynard's sideline move perfectly, Atkinson intercepted a pass from Namath and raced to the New York 5, where he was shoved out of bounds by the Jets' quarterback.

"I thought it was a good throw," Namath said, "but the kid just made a helluva play."

Oakland scored on Pete Banaszak's five-yard blast to move in front 23-20. That lead lasted three plays, all of 31 seconds.

Namath, undaunted by Atkinson's interception, threw a quick, 10-yard down-and-out to George Sauer, then sent Maynard long. With Atkinson just a half-step behind, Namath heaved a majestic, high-arcing spiral that landed in Maynard's hands at the Oakland 6, where both he and Atkinson went sprawling.

"We were both looking up at the ball while we were running," Atkinson recalled. "We both could see it fine. Then all of a sudden it moved crosswind toward the right sideline. He adjusted from the inside to the outside, took it over his right shoulder, and made a hell of a catch. I didn't think he could come up with it."

On the next play, Maynard was a safety valve. But when three other New York receivers were blanketed, Namath found Maynard open in the corner of the end zone for a touchdown and a 27-23 lead.

With six minutes remaining, Oakland reached the New York 26. On fourth-and-10, the Raiders spurned a field goal. But Lamonica was sacked by defensive end Verlon Biggs.

In the game's final minutes Lamonica drove the Raiders to the New York 24. But he threw an ill-advised pass to Charlie Smith—who was behind him and couldn't handle the ball. It was ruled a lateral, and the Jets' Baker pounced on the loose ball to defuse Oakland's final threat of the game. The Jets finally were AFL champions . . .and on their way to an appointment with destiny in Super Bowl III.

January 12, 1969

NEW YORK JETS 16
BALTIMORE COLTS 7

Joe Namath regaled the media before and after Super Bowl III. During the game, he confounded the Colts, and led the Jets to a stunning 16-7 victory.

Super Bowl III will be remembered forever as Joe Namath's Super Bowl. It should be. It was the quarterback's finest hour.

Namath's New York Jets were huge underdogs to the mighty Baltimore Colts, who had lost only once in 16 previous games, had outscored their opponents 402-144 in the regular season, had crushed Cleveland 34-0 in the NFL Championship Game, and were being proclaimed one of the greatest teams of all time.

"We didn't think they [the Jets] were really impressive," Baltimore head coach Don Shula admitted in his autobiography, *The Winning Edge.* "Their defense was awfully weak. It was tough showing the films to your squad and not having them get overconfident."

"Everyone was so sure Baltimore was going to win," CBS broadcaster Pat Summerall said, "that the previous day we rehearsed the post-

game show in the Colts' locker room...where [owner] Carroll Rosenbloom was going to stand...where Don Shula was going to stand."

When the Jets arrived in Fort Lauderdale earlier in the week to prepare for the game, Namath wasted no time invoking what Jets wide receiver George Sauer called "his genius for leadership." There was a highly publicized confrontation with Baltimore defensive end and placekicker Lou Michaels in a Fort Lauderdale restaurant. Then Namath proclaimed there were several AFL quarterbacks better than Baltimore's 34-year old Earl Morrall, who had played brilliantly all season in place of injured Johnny Unitas.

Namath's remark didn't amuse the Colts.

"Namath shouldn't talk like that," said Colts defensive end Bubba Smith. "A professional doesn't say things like that."

As it turned out, Namath hadn't even begun to talk.

Three days before the game, at a Miami Touchdown Club dinner, Namath delivered his famous called shot: "We're going to win Sunday. I'll guarantee you."

If any of the Jets' other players had said that, it probably would have received some attention. But Namath, pro football's one-man gashouse gang, attracted headlines for sending out his llama fur rug to be cleaned or for shaving his fu-manchu moustache in a television commercial. So this was mega-news.

"I've always wondered about how the Colts reacted to Joe's style," says George Sauer, who caught eight passes for 133 yards for the Jets in Super Bowl III. "There were scattered com-

---

Orange Bowl, Miami, Florida

New York	0	7	6	3 —16
Baltimore	0	0	0	7 —7

HOW THEY SCORED

NY —Snell 4 run (J. Turner kick)
NY —FG J. Turner 32
NY —FG J. Turner 30
NY —FG J. Turner 9
Balt —Hill 1 run (Michaels kick)
Attendance —75,389

---

ments expressing indignation, and I think they were somehow scandalized that anyone would approach an event of such magnitude with such an attitude. I believe it affected their preparation, making them tense without intensity. For after all, being praised as one of the best teams of the decade, they really had nothing to prove by winning.

"We had nothing to lose. I suspect the Colts thought we couldn't win, because they seemed to play with a kind of uninspired arrogance. As a team, they displayed collectively what athletes fear most: They were not on."

Baltimore dominated the early part of the first quarter, but something happened on the game's second play from scrimmage that created a tempo for the remainder of the contest.

The week before the game, Jets head coach Weeb Ewbank had stressed to his offense not to try sweeps against the Colts, because of the great pursuit of linebackers Mike Curtis and Don Shinnick, among others.

Ewbank's advice lasted for one down.

After a reliable off-tackle run by Snell on the Jets' initial offensive play from scrimmage, Namath challenged the Colts on second down.

"When we went up to the line," Snell says,

"I don't know what happened. But Namath checked off for some reason to a weakside sweep. I looked at [Emerson] Boozer, and he looked at me, and we both knew we heard it right.

"It broke clean. . . so clean it surprised me. I was ten to fifteen yards down the field when [safety] Rick Volk came up to tackle me. He ducked his head at the last second and I hit him with my knee. That knocked him out of the ball game. I went back to the huddle and said, 'These guys aren't so tough. We're supposed to be the underdogs, and there he is lying on the ground. He isn't even in the game.' The other guys said, 'You're right. They aren't Supermen in the NFL.' Then we really got after them."

Snell scored the game's first touchdown on a four-yard run for a 7-0 halftime lead.

Morrall, meanwhile, threw two interceptions that could have been touchdowns—once when he didn't see wide-open Jimmy Orr waving for the ball in the end zone. Some other well-thrown passes were bouncing off Morrall's receivers. Lou Michaels missed two first-half field-goal attempts. The Colts were pressing.

The Jets' lead had grown to 13-0 in the third quarter when Shula decided to replace Morrall with Johnny Unitas.

Unitas, who had missed much of the season with an elbow injury and had not played at all in the Colts' NFL Championship Game victory, drove the Colts 80 yards for a touchdown with 3:19 left. When Baltimore recovered an onside kick at the Jets' 44, and Unitas threw three crisp passes to reach the 19, Ewbank, who had coached Baltimore when Unitas made fourth-quarter magic against the Giants in the 1958 NFL Championship Game, felt a twinge of *deja vu*.

But this was 1969, and it was New York's day. The Jets kept Unitas and the Colts at arm's length in the remaining minutes and won 16-7.

Namath completed 17 of 28 passes for 206 yards and won the most-valuable-player award. He had many games with better statistics, but his contribution transcended numbers. In one afternoon, Namath and the Jets gave the AFL what it had sought for nine years: respect.

The headlines and MVP award went to Namath, but Super Bowl III was also Jets running back Matt Snell's finest hour. Snell picked up 121 yards on 30 carries, softening up the Colts' defense and setting up Namath's passing game.

November 8, 1970

OAKLAND RAIDERS 23
CLEVELAND BROWNS 20

During a time out late in the game, elderly miracle-worker George Blanda headed to the sideline for a strategy chat with 34-year-old Oakland Raiders head coach John Madden—nine years Blanda's junior.

In the early 1970s, television people believed that any televised game with Joe Namath meant additional ratings points. He was pro football's magnetic name, its biggest drawing card.

During the 1970 season, however, an unlikely hero in Oakland made Namath and every other NFL superstar take a back seat.

George Blanda was 43 in 1970. He had been released by the Houston Oilers at age 39 in 1967, after having been released by the Bears at 31 in 1959. Oakland picked him up in 1968, and he became the Raiders' placekicker and back-up quarterback.

The Raiders had drafted promising quarterback Ken Stabler from Alabama in 1968, but when Daryle Lamonica went out with a back injury against Pittsburgh in the sixth game of the 1970 season, the craggy old man got the call. The score was tied 7-7 when Blanda entered the game; he produced a 31-14 victory.

The following week, Blanda kicked a dramatic 48-yard field goal with three seconds left to give the Raiders a 17-17 tie with Kansas City.

The following week, the Raiders hosted Cleveland. Lamonica was fit to play; so was Blanda. Blanda harbored ill memories of losses to the Browns in the 1950s, when he was with the Bears.

"They had beaten us game after game, humiliated us, caused us terrible dressing downs from George Halas," Blanda wrote later in *Sports Illustrated.* "I remembered a game many years before when I'd had a little skirmish with some Cleveland players and on the next kickoff they sent a couple of their bully boys down the field with the sole assignment of getting me—which they did."

The Raiders jumped in front 13-0 on a touchdown pass from Lamonica to Charlie Smith and two field goals by Blanda. The Browns roared back and took a 17-13 lead when Bo Scott romped 63 yards for a touchdown on the last play from scrimmage in the third quarter.

Then the Browns did themselves in. Defensive end Ron Snidow crashed into Lamonica from the blindside, sending him to the sidelines with a shoulder injury. It was time for Blanda.

Oakland was forced to punt, then got the ball back when Nemiah Wilson intercepted a pass in the Raiders' end zone. Blanda promptly threw an interception. It looked as if Blanda's magic had vanished.

Four plays later Don Cockroft kicked a

Oakland-Alameda County Coliseum, Oakland, California				
Cleveland	0	10	7	3 —20
Oakland	3	10	0	10 —23

HOW THEY SCORED

Oak —FG Blanda 9
Oak —Smith 27 pass from Lamonica (Blanda kick)
Oak —FG Blanda 42
Cle —Kelly 10 pass from Nelsen (Cockroft kick)
Cle —FG Cockroft 42
Cle —Scott 63 run (Cockroft kick)
Cle —FG Cockroft 32
Oak —Wells 14 pass from Blanda (Blanda kick)
Oak —FG Blanda 52
Attendance—54,463

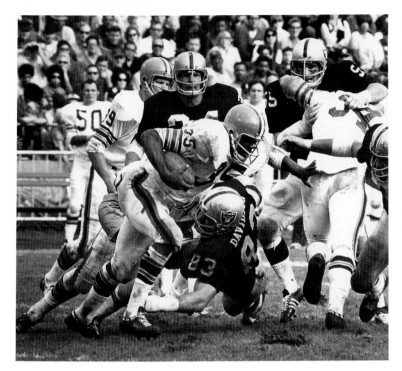

A 63-yard touchdown run on the final play of the third quarter by Cleveland's Bo Scott (35) put the Browns ahead 17-13.

32-yard field goal, and Cleveland led 20-13.

With 4:11 left, assuming it would be the Raiders' last chance, Blanda began a drive. After completions to Warren Wells, Smith, and Hewritt Dixon, Blanda faced fourth-and-16 on the Browns' 31. Throwing off-balance as he was being tackled, Blanda hit Fred Biletnikoff for a 17-yard gain and a first down.

Blanda immediately went for six points, and got them with a 14-yard pass to Wells. Blanda's extra point tied the game 20-20.

Oakland already had two ties in 1970, and, with just 1:19 remaining, this looked like number three. (Sudden-death overtime in regular-season games would not be adopted until 1974.) But cornerback Kent McCloughan intercepted a pass by Cleveland quarterback Bill Nelsen at the Oakland 46. With 34 seconds left, the Raiders had another last chance to win.

Blanda had no time outs. He threw incomplete twice, and also was decked twice by defensive end Jack Gregory. The second time, when Gregory came in from the blindside, Blanda took a swing at him. Then he completed a pass to Wells for a nine-yard gain. Suddenly, there were just three seconds left. It was fourth-and-16, the ball on the Cleveland 45. Just minutes earlier Blanda had been sucking oxygen from an inhalator on the bench. Now he was stepping off a 52-yard field-goal attempt—the longest he ever had tried with Oakland.

No one ever described a kick better than Bill King, the Raiders' ebullient radio play-by-play announcer, did that afternoon:

"Waiting for the snap...fourth down... here it is...snap...spotted down...it's kicked. That's got a *chance*! That is—good! It's good! Holy Toledo! The place has gone wild! Wheee-e-e-U! I don't believe it! I do not believe it! There are three seconds left in the game. Well, if you can hear me, this place has gone wild...the Oakland Raiders 23!...the Cleveland Browns 20. George Blanda has just been elected king of the world. I don't believe it! Holy Toledo! It went 53...no...52 yards! George Blanda has just been elected king of the world!"

At any rate, "Blanda for Mayor" buttons began popping up in the San Francisco Bay Area, and he became the darling of the Geritol generation.

NBC reported record numbers of television viewers for Oakland games, and the editor of the *Catholic Voice* wrote that church attendance was on the rise "because so many Oakland fans were saying 'If he makes this one, I'll go back to church.' "

After two more Blanda Specials—come-from-behind victories against Denver and San Diego the following two weeks—the producers of the hit television series "Mission: Impossible" sent Blanda, who was named NFL player of the year in 1970, a telegram "complaining" that he was pirating and plagiarizing their show.

The Pro Football Hall of Fame sent for one of his game jerseys to display in its rotunda. Eventually it sent for Blanda himself. He was inducted into the Hall of Fame in 1981.

Oakland wide receiver Warren Wells (81) got a 20-20 tie with this 14-yard touchdown catch. George Blanda's game-winning 52-yard field goal followed.

December 25, 1971

MIAMI DOLPHINS 27
KANSAS CITY CHIEFS 24

Garo Yepremian, an Armenian immigrant from Cyprus via Great Britain, kicked six field goals for the Detroit Lions in a 1966 game against the Minnesota Vikings. That prompted Minnesota head coach Norm Van Brocklin to say, "They ought to tighten the immigration laws." Yepremian, delighted with his new-found success, yelped, "I kick a touchdown."

The little Cypriot eventually was released by the Lions. He had been too erratic to suit head coach Joe Schmidt, who called Yepremian a "coach-killer." But Miami head coach Don Shula signed Yepremian in 1970, and Shula was glad to have him in Miami's 1971 divisional playoff game against the Kansas City Chiefs on Christmas Day.

Both teams had finished 10-3-1 in the regular season, but Miami never had beaten Kansas City. Since entering the AFL as an expansion team in 1966, the Dolphins had lost all six meetings with the Chiefs. The aggregate point differential was 213-47.

That was all B.Y.—Before Yepremian.

On Christmas Eve in 1971, Yepremian learned Kansas City's Jan Stenerud had been selected to represent the AFC in the second AFC-NFC Pro Bowl game. Yepremian, who led the AFC in scoring in 1971, resented the slight.

"It was the coaches' fault," Yepremian said. "I decided I'd show them and Stenerud that there had been a mistake... that I would kick better than he did all day."

Christmas didn't begin as Yepremian's—or Miami's—day. The Chiefs grabbed a 10-0 first-quarter lead on a 24-yard field goal by Stenerud and a 7-yard touchdown pass from quarterback Len Dawson to running back Ed Podolak.

Meanwhile, the Dolphins' power-running game, featuring Larry Csonka and Jim Kiick, was being handcuffed by Kansas City's brutish defense, particularly by linebacker Willie Lanier. ("It's one thing to run against a grizzly

Municipal Stadium, Kansas City, Missouri							
Miami	0	10	7	7	0	3	—27
Kansas City	10	0	7	7	0	0	—24

HOW THEY SCORED

KC —FG Stenerud 24
KC —Podolak 7 pass from Dawson (Stenerud kick)
Mia—Csonka 1 run (Yepremian kick)
Mia—FG Yepremian 14
KC —Otis 1 run (Stenerud kick)
Mia—Kiick 1 run (Yepremian kick)
KC —Podolak 3 run (Stenerud kick)
Mia—Fleming 5 pass from Griese (Yepremian kick)
Mia—FG Yepremian 37
Attendance—50,374

Kansas City's Ed Podolak (14) was a multi-purpose mainstay. He gained exactly 100 yards rushing and 100 yards receiving, and added another 150 on returns—including a 78-yard kickoff return in the fourth quarter.

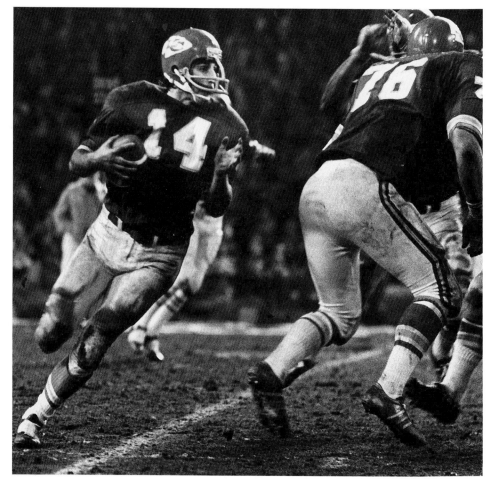

Bob Griese (12) beat a blitz by Bobby Bell (78) by tossing a 5-yard touchdown pass to Marv Fleming to force overtime.

Jan Stenerud stared at the ground in total disbelief after missing game-winning field-goal attempt.

Yepremian took a victory trot to the sideline after ending the longest game in NFL history with a 37-yard field goal in the sixth quarter.

midway through the fourth quarter put the Chiefs on top 24-17.

Miami responded with a 76-yard drive, which Griese completed with a five-yard touchdown pass to tight end Marv Fleming. It was 24-24 with 1:26 left.

Yepremian kicked off. He watched in horror as Podolak fielded the ball at his goal line, burst through the Miami coverage, and broke free near midfield. All that stood in Podolak's way was the 5-foot 7-inch, 170-pound Yepremian. Yepremian got in Podolak's way just enough to disrupt his momentum, and cornerback Curtis Johnson forced him out of bounds at the Miami 22-yard line.

Kansas City needed just a field goal to win. Four plays later, Dawson was down on one knee at the 31-yard line, waiting to spot a potential game-winning kick. Stenerud missed.

"There was no question in my mind that I was going to make it," Stenerud said later, "and I still don't know to this day how I missed it. I hit the ball perfectly. The angle was unusual, though. It wasn't in the middle and it wasn't on the hashmark. So I think the only thing I could have done was to line it up a little wrong."

The game entered sudden-death overtime. Only sudden death was not that sudden.

Kansas City won the coin toss, elected to receive, and Podolak tore off on another great return to the Chiefs' 46. (The game was virtually an Ed Podolak highlight film; he gained a total of 350 yards rushing, receiving, and on returns.)

Kansas City moved into range for Stenerud to try another field goal, this time from 42 yards. Miami linebacker Nick Buoniconti blocked it. Yepremian missed from 52 yards. The game entered a second overtime.

By this time, both clubs were exhausted. But Csonka had one big burst left in him. Early in the sixth quarter, he thundered for 29 yards on a misdirection play to put Miami on the Kansas City 36.

Griese maneuvered Miami to the middle of the field at the 30, to give Yepremian a perfect angle for a 37-yard field-goal attempt. Yepremian nailed it, ending the longest game in NFL history at 82 minutes and 40 seconds.

bear," Csonka said of Lanier, "but he's a smart grizzly bear.")

Miami quarterback Bob Griese, playing with a painful left shoulder, was forced to the air, and began softening up the Chiefs with passes to all-pro wide receiver Paul Warfield. Miami scored in the second quarter on Csonka's one-yard run, then got a 14-yard field goal by Yepremian. The first half ended 10-10.

Kansas City's Jim Otis and Miami's Kiick traded one-yard touchdown runs in the third quarter, but following a 63-yard reception by rookie Elmo Wright, Podolak's three-yard run

December 23, 1972

PITTSBURGH STEELERS 13
OAKLAND RAIDERS 7

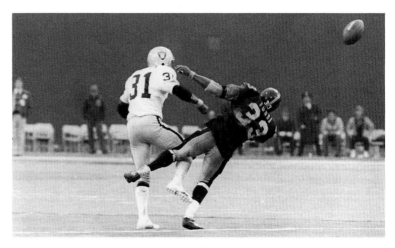

Cursed by more than four decades of mediocrity (and sometimes worse), owner Art Rooney's Pittsburgh Steelers were on the path to their National Football League dynasty in 1972.

Chuck Noll had been named head coach of the Steelers in 1969; his first team went 1-13. There was a silver lining, however. Armed with high draft picks, Noll began stocking talent for four future Super Bowl championship squads—players such as Mean Joe Greene, Terry Bradshaw, Mel Blount, Jack Ham, Larry Brown, Dwight White, Mike Wagner, and running back Franco Harris.

The Steelers hadn't planned to draft Harris. They were comfortable with running backs John (Frenchy) Fuqua and Preston Pearson, and were in desperate need of more secondary help. They wanted San Diego State's Willie Buchanon, who was projected as a solid pro cornerback.

When the Green Bay Packers, drafting ahead of Pittsburgh, took Buchanon, there was some sentiment (much of it Noll's) in the Steelers' front office to draft Robert Newhouse of the University of Houston. But Art Rooney, Jr., lobbied hard for Harris, who had been overshadowed during his Penn State career by teammate Lydell Mitchell.

Along with placekicker Roy Gerela, who developed a legion of loyalists known as Gerela's Gorillas, Harris quickly became a Pittsburgh folk hero. With his mixed ancestry (he was the son of a black army sergeant and his Italian World War II bride), he united Pittsburgh's ethnic neighborhoods, and inspired the

Probably the NFL's single most famous play, the Immaculate Reception, began when a pass from Terry Bradshaw ricocheted from a collision between Oakland safety Jack Tatum and Pittsburgh running back John (Frenchy) Fuqua (above) into the hands of Steelers running back Franco Harris (middle), who raced 60 yards for a game-winning touchdown (below).

Three Rivers Stadium, Pittsburgh, Pennsylvania

Oakland	0	0	0	7	—7
Pittsburgh	0	0	3	10	—13

HOW THEY SCORED

Pitt —FG Gerela 18
Pitt —FG Gerela 29
Oak— Stabler 30 run (Blanda kick)
Pitt —Harris 60 pass from Bradshaw (Gerela kick)
Attendance—50,327

---

birth of Franco's Italian Army, another group of fanatic followers. Harris also provided the backfield punch that led Pittsburgh to the 1972 AFC Central Division title and its first playoff berth ever. He rushed for 1,055 yards as a rookie.

Before becoming a footnote to Miami's perfect season in the AFC Championship Game, Pittsburgh stunned the Oakland Raiders in an AFC Divisional Playoff Game on a bizarre, magical play involving Bradshaw and Harris. The game touched off an intense, bitter rivalry between the two clubs that lasted for the remainder of the decade.

Some of the seeds were planted the day before the game. The Raiders, fanatically secretive about their practices, were about to end their final "closed" workout at Three Rivers Stadium. Suddenly someone with the Raiders discovered that high atop the stadium, in the private Allegheny Club, more than 100 people had spent a pleasant afternoon dining and drinking and watching Oakland prepare.

Later that night, Oakland tight end Bob Moore, trying to break through a Steelers pep rally being conducted outside the Raiders' hotel, got into a scuffle and was roughed up by a Pittsburgh policeman. Moore showed up for the game with his head covered in bandages.

Things would get worse for the Raiders.

The first 59 minutes and 44 seconds of the game were not especially memorable for either team. Pittsburgh had managed only two field goals by Gerela. The second one, with 3:50 left in the game, gave the Steelers a 6-0 lead.

Young Oakland quarterback Ken Stabler, who replaced an ineffective Daryle Lamonica in the fourth quarter, answered Gerela's field goal by scrambling 30 yards for a touchdown to put the Raiders in front 7-6 with 1:13 remaining. (It was only the second touchdown permitted by the Steelers in five games.)

With 22 seconds left, the Steelers looked beaten. They had the ball on their own 40,

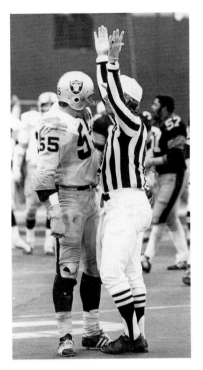

Official Fred Swearingen's touchdown signal after Harris's controversial catch enraged the Raiders, and linebacker Dan Conners let Swearingen know what he thought of the call.

fourth-and-10. Bradshaw dropped back to pass under heavy pressure. Scrambling to his right, he launched a rocket to Fuqua over the middle. The ball, Fuqua, Raiders safety Jack Tatum, and history all collided at the Oakland 35-yard line. The ball ricocheted back to the Steelers' 40, where Harris—racing upfield—caught it on a dead run at his shoetops. He never broke stride, and raced nearly untouched for 60 yards to the winning touchdown with five seconds left.

"That wasn't fate or luck or football," Art Rooney, Jr., said. "That was my father's seventy years of good Christian living."

The Raiders thought it was something else: an illegal play. Oakland head coach John Madden howled vehemently that the ball had bounced off Fuqua—not Tatum—and that the pass should have been ruled incomplete, having caromed directly from one offensive player to another. (Since 1978, that has been legal.)

Referee Fred Swearingen used the field-level phone to consult with NFL supervisor of officials Art McNally in the press box before officially signaling touchdown and touching off the city of Pittsburgh's celebration of what Steelers' radio announcer Myron Cope called "The Immaculate Reception."

"Tomorrow morning when I wake up and read it in the paper, I still won't believe it," Madden moaned.

"It hit Frenchy and he knows it," Tatum said.

Fuqua chose to keep the answer a mystery for the ages. "I put the answer in a time capsule," he said. "I'm not chopping down any cherry trees."

Later that night, Harris drove to the Greater Pittsburgh Airport to catch a plane home for Christmas. With a little time to kill before his flight, Harris walked alone into the terminal bar. He instantly recognized several Oakland players waiting for their flight back to Oakland.

"Nothing was said," Harris recalled. "But even in the darkness, I could feel their eyes on me. It made me feel like I stole their game. I guess I had, and it made me feel a little guilty.

"But not for long."

December 23, 1972

DALLAS COWBOYS 30
SAN FRANCISCO 49ERS 28

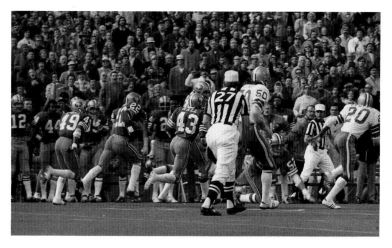

It was almost as if some sadist had a detailed map of the Bay Area and was pricking it with voodoo pins, puncturing logic in the process.

Then again, pro football often has little to do with logic, and it certainly offers no guarantees. Case in point: the events of Saturday, December 23, 1972.

When the day began, hopes were high in San Francisco and Oakland for a "Bay Area Super Bowl" between the Raiders and 49ers. Franco Harris's "Immaculate Reception" against the Raiders at Three Rivers Stadium earlier in the day eliminated half of that notion.

In San Francisco nearly three hours later, however, things were looking good for the 49ers. They were leading Dallas 28-13 with a little more that half the fourth quarter remaining in an NFC Divisional Playoff Game.

The Cowboys and 49ers were not playoff strangers. They had met in the NFC Championship Game in both 1970 and 1971. Dallas won both times, twice stranding San Francisco just one game short of the Super Bowl.

For 3½ quarters in the 1972 game, the 49ers had turned on their tormentors. The 49ers' Vic Washington set the early tone by returning the opening kickoff 97 yards for a touchdown and a 7-0 San Francisco lead.

The 49ers were opportunists most of the game. Fumbles by Dallas quarterback Craig Morton and running back Calvin Hill, plus linebacker Skip Vanderbundt's interception of one of Morton's passes, all resulted in one-yard touch-

San Francisco's Vic Washington (22) bolted 97 yards for a touchdown on the game's opening kickoff to give the 49ers an instant 7-0 lead.

Running back Larry Schreiber (35, above right) scored three times on one-yard runs to help the 49ers mount a 28-13 fourth-quarter lead.

One of Schreiber's touchdowns was set up when 49ers linebacker Skip Vanderbundt (52, right) intercepted a pass from Dallas quarterback Craig Morton.

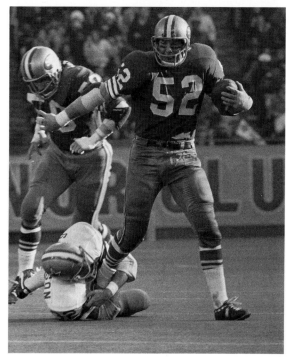

down runs by San Francisco's Larry Schreiber.

Through the first three quarters, Dallas responded only with Morton's 28-yard touchdown pass to Lance Alworth and a pair of field goals by Toni Fritsch.

Three plays from the end of the third quarter, Dallas head coach Tom Landry replaced Morton with Roger Staubach, whose preseason shoulder separation had relegated him to limited playing time in 1972.

"When coach Landry told me to go in," Staubach said, "Craig came over and hugged me and said, 'I have confidence in you. You can

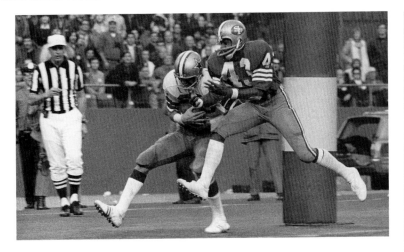

Dallas wide receiver Ron Sellers came up with a 10-yard touchdown catch to cap the Cowboys' stunning comeback; San Francisco cornerback Windlan Hall (43) and the 49ers came up empty.

The man with the miracle touch was Dallas quarterback Roger Staubach (12, right), who threw two touchdown passes in the final two minutes.

win.' I think that gave me as much confidence as anything that happened. . .that Craig would feel and act like that after he'd been pulled."

Morton's confidence at first looked misplaced. Staubach's first pass was incomplete. He lost 10 yards on another attempt. Then he fumbled as he was flattened by Bob Hoskins—the fifth turnover forced by the 49ers.

A score of any kind might have finished Dallas, but Bruce Gossett missed a field goal.

Staubach's problems continued; he was being pressured by the 49ers' fierce pass rush. But Dallas inched closer when Hill blasted 48 yards up the middle to set up Fritsch's third field goal.

The score was 28-16 two seconds before the two-minute warning. Suddenly, Staubach uncapped bottled lightning. He started completing everything—a pass to Walt Garrison, another to Garrison, one to Billy Parks, and to Parks again for a 20-yard touchdown. It took Staubach just 32 seconds to airlift Dallas 55 yards. It was 28-23. Ninety seconds remained.

Longtime 49ers fans began squirming. Was this going to be some ghoulish sequel to the 1957 Western Conference playoff disaster at Kezar Stadium, when the 49ers blew a 24-7 half-

time lead and lost to the Detroit Lions 31-27?

As expected, the Cowboys tried an onside kick. Fritsch, a former soccer standout from Austria who hadn't begun kicking footballs until 1971, approached the ball, and appeared to run past it. Using an old soccer ploy, he dragged his foot behind him and sliced the ball on a sharp diagonal path across the field. San Francisco's Preston Riley got his hands on the wildly spinning ball but was belted by rookie Ralph Coleman. The ball popped loose—into the hands of Dallas's Mel Renfro.

"The kick Toni made gave us the chance we needed," Landry said. "It was unbelievable. You have to wonder if he could do it again, even if he had a million chances."

There was no denying Staubach now. He ran for 21 yards, picked up 19 more on a pass to Parks, and then, just as he was being hit on a blitz, he rifled a 10-yard pass to Ron Sellers in the end zone. Dallas led 30-28.

There were still 52 seconds left. Quarterback John Brodie completed three quick passes and rushed the 49ers to the Dallas 22 with 10 seconds left. But the third completion, a great 23-yard catch by Riley, was nullifed by a holding penalty. The ball was brought back beyond field-goal range. On the next play, Brodie's pass was intercepted. The Cowboys had won.

Wrote the *San Diego Union's* Jerry Magee: "Dallas scored 14 points with less than two minutes to play to beat San Francisco 30-28 in the most miraculous playoff finish staged in the NFL in the last three hours."

Candlestick Park, San Francisco, California

Dallas	3	10	0	17	—30
San Francisco	7	14	7	0	—28

HOW THEY SCORED

SF —V. Washington 97 kickoff return (Gossett kick)
Dall —FG Fritsch 37
SF —Schreiber 1 run (Gossett kick)
SF —Schreiber 1 run (Gossett kick)
Dall —FG Fritsch 45
Dall —Alworth 28 pass from Morton (Fritsch kick)
SF —Schreiber 1 run (Gossett kick)
Dall —FG Fritsch 27
Dall —Parks 20 pass from Staubach (Fritsch kick)
Dall —Sellers 10 pass from Staubach (Fritsch kick)
Attendance—61,214

November 28, 1974

DALLAS COWBOYS 24
WASHINGTON REDSKINS 23

The Bible says, "Be not faithless, but believing."

That should also have been an official commandment for Dallas Cowboys fans during the era of Roger Staubach, the NFL's all-time grand master of the fourth-quarter rally.

Perhaps Dallas's most implausible comeback victory ever, though, occurred on Thanksgiving Day in 1974—with Staubach watching from the sideline. With millions of turkey dinners on standby, a nationwide television audience watched an unknown back-up quarterback named Clint Longley blaze across their screens to rescue the Cowboys from certain defeat at the hands of their most bitter adversary, the Washington Redskins.

Dallas had a 6-5 record going into the game, and trailed both the Redskins and the St. Louis Cardinals in the NFC East. The Cowboys had lost to the Redskins 12 days earlier. Another loss would end Dallas's barely glimmering playoff hopes.

Before the game, Washington defensive tackle Diron Talbert was in a talkative mood. Talbert said he hoped Staubach would try to run with the ball against Washington. That would give Talbert and his mates a chance to delete Staubach, and then have some fun with Longley, a rookie from Abilene Christian who never had appeared in an NFL game. That idea seemed sound enough; at one time, so did booking passage on the Titanic.

With Dallas trailing 9-3, Cowboys running back Walt Garrison fumbled on the opening play of the third quarter. Former Cowboy Duane Thomas made Dallas pay for the turnover when he scored on a nine-yard swing pass from Billy Kilmer. Washington now led 16-3.

Talbert's pregame wish came true with 9:57 left in the third quarter when Staubach was assisted to the sideline in a daze after absorbing a seismic hit by Washington linebacker Dave Robinson.

Enter Longley, who had earned the nickname "The Mad Bomber" for bouncing a pass off Tom Landry's coaching tower in training camp, for his first regular-season snap.

Things looked grim for Dallas, but Longley had the coolest hand—and head—on the field.

"He was a very poised cat," said Cowboys offensive tackle Rayfield Wright. "He came in as

The Redskins knocked Dallas quarterback Roger Staubach out of the game, but Staubach's replacement, Clint Longley (19), had a knockout punch of his own.

Texas Stadium, Irving, Texas					
Washington	3	6	7	7	—23
Dallas	3	0	14	7	—24

HOW THEY SCORED

Dall —FG Herrera 24
Wash—FG Moseley 45
Wash—FG Moseley 34
Wash—FG Moseley 39
Wash—Thomas 9 pass from Kilmer (Moseley kick)
Dall —DuPree 35 pass from Longley (Herrera kick)
Dall —Garrison 1 run (Herrera kick)
Wash—Thomas 19 run (Moseley kick)
Dall —Pearson 50 pass from Longley (Herrera kick)
Attendance—63,243

if he'd started the game. When Garrison came in the huddle and was trying to explain which way and what the formation was, Longley told him to shut up, that he was calling the game and knew what to do. I think that's the sign of a poised quarterback."

Longley moved the Cowboys down the field and threw a 35-yard touchdown pass to tight end Billy Joe DuPree. That whittled the Redskins' lead to 16-10.

A few minutes later, Longley again maneuvered Dallas deep into Washington territory, and Garrison scored on a one-yard plunge to put Dallas in front 17-16.

Texas Stadium was rocking. But Washington regained the lead 23-17 on a 19-yard run by Thomas early in the fourth quarter. The Redskins recovered another Dallas fumble, and moved into position for a field goal.

Another Dallas rookie rose to the occasion. Ed (Too Tall) Jones extended his 6-foot 9-inch frame to block Mark Moseley's 24-yard field-goal attempt. Dallas had the ball back with five minutes to go.

The Cowboys gave it right back to Washington when Drew Pearson fumbled. But the Cowboys' defense held the Redskins. Longley had one more crack with 1:45 to play and no time outs.

Relying mostly on nerve, Longley got a first down on the 50 with a fourth-and-six completion to veteran wide receiver Bob Hayes.

There were 35 seconds left. Landry sent in a play calling for Pearson to run a 20-yard down-and-in pattern. In the huddle, Pearson suggested a variation to go deep instead. Since he'd be facing seven defensive backs in a prevent defense, the odds were astronomical. "What have we got to lose?" Longley asked.

Longley pinpointed his pass to Pearson, who eluded his coverage, caught the ball on the 4, and stepped into the end zone.

Washington still had 28 seconds, but Dallas recovered a fumble and held on 24-23.

"I wasn't nervous—there was no time for that—but I sure was excited," Longley said. "I

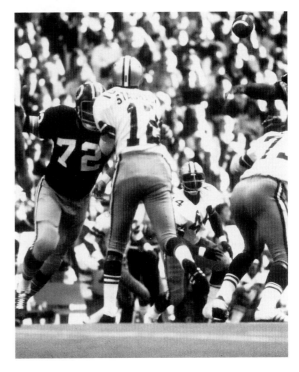

Duane Thomas (47, above), who had starred for Dallas in 1970 and 1971, was a 1974 Thanksgiving Day thorn for the Cowboys; he scored both of Washington's touchdowns.

As Roger Staubach unloaded a pass, Washington's Diron Talbert (72) was about to unload on Staubach.

tried to guess with them. I knew what I would do to a rookie quarterback if I was the Redskins. On that last pass, when the ball was halfway there, I saw Drew had got the defensive back turned around, and I knew we had a shot at it. Well, after all, this is what I've been training for."

Dallas guard Blaine Nye came up with the game's definitive summation. Alluding to Longley's total inexperience and his reliance on instinct over preparation, Nye said, "It was a triumph of the uncluttered mind."

A footnote: Just two years later, after returning to semi-oblivion on the bench, Longley was involved in several training camp altercations with Dallas's first-string miracle-worker, Staubach. He quickly was waived by the Cowboys.

For one Thanksgiving afternoon, however, Clint Longley earned a permanent place in football folklore.

December 21, 1974

OAKLAND RAIDERS 28
MIAMI DOLPHINS 26

This was a mercurial game of fluctuating scores and emotions. At left, a Miami celebration erupted after a touchdown by Benny Malone (32), which gave the Dolphins a 26-21 lead with 2:08 left. But it was Oakland coach John Madden (right) who took a victory ride.

It was billed as "Super Bowl 8½."

The Oakland Raiders, with the best regular-season record in the NFL (12-2), were hosting the two-time defending Super Bowl champion Miami Dolphins in a 1974 AFC Divisional Playoff Game. It was widely presumed the winner of the game would go on to win Super Bowl IX.

As it turned out, neither team even made it to the Super Bowl. But on December 21, 1974, the Raiders and Dolphins played a game for the ages.

Oakland-Alameda County Coliseum was a madhouse. Every fan seemed to have brought something black to wave—black pennants, black socks, black handkerchiefs...even black bras. "I've never seen the Coliseum more electric," said Raiders executive assistant Al Lo-Casale.

The two teams wasted no time getting things started. Miami rookie Nat Moore bolted 89 yards for a touchdown on the opening kickoff. With just 15 seconds elapsed, Miami led 7-0.

It stayed that way until early in the second quarter, when Oakland quarterback Ken Stabler fired a 31-yard touchdown pass to running back Charlie Smith.

Miami consumed much of the second quarter by keeping the ball on the ground—and in the hands of running backs Larry Csonka and Benny Malone. A field goal by Garo Yepremian gave the Dolphins a 10-7 halftime lead.

The Raiders took a 14-10 lead on their first possession of the second half when Fred Biletnikoff made an amazing 13-yard touchdown catch. Miami cornerback Tim Foley was all over Biletnikoff, pinning his right hand. But Biletnikoff caught the ball with the his left hand as he tightroped the sideline in the right corner of the end zone.

Bob Griese came right back with a 16-yard touchdown pass to Paul Warfield, but Yepremian's extra-point attempt was low, and Oakland defensive end Bubba Smith blocked it.

With his right hand pinned by Miami's Tim Foley, Fred Biletnikoff used his left for a brilliant scoring catch.

The Dolphins added three more points three minutes into the fourth quarter on Yepremian's 46-yard field goal, his longest of the season.

Trailing 19-14 with 4:54 left in the game, Stabler launched a quick air raid against the depleted Miami secondary, which had lost safety

Jake Scott and cornerback Curtis Johnson to injuries earlier in the game. After an 11-yard completion to Biletnikoff, he went deep to Branch. The ball was underthrown, but Branch came back for it and caught it just before it hit the ground at the Miami 28. Dolphins reserve cornerback Henry Stuckey slid by Branch without touching him. Branch got up and raced 72 yards into the end zone, for a 21-19 lead.

Now it was Griese's turn. After a completion to Moore and two runs by Csonka, the Dolphins reached the Oakland 23 with just under 2½ minutes to play. The Raiders braced for another Csonka explosion up the middle. Instead, Griese pitched to Malone, who raced to the end zone. Miami was back on top 26-21.

There was 2:08 remaining. Following the kickoff, Stabler quickly hit Biletnikoff twice for gains of 18 and 20 yards. Two more completions (to Branch and Frank Pitts), and running

Banners, fans, an official, and Cliff Branch all verified a theatrical touchdown by Branch.

Even seeing this play wasn't believing it, but a remarkable desperation catch by Clarence Davis (28) with 26 seconds left beat Miami.

Oakland-Alameda County Coliseum, Oakland, California

Miami	7	3	6	10	—26
Oakland	0	7	7	14	—28

HOW THEY SCORED

Mia —N. Moore 89 kickoff return (Yepremian kick)
Oak —C. Smith 31 pass from Stabler (Blanda kick)
Mia —FG Yepremian 33
Oak —Biletnikoff 13 pass from Stabler (Blanda kick)
Mia —Warfield 16 pass from Griese (kick failed)
Mia —FG Yepremian 46
Oak —Branch 72 pass from Stabler (Blanda kick)
Mia —Malone 23 run (Yepremian kick)
Oak —Davis 8 pass from Stabler (Blanda kick)
Attendance—53,023

back Clarence Davis's six-yard inside slant put the Raiders on the Miami 8 with 35 seconds left. The Raiders used their final time out.

What happened next will be included in film anthologies of all-time great finishes.

"The play we called was '91 flare 7,'" said Tom Flores, then the Raiders' receivers coach. "We expected to have either [tight end] Bob Moore or Biletnikoff open on the right side."

The Dolphins smothered Biletnikoff with double coverage. Stabler looked for Moore. He was covered. Stabler looked for running back Marv Hubbard. He couldn't break free. The pocket crumbled, and Stabler scrambled to the left, desperately looking for someone to get open. Branch and Davis were bottled up together in the end zone. Miami defensive end Vern Den Herder, chasing Stabler from behind, lunged and grabbed his ankles. As Stabler began to topple—and the Raiders' season with him—he flipped a knuckleball toward Davis, who was cutting across the end zone.

Miami linebacker Mike Kolen was with Davis. For an instant, they both had the ball. Then they collided with Miami defensive back Charles Babb, and the ball wedged into Davis's chest. He finally wrested it away from Kolen, and held on for the game-winning touchdown.

"I didn't know I was that strong," Davis said. "I did it by the grace of God—and a little good luck."

"When you lose like that," said Miami head coach Don Shula, "you know it wasn't meant to be. Your dreams just go down the drain."

December 28, 1975

DALLAS COWBOYS 17
MINNESOTA VIKINGS 14

Dueling each other in a 1975 NFC Divisional Playoff Game were two of the NFL's all-time best scrambling quarterbacks: the Vikings' Fran Tarkenton (left) and the Cowboys' Roger Staubach (right). On this day, Staubach delivered victory.

There have been hundreds of NFL games with last-second, desperation Hail Mary passes. One stands apart from the rest: the 1975 NFC Divisional Playoff Game between the Minnesota Vikings and the Dallas Cowboys.

It was a longshot that Dallas had even made the playoffs that year. With 12 rookies on the squad, the team's operative word was "rebuilding."

But head coach Tom Landry coaxed a 10-4 record and a wild-card playoff berth from his new-look team, which included hard-hitting rookies Randy White, Pat Donovan, Herb Scott, Bob Breunig, and Thomas Henderson.

Minnesota didn't sneak up on anyone; the Vikings (12-2) were two-time defending NFC champions, solid everywhere, and eager to atone for two consecutive Super Bowl losses.

The setting was Metropolitan Stadium in Bloomington. The day was gloomy and overcast with a threat of snow, but for December in Minnesota, it was a mild 27 degrees.

The game's first break went to the Vikings early in the second quarter. Dallas's Cliff Harris attempted to field a punt deep inside the Dallas 10, but he was unable to catch the ball as it descended. An official ruled the ball had touched Harris, however, and Minnesota's Fred McNeill recovered at the 4. Three plays later, running back Chuck Foreman burst into the end zone and the Vikings took a 7-0 lead.

With 6:41 gone in the third quarter, Landry outfoxed the Vikings. The Cowboys had driven 68 yards, with a third-and-four on the Minne-sota 4. Landry called for a run up the middle—uncharacteristic of Dallas in that situation. With the Vikings expecting a pass, Doug Dennison tore through the middle for a game-tying touchdown.

The fourth quarter opened with a field goal by Toni Fritsch, and the Cowboys clung to a 10-7 lead for nearly 10 minutes. But with Foreman gaining 57 yards on runs and catches, the Vikings, under the guidance of quarterback Fran Tarkenton, drove 70 yards in 11 plays. Brent McClanahan's gritty one-yard touchdown run made it 14-10.

The Dallas offense responded weakly, and was forced to punt with a little more than three minutes remaining.

There was a big moment just before the two-minute warning, when Minnesota faced a third-and-two on the Dallas 47. Tarkenton called a rollout option, knowing that Dallas would stack the line to stop a run. But strong safety Charlie Waters blitzed on the play and buried Tarkenton for a three-yard loss. Minnesota had to punt the ball back to Dallas.

Dallas got into fourth-and-16 trouble on its own 25. Staubach and Drew Pearson conferred in the huddle. "Go to the corner," Staubach told Pearson.

Pearson faked a post and broke for the sideline. Cornerback Nate Wright was just a step away, and when Pearson leaped to catch Staubach's pass, Wright hit him in the air and knocked him over the sideline. Pearson's own impetus might have carried him out of bounds, but the official judged he had been forced out

---

Metropolitan Stadium, Bloomington, Minnesota

Dallas	0	0	7	10	—17
Minnesota	0	7	0	7	—14

HOW THEY SCORED

Minn—Foreman 1 run (Cox kick)
Dall —Dennison 4 run (Fritsch kick)
Dall —FG Fritsch 24
Minn—McClanahan 1 run (Cox kick)
Dall —D. Pearson 50 pass from Staubach (Fritsch kick)
Attendance—46,425

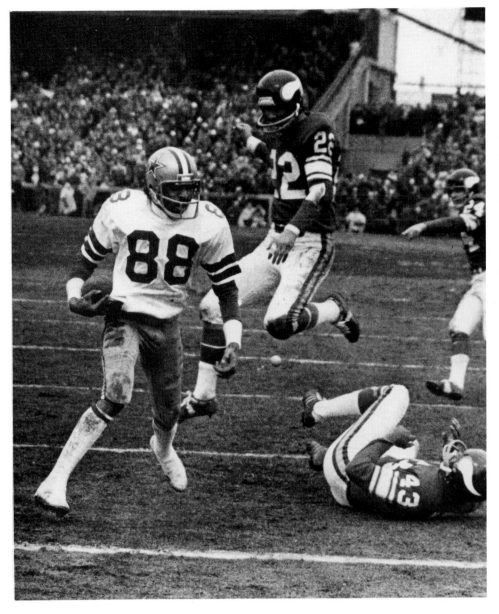

Minnesota's Nate Wright (43) tumbled to the ground, teammate Paul Krause (22) arrived too late, and Dallas's Drew Pearson answered a prayer with a game-winning touchdown catch. Note the orange (see game story) just to the right of Pearson's left hand.

by Wright, and it was ruled a reception.

Staubach later labeled that pass the "Mini-Hail Mary."

Dallas had a first down at the 50 with 37 seconds left. After an incomplete pass to running back Preston Pearson, Drew Pearson told Staubach in the huddle he thought he could beat Wright deep again. Staubach told him to first fake in, then break deep.

This was the big "Hail Mary."

"I was just standing on the sideline feeling very disappointed that we had played so well and were going to lose," Landry said. "I knew our only chance was to throw one long and hope for a miracle."

From the Shotgun, Staubach waited as long as he could. He gave a pump-fake that froze safety Paul Krause, then lofted a long pass to Pearson. The pass was underthrown, and Pearson had to pull up slightly. As Wright slipped—or

was pushed—at the 5, Pearson grabbed the ball at his waist. It began to slip away but miraculously got wedged in between his elbow and his hip, and he lunged into the end zone. The Minneosta players screamed for offensive interference. There was no call. Dallas won 17-14.

"It was the kind of catch only heaven can understand, or ordain," wrote Jim Klobuchar in *Tarkenton*. "But Pearson had the ball and was stepping into the end zone in astonishment, almost in guilt, because even the pro flankers with all their big talk about catching everything in sight don't catch a football like that."

"When I lined up for the play, I noticed that Wright was playing pretty close to a prevent-defense situation," Pearson says. "When I came off the ball, I tried to get on top of him quickly. He had to respect my post move, and I drew even with him running down the sideline. The pass was a little underthrown, but I saw it before he did. The ball hit my hand, and I thought I had dropped it. It slid to my hip, and I hung on with my elbow.

"I still didn't think the play was over. I saw something fly by, and I thought it might have been a flag. But then I saw it was an orange rolling on the ground, and I knew I was home free."

"I never had a more eerie sensation on a football field than during the aftermath of our touchdown," Staubach said. "The crowd was so shocked there wasn't a sound from the stands. It was as though all of a sudden we were playing in an empty stadium."

There was a sad epilogue. Fran Tarkenton's father suffered a heart attack while watching the game on television and died before it was over. Ironically, his father's first name was Dallas.

January 18, 1976

PITTSBURGH STEELERS 21
DALLAS COWBOYS 17

The Super Bowl had an identity crisis in the mid-1970s. None of the first nine games actually had been very super. Not that there hadn't been exciting moments. The sheer magnitude of the Jets' upset of the Colts made Super Bowl III a classic, and Super Bowl V was won on a last-second kick by Baltimore's Jim O'Brien. But there hadn't been a well-played, start-to-finish spine-chiller.

Super Bowl X, which paired the big-thrill Dallas Cowboys and the big-play Pittsburgh Steelers, changed that.

The big thrills for Dallas, the first wild-card team to reach the Super Bowl, usually originated with quarterback Roger Staubach. But the daring Cowboys didn't wait for Staubach to get Super Bowl X off to a scintillating start. Linebacker Thomas (Hollywood) Henderson picked up 53 yards with a reverse on the opening kickoff. Henderson would have scored if Pittsburgh kicker Roy Gerela hadn't made a saving tackle — at the cost of bruised ribs. The injury affected Gerela's kicking the rest of the game.

Dallas was forced to punt on its first series, but the Cowboys quickly regained possession when Pittsburgh punter Bobby Walden bobbled a long fourth-down snap and was buried by Dallas's Billy Joe DuPree at the Steelers' 29.

Staubach, who was hampered by badly bruised ribs and played with a rib cage protector, immediately whipped a 29-yard touchdown pass to wide receiver Drew Pearson.

Pittsburgh got those points back in a hurry, with the help of a gravity-defying catch by wide receiver Lynn Swann.

Swann, who had suffered a concussion in the AFC Championship Game against the Raiders, hadn't even been a definite Super Bowl starter. The Cowboys, suspecting Swann might be a little tentative because of the injury, also made it known that he would be targeted for special attention if he did play.

On the Steelers' first touchdown drive Swann soared over Dallas safety Cliff Harris for a 32-yard reception — somehow levitating himself in midair to keep his feet in bounds while seemingly leaning into the box seats.

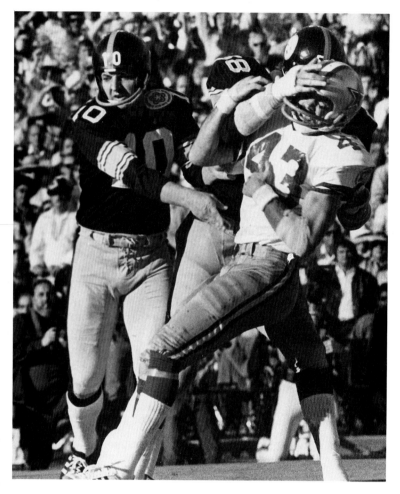

The Steelers cashed-in three plays later with Terry Bradshaw's seven-yard touchdown pass to tight end Randy Grossman.

Dallas opened the second quarter with a 36-yard field goal by Toni Fritsch, which concluded the scoring until the fourth quarter.

But an incident early in the third quarter, following Gerela's second missed field goal of the game, changed the complexion of the game. After Gerela missed, Cliff Harris mockingly patted him on the helmet. Pittsburgh linebacker Jack Lambert was incensed, and he flung Harris to the ground. "When I see injustice," Lambert said later, "I try to do something about it."

Lambert played the rest of the game at tornado strength. He delivered crushing tackles (14 in all), gave his teammates a spark, and generally agitated the Cowboys.

"I felt we were intimidated a little bit in the

Linebacker Jack Lambert (58) laid down the law, Pittsburgh Steelers style, by decking Dallas safety Cliff Harris (43). Lambert's fury was piqued when Harris mocked placekicker Roy Gerela (10) for missing a field goal.

Reggie Harrison (46) rerouted a punt by Mitch Hoopes. The ball went through the end zone for a safety.

first half," Lambert said. "The Pittsburgh Steelers aren't supposed to be intimidated. We're supposed to do the intimidating. I decided to do something about it."

The Steelers did something about the score early in the fourth quarter when reserve back Reggie Harrison blocked a punt by Dallas's Mitch Hoopes. The ball rolled through the end zone for a safety.

Gerela also sandwiched two field goals around Mike Wagner's interception of Staubach. With 6:37 left, Pittsburgh led 15-10.

After stopping Dallas again, Swann caught a 64-yard touchdown pass from Bradshaw—who was decked by blitzing Cliff Harris as he released the ball, and had to leave the game. Although Gerela missed the conversion, the score by Swann, who was named the game's most valuable player, gave the Steelers a 21-10 lead.

Pittsburgh, which had turned Dallas's Shotgun offense into a popgun, was in control.

Then Staubach struck. Less than three minutes remained when he began a drive at the Dallas 20. It took him just five plays and 1:07 to air express the Cowboys 80 yards. A 34-yard scoring pass to rookie wide receiver Percy Howard cut the deficit to 21-17, and started everyone thinking about another miracle. After all, spectacular finishes were *de rigueur* for Staubach.

Pittsburgh recovered Fritsch's onside kickoff at the Dallas 42, but with Terry Hanratty re-

Pittsburgh quarterback Terry Bradshaw paid for a safety blitz by Dallas's Cliff Harris (above), and had to leave the game, but not before he launched a game-winning 64-yard touchdown pass to Lynn Swann.

Swann's routine brilliance resulted in a diving second-quarter catch over sprawled Dallas cornerback Mark Washington (left), and selection as the game's MVP.

placing the woozy Bradshaw, netted only one yard on three runs. It was fourth-and-nine on the Dallas 41 with 1:28 left. It was a punting situation, and because several previous punts had been misadventures, Pittsburgh head coach Chuck Noll ordered another running play, taking precious seconds off the clock.

"We didn't want to give them a big play again," Noll said. "They needed a touchdown to win. I felt our defense could prevent that."

Staubach ran 11 yards for a first down to the 50, then passed 12 yards to former Steeler Preston Pearson at the Pittsburgh 38. Pittsburgh fans were sweating all over their Terrible Towels.

After two incompletions, and with time running out, Staubach tried another Hail Mary pass to Drew Pearson in the end zone. This time the prayer wasn't answered. Safety Glen Edwards intercepted in the end zone. Time—and the Cowboys—expired.

Orange Bowl, Miami, Florida

Dallas	7	3	0	7	—17
Pittsburgh	7	0	0	14	—21

HOW THEY SCORED

Dall—D. Pearson 29 pass from Staubach (Fritsch kick)
Pitt—Grossman 7 pass from Bradshaw (Gerela kick)
Dall—FG Fritsch 36
Pitt—Safety, Harrison blocked Hoopes's punt through end zone
Pitt—FG Gerela 36
Pitt—FG Gerela 18
Pitt—Swann 64 pass from Bradshaw (kick failed)
Dall—P. Howard 34 pass from Staubach (Fritsch kick)
Attendance—80,187

December 24, 1977

OAKLAND RAIDERS 37
BALTIMORE COLTS 31

The AFC Divisional Playoff Game between the Oakland Raiders and the Baltimore Colts on Christmas Eve in 1977 was not for the faint of heart.

The two teams spent the entire game playing tug o' war with the lead and with the nervous systems of a deafening sellout crowd at Baltimore's Memorial Stadium.

One team would gain an inch, the other would gain it right back. There were two ties and eight lead changes. First Oakland led, then Baltimore tied it. Then it was Baltimore. . . then Oakland. . .then Baltimore. . .then Oakland. . .then Baltimore. . .then Oakland. . . then Baltimore. Then it was tied again. The game went into overtime. Then it went into a second overtime.

When it was over, the players must have felt like people who had just spent three straight hours in Space Mountain.

"In the textbook," said Raiders tight end Dave Casper, "it would have to be considered a great game. It fills a computer readout of what a great game is. But anytime you have a situation where you score, then they score, and it goes back and forth—that's no fun. It was a test, a matchup. Checkers with your daughter is fun. This wasn't."

It was highly entertaining for fans, though.

The first half was marked by probing play

In a game of big plays, the biggest was an over-the-shoulder, 42-yard catch on the fly by Oakland tight end Dave Casper (87), who beat Colts cornerback Nelson Munsey (31) and set up a field goal to force overtime.

and turnovers. A 30-yard run by Oakland running back Clarence Davis late in the first quarter gave the Raiders a 7-0 lead.

Baltimore drew even on strong safety Bruce Laird's 61-yard interception return for a touchdown, and went ahead 10-7 just before halftime on a field goal by Toni Linhart.

Then came an explosion of thrills in the opening minutes of the third quarter, beginning with an eight-yard touchdown pass from Stabler to Casper on the Raiders' first possession.

Baltimore's response: Marshall Johnson returned the kickoff 87 yards for a touchdown, giving the Colts a 17-14 lead.

"A whole new world had opened," said Laird. "Things just went crazy."

Oakland linebacker Jeff Barnes recovered a Baltimore punt blocked by teammate Ted Hendricks; Stabler and Casper immediately connected again for a 10-yard touchdown pass to give

---

Memorial Stadium, Baltimore, Maryland

Oakland	7	0	14	10	0	6 —37
Baltimore	0	10	7	14	0	0 —31

HOW THEY SCORED

Oak —Davis 30 run (Mann kick)
Balt —Laird 61 interception return (Linhart kick)
Balt —FG Linhart 36
Oak —Casper 8 pass from Stabler (Mann kick)
Balt —Johnson 87 kickoff return (Linhart kick)
Oak —Casper 10 pass from Stabler (Mann kick)
Balt —R. Lee 1 run (Linhart kick)
Oak —Banaszak 1 run (Mann kick)
Balt —R. Lee 13 run (Linhart kick)
Oak —FG Mann 22
Oak —Casper 10 pass from Stabler (no PAT attempted)
Attendance —59,925

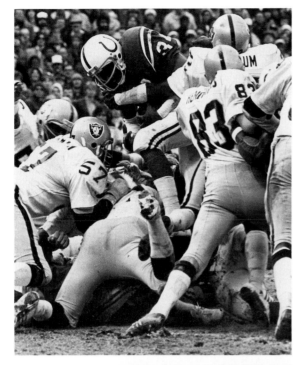

Baltimore running back Ronnie Lee (34 above) hurdled an obstacle course of Raiders to score the first of his two fourth-quarter touchdowns.

Oakland's Ken Stabler (12, above) hit 21 of 40 passes for 345 yards and 3 touchdowns—all to Dave Casper.

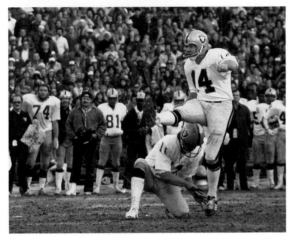

With just 29 seconds left in regulation time, Oakland kicker Errol Mann tied the game 31-31 with a 22-yard field goal.

the Raiders a 21-17 third-quarter advantage.

Early in the fourth quarter, the Colts drove 79 yards to the Oakland 1, helped by a pass interference call against rookie cornerback Lester Hayes in the end zone. The Raiders stopped three consecutive power runs, Ron Lee plunged for a touchdown on fourth down, and Baltimore was back in front, 24-21.

The point-counterpoint continued on the next series when Raiders running back Pete Banaszak powered for a one-yard touchdown. Oakland led 28-24. But leads in this game were fleeting; this one fled 78 seconds later.

Colts quarterback Bert Jones, who was sacked six times and hit just 12 of 26 passes for 164 yards, covered 46 yards on passes to Lee and tight end Raymond Chester, a former Raider. Lee scored another touchdown on a 13-yard run, and Baltimore had a 31-28 lead.

Just before the two-minute warning, Raiders'

ball on their 44. Head coach John Madden sent running back Mark van Eeghen in with the play. "Look for Ghost to the Post," Madden said. ("Ghost" was Casper, who was nicknamed after television's friendly little apparition.)

As Stabler dropped back, he noticed that the Colts' coverage was jamming Casper's intended path to the left goal post. So Stabler wobbled a long pass toward the right corner of the field instead. Casper picked up the ball's flight pattern, altered his route, and ran under it. He made a basket catch over his shoulders, like a centerfielder chasing a long fly ball to the wall.

"I was covering Biletnikoff on the other side of that play," Laird said. "When I looked back and saw Casper make that catch, I thought to myself, 'Here we go again.'"

Casper's brilliant 42-yard reception gave Oakland a first down on the Baltimore 14. But three running plays left the Raiders short of a first down, so Madden decided to go for the tie rather than an immediate victory. Errol Mann's 22-yard field goal with 29 seconds left sent the game into overtime.

"The easiest thing to do is say, 'Go for it' in that situation," Madden said. "Emotionally, I wanted the first down and the victory. But I couldn't let the whole season hinge on going for a first down. You can't get caught up in emotion and that stuff. You have to do what you know is right, even though it's more difficult. And what was right was to kick the field goal, tie the game up, and start all over."

Neither team scored in the first overtime, but the Raiders did begin a game-winning drive late in the "fifth quarter." They reached the Baltimore 10 early in the second overtime. On second-and-7, Stabler used a play-action fake to isolate Casper in the corner of the end zone. The Oakland quarterback lobbed the ball over Casper, who pulled it in for a 37-31 triumph. It was the NFL's third-longest game ever.

Victory was sweet. "It was like getting cleansed in a religious ceremony," said linebacker Ted Hendricks. "An ecstatic feeling comes over you, and celebration is in order."

November 20, 1978

HOUSTON OILERS 35
MIAMI DOLPHINS 30

Miami running back Delvin Williams (24), who entered the game as the NFL's leading rusher, carried 18 times for 73 yards and one touchdown—and attracted the Oilers' attention throughout the game.

Houston defensive end James Young (77) gave Miami quarterback Bob Griese one of his few bad moments of the night. Griese completed 23 of his 33 passes for 349 yards and two touchdowns.

Don Shula was looking forward to a Monday night game at Houston in late November of 1978. His Miami Dolphins were 8-3 and bound for the playoffs. Playing the Oilers in front of a hostile crowd at the Astrodome figured to be good playoff preparation.

"I felt we had to win a big game in that kind of atmosphere—the frenzied fans against a hot team," Shula said. "We did that during the Super Bowl years."

The Oilers qualified as hot. Homespun head coach O.A. (Bum) Phillips, with his colorful sideline wardrobe that featured boots (armadillo and powder-blue anteater were two of the many styles in his collection), western shirts, tailored Levis and a cowboy hat, had stoked his team into playoff contention. The Oilers were 7-4, had won four of their previous five games, and were coming off a semi-miraculous 26-23 victory over New England, having overcome a 23-0 deficit in the process.

No Oiler was hotter than rookie running back Earl Campbell, the 1977 Heisman Trophy winner from Texas. Houston's acquisition of Campbell (he was the first player selected in the 1978 draft) was roughly equivalent to giving a Third World country The Bomb. Except for a fluky 10-4 record in 1975 ("We were lucky," Phillips said), the Oilers had been on pro football's skid row for most of the 1970s. But Campbell gave them a Doomsday weapon.

"He plays like he's got a rocket tied to his back and a gyroscope in his stomach," said Houston quarterback Dan Pastorini.

"Dan Pastorini now has some weapons to fight with," Phillips said after Campbell's arrival in Houston. "Used to be that Dan was a sword fighter with a pocket knife. Now he has his sword."

Campbell-watchers were eager to see how he would fare against the rugged Dolphins defense. Miami also had a productive back of its own: league-leading rusher Delvin Williams.

The teams traded touchdowns in each of the first three quarters. Miami quarterback Bob Griese's deft passing (23 of 33 for 349 yards) produced a 10-yard touchdown pass to Nat Moore and set up one-yard touchdown runs by Williams and Leroy Harris.

Pastorini also was impressive. His 15-yard touchdown pass to tight end Mike Barber and a pair of short touchdown runs by Campbell

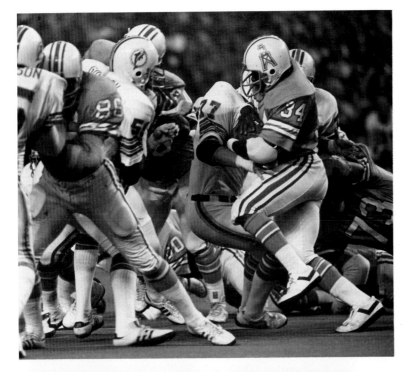

matched Miami's output. It was 21-21 when a classic fourth quarter began.

Pastorini was dumped in the end zone for a safety by defensive end A.J. Duhe to give Miami a 23-21 lead early in the period, and it stayed that way until Campbell took a pitch and swept around right end for a 12-yard touchdown with 4:46 left.

Miami was threatening again when safety Mike Reinfeldt stepped in front of Dolphins tight end Andre Tillman at the Houston 11 and deflected a pass to linebacker Steve Kiner with just over three minutes left.

Kiner's interception set the stage. Then Campbell, who had a fuse that was constantly hissing, exploded to knock out the Dolphins.

On his twenty-eighth carry of the game, Campbell turned the corner of the Dolphins' line and whirled 81 yards for a touchdown.

"What everyone in the stadium noticed," wrote Mickey Herskowitz in *GameDay*, "was one gesture—Earl's hugging the sideline and looking back over his shoulder to check out the pursuing linebacker, Steve Towle. He actually *measured* him and paced his step, the way a mailman does when he wants to walk away from a dog of questionable character without appearing desperate."

On the Houston sideline, Phillips went berserk. He planted a kiss on the cheek of his big rookie, who rushed for a total of 199 yards and wrested the AFC rushing lead from Williams. In one game, Campbell firmly established himself as the NFL's brightest new superstar.

"We knew he'd get the call," said defensive end Doug Betters, "but obviously we couldn't do a damn thing about it. He's unbelievable."

"Earl knew where he was going and so did we," said Dolphins linebacker Kim Bokamper. "A lot of good it did us."

The Dolphins, who outgained the Oilers 447 yards to 406 in the total offense duel, scored an academic touchdown as time expired. That didn't dent the joyous celebration by the 50,290 delirious, pom-pon waving fans in the Astrodome. The Oilers had a victory, a new hero, and were heading into an exciting new era summed up by three short words: Luv Ya Blue.

Campbell, the former Heisman Trophy running back from Texas, flashed a "Hook 'em Horns" sign after taking over the AFC rushing lead against the Dolphins. Or maybe it was "Hook 'em Oilers."

Astrodome, Houston, Texas

Miami	7	7	7	9	—30
Houston	7	7	7	14	—35

HOW THEY SCORED

Mia —Moore 10 pass from Griese (Yepremian kick)
Hou —Campbell 1 run (Fritsch kick)
Hou —Barber 15 pass from Pastorini (Fritsch kick)
Mia —Williams 1 run (Yepremian kick)
Hou —Campbell 6 run (Fritsch kick)
Mia —Harris 1 run (Yepremian kick)
Mia —Safety, Pastorini tackled in end zone by Duhe
Hou —Campbell 12 run (Fritsch kick)
Hou —Campbell 81 run (Fritsch kick)
Mia —Cefalo 11 pass from Griese (Yepremian kick)
Attendance —50,290

January 21, 1979

PITTSBURGH STEELERS 35
DALLAS COWBOYS 31

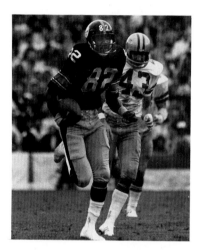

Dallas's Tony Hill (80, far left) sprinted past safety Donnie Shell en route to a 39-yard touchdown.

Left: Ambushed by Thomas Henderson (56) and Mike Hegman (58), Steelers quarterback Terry Bradshaw lost a fumble.

After catching a short pass from Terry Bradshaw at the Steelers' 35, wide receiver John Stallworth left Dallas defenders looking at the back of his jersey on his second-quarter 74-yard touchdown.

The virtuoso performance by Dallas and Pittsburgh in Super Bowl X begged for a sequel. So when the two teams both qualified for Super Bowl XIII, the nation's sportswriters spent the two weeks prior to the game tripping over their own superlatives. Most of them predicted another stirring epic at the Orange Bowl.

It was. The Cowboys and Steelers played a game at the mountain top, a high-scoring, thrill-a-minute spectacle worthy of all the pregame word-rain.

Repeating a scene from Super Bowl X, Steelers fans were the clear winners of the crazed-zealot competition in the carnival atmosphere outside the Orange Bowl before the game.

The pregame rhetoric award, however, went to the Cowboys, in particular linebacker Thomas (Hollywood) Henderson, who taunted Pittsburgh quarterback Terry Bradshaw. "He's so dumb," Henderson said, "that he couldn't spell 'cat' if you spotted him the 'c' and the 'a.'"

In the end, actions scored their customary victory over words—but just barely.

Pittsburgh struck first on the first of Bradshaw's four touchdown passes, a 28-yard first-quarter strike to wide receiver John Stallworth.

Following a fumble recovery by defensive end Ed (Too Tall) Jones, quarterback Roger Staubach pulled Dallas even on the last play of the period with a 39-yard scoring pass to wide receiver Tony Hill.

The second quarter ebbed and flowed with enough pure football emotion to supply most full games. By halftime the two teams had put together the highest-scoring 30 minutes in Super Bowl history: 35 points.

Dallas went ahead 14-7 when Henderson roared in from the strongside and slammed into Bradshaw as fellow linebacker Mike Hegman stripped the ball from Bradshaw (who suffered a wrenched shoulder) and raced 37 yards for a touchdown.

Less than two minutes later, Bradshaw

Orange Bowl, Miami, Florida					
Pittsburgh	7	14	0	14	—35
Dallas	7	7	3	14	—31

HOW THEY SCORED

Pitt —Stallworth 28 pass from Bradshaw (Gerela kick)
Dall —Hill 39 pass from Staubach (Septien kick)
Dall —Hegman 37 fumble return (Septien kick)
Pitt —Stallworth 75 pass from Bradshaw (Gerela kick)
Pitt —Bleier 7 pass from Bradshaw (Gerela kick)
Dall —FG Septien 27
Pitt —Harris 22 run (Gerela kick)
Pitt —Swann 18 pass from Bradshaw (Gerela kick)
Dall —DuPree 7 pass from Staubach (Septien kick)
Dall —B. Johnson 4 pass from Staubach (Septien kick)
Attendance—79,484

caught Stallworth in full stride on a short first-down pass. Stallworth eluded a tackle by cornerback Aaron Kyle and accelerated for a record-tying 75-yard touchdown play.

Running back Rocky Bleier gave Pittsburgh a 21-14 halftime lead with a spectacular, leaping seven-yard touchdown catch.

"It was a game where we could never catch our breath," said Steelers safety Mike Wagner. "It was back and forth, back and forth, like a basketball game. It was one of those days when you knew no lead was gonna be safe."

A light rain fell amid punt exchanges for half of the third

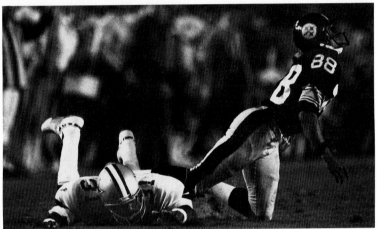

period, until Dallas began a march climaxed by one of the most poignant moments in Super Bowl history: 38-year old tight end Jackie Smith dropping a "certain" touchdown pass in the end zone.

The Cowboys were forced to settle for a 27-yard field goal by Rafael Septien.

Bradshaw then sent Lynn Swann sprinting down the right side, one-on-one against cornerback Benny Barnes. The ball was thrown high, toward the middle of the field. Swann curled toward the line of flight, and Barnes curled in pursuit. A tangle of legs left both players stretched flat on the turf alongside field judge Fred Swearingen's yellow flag. Barnes complained that Swann had shoved him and knocked him down. Swearingen ruled pass interference against Barnes.

Four plays later, Franco Harris broke up the middle for 22 yards, Pittsburgh's fourth touchdown, and a 28-17 advantage.

Roy Gerela's ensuing kickoff was too hot to handle for Dallas's Randy White, whose hand was in a cast because of a broken thumb. White lost the ball when he was hit by Tony Dungy, and Dennis (Dirt) Winston recovered at the Dallas 18. Seven seconds later, Swann sailed

above Cliff Harris to catch another dart from Bradshaw. Suddenly, the Steelers' lead had ballooned to 18 points.

"Our guys started celebrating when it was 35-17," Bradshaw said, "and it made me mad. They were slapping hands and shaking hands and saying how great it was. But it wasn't so great because the game wasn't over."

Staubach didn't think it was over, either. He drove the Cowboys 89 yards in eight plays, passing to tight end Billy Joe DuPree for a seven-yard touchdown. The drive took 4:24 and left Dallas 11 points behind with 2:27 to play. The Cowboys weren't finished. With Staubach on the field, there always was a chance.

Septien hooked an onside kick through the hands of Dungy, and Dennis Thurman recovered for Dallas at the Cowboys' 48. Nine plays and 2:05 later, Staubach threw four yards to Johnson for another touchdown.

It was 35-31, only 22 seconds remained, and the Cowboys were out of time outs. Septien tried another onside kick, but Bleier recovered. Bradshaw—named the game's most valuable player—fell on the ball twice, then stood up to celebrate what no team had accomplished before: three Super Bowl victories.

Dallas's Jackie Smith missed a can't-miss touchdown pass (above). "He was so open I could have punted it to him," said Roger Staubach.

Super Bowl XIII may have turned on one key matchup. Dallas cornerback Benny Barnes (31) was called for interference against Lynn Swann (left), which set up a Pittsburgh touchdown.

December 16, 1979

DALLAS COWBOYS 35
WASHINGTON REDSKINS 34

In November, 1979, Washington had a 31-20 lead against Dallas with nine seconds left when Redskins head coach Jack Pardee called time out and ordered Mark Moseley to kick a field goal. The Cowboys thought the Redskins were rubbing it in. Even though Pardee correctly defended the move because a playoff berth might (and did) hinge on the NFL's point-differential tie-breaker criterion, it still peeved the Cowboys.

"It had a big impact on us," said Dallas quarterback Roger Staubach, "because it simmered in everyone's mind for a month. Regardless of Washington's motivation for sending out Moseley, his kick dominated our thoughts toward the Redskins before the second game."

Staubach claims the second game, which was played at Texas Stadium on December 16, 1979, was the greatest he ever played in.

"Up to that point," he said, "I felt sure the high point had been reached somewhere in my career. But that one was like no other game I've ever been a part of. We were out of it...then we were in it...then we were out of it...then in it. It was, to put it simply, the most thrilling sixty minutes I ever spent on the football field."

Both Washington and Dallas entered the final game of the 1979 season with 10-5 records. Dallas could clinch the NFC East title with a victory and already was assured no worse than a wild-card spot. The Redskins could least afford defeat. If they won, they would be the NFC East champions. If they lost, a playoff berth hinged on their point differential over the Chicago Bears, who were playing St. Louis.

Two days before the game, a funeral wreath was delivered to Dallas defensive end Harvey Martin, presumably by one of the Redskins. (Martin later learned it had been sent by a Cowboys fan as a psych maneuver.) The wreath seemed appropriate two minutes into the second quarter, when the Redskins led 17-0 (on a field goal by Moseley, a one-yard touchdown run by quarterback Joe Theismann, and Theismann's 55-yard scoring pass to Benny Malone). In its 20-year history, Dallas never had made up a 17-point deficit to win.

The Cowboys began the road back with a one-

yard touchdown dive by Ron Springs, who was playing for injured running back Tony Dorsett.

Nine seconds before halftime, after dueling the clock on an 85-yard drive, the Cowboys came out in Shotgun formation on third-and-20 from the 26, and Staubach threw a touchdown pass to running back Preston Pearson.

Dallas took a 21-17 lead on its first possession of the third period when Robert Newhouse plunged two yards for a touchdown.

But Washington came roaring back in the fourth quarter, scoring 17 consecutive points on a field goal by Moseley, and touchdown runs

All Washington free safety Mark Murphy could do was watch Dallas's Preston Pearson catch a 26-yard touchdown pass just before halftime.

John Riggins (44) shook off Dallas corner-back Dennis Thurman on a one-yard touchdown burst in fourth quarter.

Riggins finished off a 66-yard touchdown run to give the Redskins an imposing 34-21 lead. But the Cowboys weren't finished.

Disconsolate Redskins head coach Jack Pardee couldn't wipe away the sting of his team's season-ending loss to Dallas.

of 1 and 66 yards by John Riggins, who rushed for 151 yards on 22 carries.

Riggins's 66-yard touchdown trip gave the Redskins a 34-21 lead with 6:54 left.

"He ran right past our bench," said Staubach. "He didn't say hello, and to us it looked like goodbye to the game."

Three minutes later, Washington still had its 13-point lead, the ball, and an apparent victory—or so thought the disappointed thousands who began to file out of Texas Stadium.

But Dallas defensive tackle Randy White recovered a fumble. Then Staubach went to work, hitting three passes in a row—to Butch Johnson for 14 yards, to Tony Hill for 19, and to Springs for 26 and a touchdown. Now Dallas trailed 34-28 with 2:20 remaining.

At the two-minute warning, Washington faced third-and-2 from its 33. Riggins took a handoff and swung wide to the right with the same move he had used on his 66-yard touchdown. This time Dallas defensive end Larry Cole knifed into the backfield and nailed Riggins for a two-yard loss. Washington punted.

With two time outs and 1:46 left, Staubach

had 75 yards to cover. He got 67 of them on a 20-yard pass to Hill, and completions of 22 and 25 yards to Preston Pearson. Suddenly, Dallas was on the Washington 8 with 45 seconds left.

Staubach wanted to pass to tight end Billy Joe DuPree, but, when the Redskins blitzed, he instead lobbed a semi-Alley-Oop pass to Hill, who had broken loose from cornerback Lemar Parrish near the corner of the end zone. Hill ran under the ball and caught it for the tying touchdown. Septien's extra point gave the Cowboys a 35-34 lead.

"It was a perfect play," Parrish said. "Anything else, I could have covered."

There still were 39 seconds left, but the Redskins had only reached the Dallas 42 when time—and their season—expired. Chicago had crushed St. Louis 42-6 to overcome Washington's 33-point tie-breaker edge, giving the Bears the remaining NFC wild-card berth.

"In the back of my mind," said Washington cornerback Joe Lavender, "even when we had that big lead, I knew what the Cowboys were going to do."

"This puts Hail Mary [against Minnesota] in second place," said Drew Pearson, Staubach's Hail Mary receiver.

Texas Stadium, Irving, Texas

Washington	10	7	0	17	—34
Dallas	0	14	7	14	—35

HOW THEY SCORED

Wash—FG Moseley 24
Wash—Theismann 1 run (Moseley kick)
Wash—Malone 55 pass from Theismann (Moseley kick)
Dall —Springs 1 run (Septien kick)
Dall —P. Pearson 26 pass from Staubach (Septien kick)
Dall —Newhouse 2 run (Septien kick)
Wash—FG Moseley 24
Wash—Riggins 1 run (Moseley kick)
Wash—Riggins 66 run (Moseley kick)
Dall —Springs 26 pass from Staubach (Septien kick)
Dall —Hill 8 pass from Staubach (Septien kick)
Attendance—62,867

January 2, 1982

SAN DIEGO CHARGERS 41
MIAMI DOLPHINS 38

A lasting image: Kellen Winslow—dehydrated, nearly swooning from heat cramps, and suffering from a painful shoulder injury—being helped off the field after the game after an immense performance. "I felt as if I was dead," said the Chargers' tight end, who caught 13 passes for 166 yards and also blocked a field-goal attempt.

It was a contest that will be paid homage for as long as pro football is played.

For nearly five quarters of a 1981 AFC Divisional Playoff Game at the Orange Bowl, the San Diego Chargers and Miami Dolphins stood chest-to-chest, locked in a staggering, exhausting struggle.

What began as a rout turned into a molten crucible of heart and desire. The struggle took four hours and three minutes, and was played in dizzying, humid heat. In the end, neither team crumbled; one simply outlasted the other.

San Diego bounded to a 24-0 lead in an incredible first quarter. A field goal by Rolf Benirschke, a 56-yard punt return by Wes Chandler, a one-yard touchdown run by Chuck Muncie, and an 8-yard touchdown reception by James Brooks left the Dolphins reeling.

"When it was 24-0," said Miami wide receiver Duriel Harris, "I wanted to stick my head in a hole somewhere and hide. We were just totally embarrassed and humiliated."

But there was no quit in the Dolphins.

"We knew we couldn't get it back in one lump sum," said running back Tony Nathan. "We had to take it a step at a time. We knew we had to do it the hard way, and that's what

we did—inch by inch and yard by yard."

The first step was Miami head coach Don Shula's decision to replace ineffective starting quarterback David Woodley with nine-year veteran Don Strock, who lit up the Orange Bowl with the performance of his career (403 yards and four touchdown passes).

The Dolphins got their first points on a field goal from Uwe von Schamann. With 2:46 left in the first half, Strock tossed a one-yard touchdown pass to tight end Joe Rose.

Miami regained possession with 30 seconds left in the half when Benirschke missed a 55-yard field-goal attempt. The Dolphins were on the San Diego 40 with six seconds remaining when Strock called for an "86 circle-curl-lateral to the halfback."

The result: Strock threw a pass covering 15 yards to Harris, who lateraled the ball to Nathan, who sped untouched into the end zone. It was a mind-blowing finale to the first half, and left the Dolphins trailing only 24-17.

Orange Bowl, Miami, Florida

San Diego	24	0	7	7	3	—41
Miami	0	17	14	7	0	—38

HOW THEY SCORED

SD —FG Benirschke 32
SD —Chandler 56 punt return (Benirschke kick)
SD —Muncie 1 run (Benirschke kick)
SD —Brooks 8 pass from Fouts (Benirschke kick)
Mia —FG von Schamann 34
Mia —Rose 1 pass from Strock (von Schamann kick)
Mia —Nathan 25 run with lateral from Harris after 15 pass from Strock (von Schamann kick)
Mia —Rose 15 pass from Strock (von Schamann kick)
SD —Winslow 25 pass from Fouts (Benirschke kick)
Mia —Hardy 50 pass from Strock (von Schamann kick)
Mia —Nathan 12 run (von Schamann kick)
SD —Brooks 9 pass from Fouts (Benirschke kick)
SD —FG Benirschke 29
Attendance—73,735

"We'd worked on it [the pass-lateral play], but never really had taken it seriously," Harris said. "I can remember coach Shula getting on us about it, saying, 'You've got to get into it, because one day you'll need it.' This was the day we needed it."

The fired-up Dolphins drove 74 yards with the second-half kickoff and tied the game on Strock's 15-yard touchdown pass to Rose.

Quarterback Dan Fouts rekindled the Chargers. He threw a 25-yard touchdown pass to tight end Kellen Winslow late in the third quarter, and San Diego led once more, 31-24.

Miami clawed back to another tie when Strock gunned a 50-yard scoring pass to tight end Bruce Hardy.

On the first play of the fourth quarter, the Dolphins capitalized on Lyle Blackwood's interception with a 12-yard touchdown run by Nathan. Once trailing 24-0, Miami now led 38-31.

The Dolphins muffed a chance to pad their advantage when Chargers defensive tackle Louie Kelcher stripped the ball from rookie running back Andra Franklin at the San Diego 18.

Fouts, who passed for 433 yards and three touchdowns, subsequently tied the game with a nine-yard touchdown pass to Brooks.

With four seconds left in regulation, the two teams assembled for a dramatic 43-yard field-goal attempt by von Schamann. The Chargers put their best leaper, the 6-foot 5-inch Winslow, just behind the line of scrimmage. He blocked the kick.

"I was very fortunate to get my pinkie on the ball—my pinkie and the outside edge of my right hand," Winslow said. "That's all I got. It was the biggest thrill of my life. I felt like I had scored three touchdowns."

In overtime, San Diego got the first crack, and marched from its 13 to Miami's 8, where Benirschke missed a 27-yard field goal.

With 3:42 left, von Schamann attempted another field goal, from 34 yards. San Diego's Leroy Jones blocked it.

"When we blocked that second field goal," said Chargers linebacker Jim Laslavic, "I swear, I started to cry. That's the kind of stuff they make in Hollywood."

Fouts went back to work, and after a 20-yard completion to Chandler and a 29-yard toss to Charlie Joiner, the Chargers had a first down on the Miami 10.

Benirschke ended the melodrama by kicking a 29-yard field goal with 1:08 left in the overtime, giving the Chargers a 41-38 victory.

"After it was over," said San Diego special teams captain Hank Bauer, "everyone kind of looked at the skies and said, 'Thank God it's over.' Normally, after you win a game on a field goal, everybody's going crazy."

"We fought 'em tooth and nail all the way, literally fought our guts out," said Dolphins defensive end Doug Betters. "In the overtime, it had gotten to the point where physical conditioning had taken us as far as it could. We reached a point where we were going on emotion, and all of us had to look down and see how much heart we had."

San Diego's Dan Fouts (above left) set playoff records by completing 33 of his 53 passes for 433 yards and three touchdowns. A companion in greatness was Miami's Don Strock (above right), who replaced starter David Woodley in the second quarter and was 29 of 43 for 403 yards and four touchdowns. "He played one of the best games I've ever seen any quarterback play," said Fouts. "He was awesome."

January 10, 1982

SAN FRANCISCO 49ERS 28
DALLAS COWBOYS 27

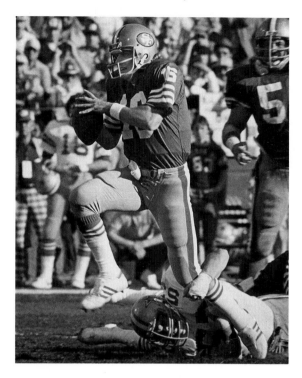

Escape artist Joe Montana eluded the minor shackle of Dallas linebacker Bob Breunig's left arm just prior to throwing a 20-yard touchdown pass to 49ers wide receiver Dwight Clark.

The San Francisco 49ers were playing host to the Dallas Cowboys in the 1981 NFC Championship Game at Candlestick Park. What better opponent to enable the 49ers to exorcise the haunting ghosts of playoff failures past?

There were those 1970 and 1971 NFC Championship Game losses to the Cowboys to avenge. There was the bedeviling memory of 1972's Black Saturday, when Roger Staubach personally pitchforked the 49ers' Super Bowl dreams in a divisional playoff game. There even

---

Candlestick Park, San Francisco, California

Dallas	10	7	0	10	—27
San Francisco	7	7	7	7	—28

HOW THEY SCORED

SF —Solomon 8 pass from Montana (Wersching kick)
Dall—FG Septien 44
Dall—Hill 26 pass from D. White (Septien kick)
SF —Clark 20 pass from Montana (Wersching kick)
Dall—Dorsett 5 run (Septien kick)
SF —Davis 2 run (Wersching kick)
Dall—FG Septien 22
Dall—Cosbie 21 pass from D. White (Septien kick)
SF —Clark 6 pass from Montana (Wersching kick)
Attendance—60,525

---

was a lingering 59-14 regular-season embarrassment against Dallas in 1980 to be considered.

Incentive? The 49ers and San Francisco—the team and its citizenry—were ready.

"From the time you got to that parking lot—it was full at 9:30—there was a nice feeling," said 49ers guard Randy Cross. "Inside the stadium it was loud, and there was kind of a building crescendo, especially on our final drive."

The final drive was the stuff of which football legends are made. Capitalize it right now: The Drive.

The 49ers had some Cinderella in them, some destiny. Under head coach Bill Walsh they had improved from 2-14 in 1979, to 6-10 in 1980, and all the way to an NFL-best 13-3 in 1981. Walsh kindled a spirit of inventiveness and resourcefulness worthy of the team's nickname, and the clock never struck midnight in 1981. Thanks to an uncharacteristic spate of six turnovers against the Cowboys, however, it did strike 11:59 P.M..

San Francisco took an early 7-3 lead, but a fumble by running back Bill Ring at the 49ers' 29 resulted in a 26-yard touchdown pass from Dallas quarterback Danny White to wide receiver Tony Hill.

Quarterback Joe Montana threw to wide receiver Dwight Clark, on his knees in the end zone, for a 20-yard touchdown in the second quarter and a 14-10 49ers lead. Dallas nudged ahead 17-14 before halftime on a five-yard sweep by running back Tony Dorsett.

San Francisco linebacker Bobby Leopold intercepted a pass from Danny White midway through the fourth quarter to set up a two-yard touchdown plunge by running back Johnny Davis, and the 49ers went ahead 21-17.

Rafael Septien's second field goal of the day, from 22 yards, cut San Francisco's lead to 21-20 with 14:08 remaining.

Another 49ers turnover, this time a fumble by running back Walt Easley, gave Dallas the ball at midfield. Four plays later, tight end Doug Cosbie caught a 21-yard touchdown pass to put the Cowboys in front 27-21.

An interception by cornerback Everson Walls ended a San Francisco comeback drive,

Freddie Solomon (88, below) scored the 49ers' first touchdown and played a feature role in the winning drive.

The Catch: Rising to the occasion, the 49ers' Dwight Clark (right) pulled down a pass with a Super Bowl payload.

but the Cowboys were forced to punt on their next series. Freddie Solomon fielded the punt at the 49ers' 11. From there, with 4:54 remaining, San Francisco launched The Drive.

Its primary ingredient was surprise. With Walsh's Machiavellian play-calling crossing up the Cowboys, Montana executing the 49ers' rhythmic passing game, and journeyman running back Lenvil Elliott sweeping and surprising, San Francisco began to move.

At the two-minute warning, Montana conferred with Walsh, and the two agreed on a reverse to Solomon. It worked for a 14-yard gain to the Dallas 35.

Shedding a furious pass rush by the Cowboys, Montana completed risky passes with zero margins for error to Clark (10 yards) and Solomon (12 yards). Elliott swept left end for 7 more.

On third-and-3 at the Cowboys' 6-yard line, with 58 seconds remaining, Walsh called a play good for the six yards and the 2,400 miles that separate San Francisco from Pontiac, Michigan —site of Super Bowl XVI. Off-balance and about to be obliterated by Dallas's Larry Bethea and Ed (Too Tall) Jones, Montana threw high and hard to the back of the end zone, where a scrambling Dwight Clark reversed his initial route to make a leaping, breathtaking catch.

"I wasn't going to take the sack," Montana said. "I couldn't see Dwight open. I knew he had to be at the back of the end zone. I let the ball go. I got hit and wound up on my back. I rolled over. I saw Dwight's feet hit the ground. I heard the crowd screaming."

Slashing sweeps by Lenvil Elliot (left), who rushed 10 times for 48 yards, helped set up the winning touchdown.

"It was over my head," Clark said. "I thought, 'Oh, oh, I can't go that high.' Something got me up there. It must have been God or something."

Ray Wersching's extra point broke the tie, and San Francisco led 28-27.

The Cowboys had one more gasp, but Lawrence Pillers forced a fumble by Danny White at the San Francisco 44-yard line. Defensive end Jim Stuckey recovered. It was over.

The celebration that spilled from Candlestick, up Third Street, and into downtown San Francisco, was orchestrated with every noise-making device available to man. People on street corners emptied cases of beer and tossed full bottles and cans into the outstretched arms of bus passengers. It turned out they only were rehearsing for the madness that would follow a Super Bowl victory over Cincinnati two weeks later.

October 2, 1983

WASHINGTON REDSKINS 37
LOS ANGELES RAIDERS 35

The Washington Redskins and Los Angeles Raiders played an extraordinary game in week five of the 1983 season. As Alan Greenberg of the *Los Angeles Times* put it, "It was art at its most uplifting, human athletic effort at its noblest, the *Chariots of Fire* of NFL '83. If only it could have been captured on canvas, surely it would be on display at the National Gallery. The Louvre, the Prado, and the Metropolitan Museum of Art would be begging to borrow it."

The Raiders were undefeated. The Redskins were 3-1, and the customary sellout crowd at

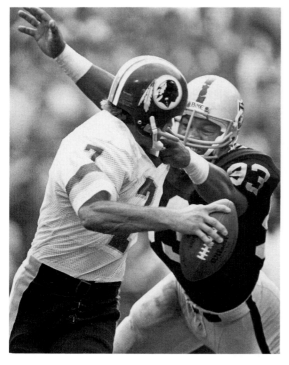

RFK Stadium was even more excited than usual. It was the Raiders' second visit ever to Washington. Except perhaps for the annual game against Dallas, this rare session with the NFL's wild bunch figured to be the Redskins' feature home game for 1983. It turned out to be one of the most incongruous professional football games ever.

Washington quarterback Joe Theismann compared it to a heavyweight fight, with each team alternately delivering—and reeling from—roundhouse punches, but neither one falling until the final bell.

"And this one," Theismann said, "went all fifteen rounds."

The early rounds went to the defending Super Bowl champion Redskins, who built a 17-7 halftime lead while the Raiders played giveaway. Assault back John Riggins scored the game's first touchdown and tore through the Raiders' line for 67 yards in the first half, while Theismann minced the Los Angeles secondary.

Quarterback Jim Plunkett, meanwhile, threw three interceptions on the Raiders' first four possessions. Two of them led to 10 points by Washington (a 28-yard field goal by Mark Moseley and a 5-yard touchdown catch by running back Joe Washington).

Plunkett's lone bright moment in the first half was a 99-yard touchdown pass to wide receiver Cliff Branch, tying the NFL record. Even that was costly; Branch pulled a hamstring muscle on the play and never returned.

A 20-yard interception return by Washington safety Curtis Jordan (22, below) set up the Redskins' first touchdown.

The Raiders kept Washington quarterback Joe Theismann company (left), sacking him six times. On this play, however, defensive end Greg Townsend was flagged for a facemask penalty.

RFK Stadium, Washington, D.C.

Los Angeles	0	7	14	14	—35
Washington	7	10	3	17	—37

HOW THEY SCORED

Wash —Riggins 2 run (Moseley kick)
Wash —FG Moseley 28
LA —Branch 99 pass from Plunkett (Bahr kick)
Wash —Washington 5 pass from Theismann (Moseley kick)
Wash —FG Moseley 29
LA —Muhammad 35 pass from Plunkett (Bahr kick)
LA —Muhammad 22 pass from Plunkett (Bahr kick)
LA —Christensen 2 pass from Plunkett (Bahr kick)
LA —Pruitt 97 punt return (Bahr kick)
Wash —Brown 11 pass from Theismann (Moseley kick)
Wash —FG Moseley 34
Wash —Washington 6 pass from Theismann (Moseley kick)
Attendance—54,016

Otherwise, the Raiders looked dreadful.

Washington padded its lead to 20-7 on Moseley's 29-yard field goal early in the third quarter. Then things went haywire for the Redskins.

Plunkett began playing as if he had made a halftime visit to a phone booth. He atoned for earlier follies with third-quarter touchdown passes of 35 yards and 22 yards to Calvin Muhammad (who had replaced Branch in the lineup) to give the Raiders a 21-20 lead. Their lead swelled to 28-20 early in the fourth quarter on Plunkett's three-yard scoring pass—his fourth of the game—to tight end Todd Christensen. Four minutes later, Greg Pruitt fielded a punt at his 3 and dashed 97 yards for a touchdown.

That's counterpunching, and it made the score 35-20 with 7:31 left. What began as a Redskins rout had turned into a Raiders runaway.

The Redskins were reeling, but straightened up when wide receiver Charlie Brown (11 receptions for 180 yards) caught an 11-yard touchdown pass with 6:15 left in the game.

Trailing 35-27, Washington needed two scores—and it needed the ball. The Raiders, knowing this, lined up with an overloaded front to thwart any onside kick. But Washington's Jeff Hayes did the thwarting with a low, hard kick that eluded the Raiders' first line. The

After four costly interceptions, Raiders quarterback Jim Plunkett (above) brought the Raiders back. Greg Pruitt (above right) put them ahead 35-20 with a club-record 97-yard punt return.

While Raiders linebacker Rod Martin (53, below) looked on in anguish, Joe Washington landed in the end zone with the winning points.

ball bounced off someone's foot, spinning crazily. Los Angeles's Dokie Williams fell on it, but it squirted loose, and Washington's Greg Williams recovered at the 32. Moseley kicked a 35-yard field goal five plays later.

"That onside kick put helium in their balloons," said Raiders strong safety Mike Davis.

This time, with 4:28 left, Hayes kicked off deep. The Raiders were forced to punt shortly after the two-minute warning.

Beginning at his own 31, Theismann plundered the Raiders' prevent defense. He completed passes to Brown for 9, 26, and 28 yards. With 33 seconds left and the ball at the Raiders' 6, Joe Washington, who had replaced Riggins for much of the second half, slipped past Raiders linebacker Rod Martin and made a diving catch in the end zone.

After surrendering 28 points in less than a quarter, the Redskins had scored 17 unanswered points in just over six minutes to defeat the Raiders 37-35.

"I wouldn't be surprised if we met them again in January," said Washington guard Mark May.

May turned out to be right, although the Raiders' stunning 38-9 victory over the Redskins in Super Bowl XVIII did surprise him.

December 2, 1984

LOS ANGELES RAIDERS 45
MIAMI DOLPHINS 34

Miami's Dan Marino doesn't chase after his own passes too often, but when Raiders corner-back Mike Haynes made a first-quarter interception (above left), Marino had no choice. The chase was futile; Haynes went 97 yards for a touchdown. In the fourth quarter, Haynes intercepted another pass (top right) and returned it 54 yards to set up another touchdown.

There are easier ways to win "must" games than to play the Dolphins in Miami. The Los Angeles Raiders don't always do things the easy way.

In this case, they had no choice. The NFL schedule showed the Raiders had an appointment with the Dolphins on December 2, 1984, at the Orange Bowl, where the Dolphins had lost one regular-season game in three years.

With 12 victories in its first 13 games (after winning its first eleven) in 1984, Miami already had clinched the AFC East championship.

The Raiders, who had won seven of their first eight games, had hit a midseason injury mine field and lost three consecutive games. Their playoff pulse had become faint. A victory against Miami was essential. But the Raiders thrive on such situations, and they turned a potential Dunkirk into the finest hour of their season.

In 80-degree heat and oppressive humidity, there was back-and forth, try-to-stop-this, try-to-top-that action between two intense teams—the defending Super Bowl champion and the AFC champion-to-be—playing a bragging-rights version of king of the hill.

The Raiders gained the first foothold midway through the first quarter when cornerback Mike Haynes intercepted a pass from record-shattering quarterback Dan Marino at the Los Angeles 3 and sprinted 97 yards for a touchdown.

Miami countered immediately with a 72-yard, 12-play drive, which Marino concluded with a four-yard touchdown pass to wide receiver Jimmy Cefalo.

The teams traded touchdown runs in the first five minutes of the second quarter. A 44-yard field goal by Chris Bahr gave the Raiders a 17-13 halftime lead.

A significant non-score occurred just before the end of the second quarter. The Dolphins had marched 89 yards to the Raiders' 1, and had a first-and-goal. Pete Johnson, Miami's massive fullback, was repelled twice by the Raiders on thrusts into the line, leaving the Dolphins with third-and-inches with just nine seconds left. Miami head coach Don Shula wanted a touchdown. Woody Bennett, the other mastodon in Miami's short-yardage backfield, dived through the left side. The Raiders stuffed him, too. Time expired, and the Dolphins went to the locker room empty.

"What was it, half a foot? Six inches?" asked Shula. "I thought we could run it in, period."

A collision with teammate Vann McElroy left Mike Haynes in pain on the ground (left), and turned Miami's Mark Clayton loose for a 64-yard touchdown romp.

Marcus Allen's 52-yard touchdown sprint (right) closed the issue.

"I was kind of surprised," said Raiders defensive end Howie Long. "It's arrogant in a way to go for a touchdown with nine seconds left before the half and not get the field goal and get some points out of a long drive like that. But who am I to second-guess Don Shula?"

Quarterback Marc Wilson, playing with an injured thumb on his passing hand, teamed with tight end Dave Casper on a seven-yard touchdown pass early in the third quarter to put the Raiders ahead 24-13.

Then Marino heated up Miami with consecutive scoring drives of 91 and 83 yards. On the first drive he threw a 64-yard touchdown pass to wide receiver Mark Clayton. He went to Clayton again for an 11-yard touchdown on the second drive, and Miami edged ahead 27-24.

Then the big-play pendulum swung to the Raiders. Wide receiver Dokie Williams converted a medium-range pass from Wilson into a 75-yard touchdown. The Raiders led 31-27.

More larceny by Haynes on the Dolphins' next possession—a 54-yard interception return—put the Raiders on the Miami 15. Three

plays later, running back Marcus Allen swept into the end zone for a six-yard touchdown to make it 38-27 with 6:07 left.

That still left time for Marino and his explosive receivers, Clayton and Duper. After a nine-play, 86-yard drive, Marino hit Duper for a nine-yard touchdown, Marino's fourth scoring pass of the game and fortieth of the season.

After gaining just four yards on their first two downs, the Raiders faced third-and-six from their own 48 with 1:53 remaining. The Dolphins still had two time outs, not to mention Marino, who was on the sideline, gearing up for a final touchdown assault.

But Allen, who rushed for 156 yards, took a handoff on what the Raiders called a sprint draw, headed to his left, saw too many Dolphins, cut back to his right, and sprinted 52 yards for a game-clinching touchdown.

Marino passed for a personal-best 470 yards, and his 14-game total of 40 touchdowns was an NFL single-season record (he would finish the season with 48).

For Miami, it was a momentary setback, a defeat with honor in a glorious season that culminated in the team's fifth Super Bowl.

The Raiders? They did what they had to do.

Dan Marino escaped this assault by defensive end Howie Long, but the Raiders sacked Marino three times.

Orange Bowl, Miami, Florida

Los Angeles	7	10	7	21	—45
Miami	7	6	14	7	—34

HOW THEY SCORED

LA —Haynes 97 interception return (Bahr kick)
Mia—Cefalo 4 pass from Marino (von Schamann kick)
Mia—Nathan 6 run (kick failed)
LA —Allen 11 run (Bahr kick)
LA —FG Bahr 44
LA —Casper 7 pass from Wilson (Bahr kick)
Mia—Clayton 64 pass from Marino (von Schamann kick)
Mia—Clayton 11 pass from Marino (von Schamann kick)
LA —Williams 75 pass from Wilson (Bahr kick)
LA —Allen 6 run (Bahr kick)
Mia—Duper 9 pass from Marino (von Schamann kick)
LA —Allen 52 run (Bahr kick)
Attendance—71,222

PART IV

WORDPLAY: FOOTBALL WIT AND WISDOM FROM 1960-1984

Novelist Irwin Shaw, a one-time quarterback for Brooklyn College, writing about New York Giants quarterback Y.A. Tittle in a 1965 story for *Esquire*: "Aside from his physical and intellectual equipment, Tittle has an added 'thing' that brings out the crowds and has made the Giants games a Sunday must on the television screens of the nation. He almost always seems to be in desperate trouble, and almost always seems to get out of it at the last fateful moment. Whether the record bears it out or not, the Giants always seem to be behind, and in the good days, at least, Tittle put them ahead when all hope seemed lost. It's the Alamo every Sunday, with Davy Crockett sighting down his long rifle with the powder running out, and Jim Bowie asking to be carried across the line with his knife in his hand. It is the Alamo every Sunday, with the Texans reversing history and the United States cavalry coming in on a long, high pass.

"Pro football is show business, and where are you going to find a better show than the Alamo?"

Tittle did his "thing" in this mud ballet with St. Louis.

The early AFL drew all comers; two would-be Los Angeles Chargers could at least tell their friends they got a "look" from head coach Sid Gillman.

Boston Patriots head coach Mike Holovak, on his first team's shortage of talent: "If you could afford a hamburger, you were afraid to go to the diner for fear the cook would want to try out for the team. When a bellhop put your bag in a motel room, you had to make sure you tipped him good; the next time you saw him he might be your starting tackle."

"[San Diego Chargers head coach] Sid Gillman said we're having our training camp at a million-dollar dude ranch, so I was expecting more than I saw when I arrived. I thought I had arrived in hell."

Walt Sweeney, guard, San Diego Chargers

Wide receiver John Jefferson, recalling his flight from San Diego to Green Bay after being traded to the Packers in 1981: "I was wondering why we were stopping. I didn't see any lights down there and I was starting to get a little worried."

Vince Lombardi's stroke of football genius produced five world titles.

"The pressures of losing are awful. It kills you eventually. But the pressure of winning is even worse, infinitely worse, because it keeps on torturing you and torturing you."

Vince Lombardi, head coach, Green Bay Packers

New Orleans Saints wide receiver Guido Merkens, recalling head coach Bum Phillips's admonition to the club prior to his 1981 "homecoming" against Houston in the Astrodome: "He felt the team was getting too tight, so he told us he lied when he said all week it wasn't important to him. He said, 'It's a matter of life and death—my life and your death.' "

CBS-TV commentator John Madden, on Denver Broncos quarterback John Elway, the first player chosen in the 1983 draft: "He's an immediate cure for coaches' burnout."

Los Angeles Raiders linebacker Matt Millen, when told before Super Bowl XVIII that Washington Redskins guard Russ Grimm had said that he'd run over his own mother to win the game: "I'd run over Grimm's mother, too."

Matt Millen brought an attitude to Super Bowl XVIII.

Washington Redskins placekicker Mark Moseley, named the NFL's most valuable player by Associated Press at the end of the 1982 season: "I didn't even think kickers were eligible."

Los Angeles Rams guard Kent Hill in early December of 1981, on the rigors of line play in the NFL: "This time of year, if you're breathing, you're healthy."

New England Patriots defensive end Julius Adams, asked to comment on the Raiders' well-publicized tendency toward offensive holding: "Let's put it this way. After every time I rushed the passer, I had to tuck my shirt back in."

Kansas City Chiefs quarterback Len Dawson, reflecting on his two Super Bowl experiences (games I and IV): "I had a taste of both winning and losing, and believe me, winning was better."

New Orleans running back George Rogers, asked about his goals for the 1984 season: "I want to gain 1,500 or 2,000 yards, whichever comes first."

Kansas City Chiefs running back Curtis McClinton, on the Chiefs' loss to the Green Bay Packers in Super Bowl I: "I felt like one of the losers at Pompeii. I was overwhelmed by the feeling that there would never be another chance, that there would never be another Super Bowl game or another football season. It was like being on a deathbed. Everything you've accomplished up to that point didn't mean a damn thing."

"To me, football is a contest in embarrassments. The quarterback is out there to embarrass me in front of my friends, my teammates, my coaches, my wife, and my three boys. The quarterback doesn't leave me any choice. I've got to embarrass him instead."

Alex Karras, defensive tackle, Detroit Lions

Karras was able to work his theory on Sonny Jurgensen (9) in this 1965 Detroit-Washington game.

Quarterback Jack Kemp, on his pre-AFL wanderings from the Detroit Lions to the Pittsburgh Steelers to the New York Giants to the San Francisco 49ers: "It was the same story every place I went. I was the guy they kept for insurance. They should have dressed me in a policy instead of a uniform."

Pittsburgh Steelers head coach Chuck Noll at the outset of the 1979 season: "We regard our Super Bowl XIII trophy as an antique."

Joe Foss, World War II hero

Joe Foss, AFL commissioner

"I traveled over 250,000 miles in my first year [1960] promoting the league. People would say to me, 'When did you get into baseball?' That was a little frustrating."

Joe Foss, *first AFL Commissioner*

Defensive back Curtis Jordan, on what he learned as a member of the Tampa Bay Buccaneers: "When we came out of the tunnel, we made sure never to stand next to coach [John] McKay, because the fans threw beer at him."

The late Norm Van Brocklin, once an NFL quarterback, later coach of the Vikings and Falcons, on his 1980 brain surgery: "It was a brain transplant. I got a sportswriter's brain so I could be sure I had one that hadn't been used."

Cleveland Browns head coach Sam Rutigliano, on his ability to endure several last-minute defeats in 1978: "It's like having heart attacks. You can survive them, but there's always scar tissue."

"When Cookie [Gilchrist] came out of the blocks, you just heard this rumbling, like an earthquake. The quarterbacks handed off to him and got the hell out of the way. We were in as much danger as the defensive linemen."

Al Dorow, quarterback, Buffalo Bills

Kansas City Chiefs owner Lamar Hunt, as the Raiders and the NFL went to court over the Raiders' move to Los Angeles in 1982: "The best description of utter waste would be for a busload of lawyers to go over a cliff with three empty seats."

"Walter Payton is the alllll-tiiiiime greatest. Remember the word alllll-tiiiiime! All-time means that he's the greatest since they started keeping records. Maybe there was some other guy, who is now unknown to man, who carried a stone for more yards. Or maybe those guys who carried messages from city to city covered more yardage. You know, the guys in Greece. But as far as we know, Payton's the greatest."

Darryl Grant, defensive tackle, Washington Redskins

Walter Payton paced Chicago's playoff victory over Washington in the 1984 NFC playoffs.

"We beat the Packers 40-0, but do you think he put his head down and ran for the tunnel? No way. He came over and congratulated us, wished us luck, and told us to stay healthy. Bart Starr has more class than any football player I've ever known."
Wayne Walker, linebacker, Detroit Lions

Ken Stabler, after completing 15 of 23 pass attempts during Houston's loss to Pittsburgh in 1981: "It doesn't matter, when you lose. It's like earrings on a pig. It doesn't make a whole lot of difference."

New Orleans linebacker Jim Kovach, recalling a moment during a game against the Los Angeles Rams in 1981: "I told [the defensive unit], 'Remember what they did to us last year.' Then I looked around the huddle, and nobody but me and Ricky Ray were even here last year. The rest of them still were in college."

"Trading quarterbacks is rare, but not unusual."

Joe Kuharich, head coach, Philadelphia Eagles

Philadelphia fans taunted coach Kuharich, whose unpopular trades included Sonny Jurgensen for Norm Snead.

"Someday, it will come down to the Dolphins and the Raiders playing for the American Conference Championship at the [Oakland] Coliseum. There will be six inches of water on the field as the Dolphins drive for the winning touchdown with ten seconds left. There we'll be, on the three-yard line. . .the clouds will part, and we'll look up to see Al Davis standing on the goal line with a garden hose."
Don Shula, head coach, Miami Dolphins

Dorothy Shula, wife of Miami Dolphins head coach Don Shula: "I'm fairly confident that if I died tomorrow, Don would find a way to preserve me until the season was over and he had time for a nice funeral."

Cincinnati defensive end Gary Burley, on how it felt to tackle running back Earl Campbell: "It's like standing blindfolded in the middle of Interstate 75, dodging the cars and trying to tackle the biggest truck out there."

Dallas Cowboys linebacker Bob Breunig, on his team's offseason aerobic workouts: "It's just another way of getting tired."

"Teams in the AFL converted third-and-fifteen situations into first downs like they were third-and-inches."

Al Ward, AFL
publicity director

The late Dan Birdwell, a defensive tackle for the Oakland Raiders in the 1960s, coming into the huddle during the fourth quarter of a 1967 preseason game against Kansas City with the Raiders trailing 42-0: "Come on guys, let's hold 'em. If we get seven quick scores, we've got 'em beat."

"Al Davis is a good guy not to play gin rummy with."

Mike Holovak, head coach,
Boston Patriots

Cincinnati wide receiver Cris Collinsworth, on finishing his rookie season with an appearance in Super Bowl XVI: "I feel like some guy who picked up a Rubik's Cube and got it right the first time."

Referee Jim Tunney, on the typical pro football fan: "He'll scream from the sixtieth row of the bleachers that you missed a marginal call in the center of the interior line, and then won't be able to find his car in the parking lot."

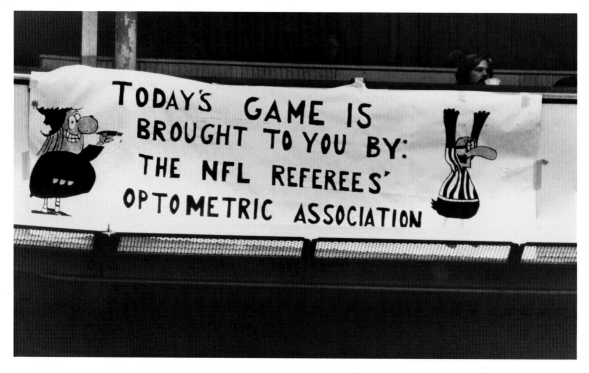

NFL fans' homemade banners included the officials' report card genre in 1975.

Cowboys coach Landry studied the situation in 1984 with quarterbacks White (center) and Hogeboom.

Dallas Cowboys back-up quarterback Gary Hogeboom, introducing starter Danny White at a banquet during the 1982-83 offseason: "It's kind of difficult to introduce a guy you hope gets the flu every week."

Dallas Cowboys running back Walt Garrison, when asked if coach Tom Landry ever smiles: "I don't know. I only played there nine years."

Dallas Cowboys quarterback Don Meredith on Dallas running back Walt Garrison: "If you needed four yards, you'd give the ball to Garrison and he'd get four yards. If you needed twenty yards, you'd give the ball to Garrison and he'd get four yards."

New York Giants linebacker Harry Carson, on learning the Giants would spend the week prior to their 1984 NFC Divisional Playoff Game against the 49ers training in Fresno, California: "Fresno? I thought that was a diet soft drink."

New York Giants journeyman guard Lou Cordileone, upon learning he had just been traded even-up for San Francisco quarterback Y. A. Tittle: "Me for Tittle? Just me? Who else?" Tittle, after hearing he had been traded for Cordileone: "Who?"

Los Angeles Raiders quarterback Jim Plunkett, on his one-kilometer leg in the 1984 Olympic Torch Relay: "That's probably the farthest I'll run this year without being hit."

Miami Dolphins all-pro guard Bob Kuechenberg, discussing the steel pin inserted in his arm after an injury: "Ever since they put it in, I've been getting great reception on my car radio."

NBC-TV's Bob Costas, calling the play-by-play of the 1980 New England-Seattle game: "Don't fix your sets. I've been waiting for this all day. Mosi Tatupu runs into the arms of Manu Tuiasosopo."

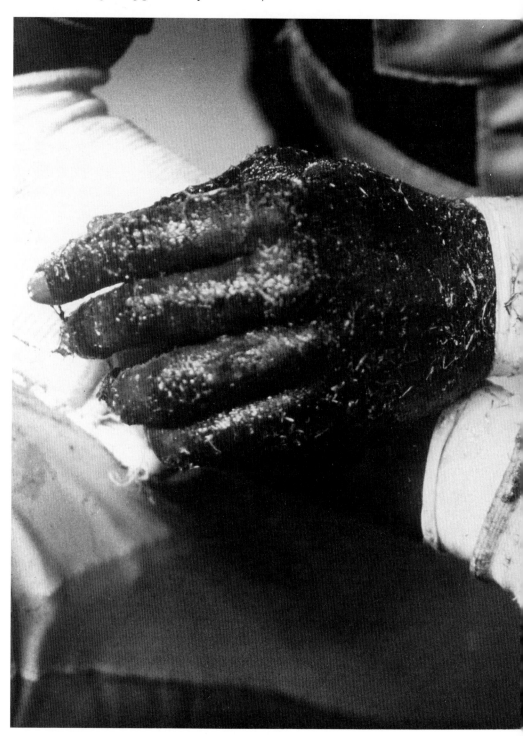

Los Angeles Rams running back Elvis Peacock: "I like my name. Not too many people have it."

Pro Football Hall of Fame end Raymond Berry: "My whole life and ambition could be summarized in one sentence: I just had to play football."

The hands of Oakland Raiders cornerback Lester Hayes revealed that in 1980, it was okay to use stickum. Those days are gone.

Los Angeles Rams head coach Ray Malavasi, when asked early in the 1978 season about Atlanta's rookie quarterback June Jones III: "He's got a great reputation, but nobody knows anything about him."

New England Patriots defensive end Richard Bishop, when asked in 1979 whether opposing players ever talked to him during a game: "Yeah. As a matter of fact, Larry Little of Miami once asked, 'Who are you, anyway?'"

Tampa Bay Buccaneers outside linebacker Cecil Johnson, on why he doesn't play middle linebacker: "Playing middle linebacker is like walking through a lion's cage in a three-piece pork-chop suit."

Kansas City Chiefs head coach John Mackovic, commenting in 1984 about how coach-player relationships had changed: "It used to be 'Go stand in the corner.' Then it got to be 'Could you go stand in the corner?' Then it was 'Is there a possibility we could discuss your going over and standing in the corner?' Now it's 'Why don't I go stand in the corner for you?'"

Los Angeles Raiders linebacker Ted Hendricks: "[The Raiders] are responsible for many rules changes. There's the no-clothesline rule. The no-spearing rule. The no-hitting out-of-bounds rule. No fumbling forward in the last two minutes of the game. No throwing helmets. The no-stickum rule. . . So you see, we're not all bad."

Philadelphia Eagles safety Don Burroughs, on a sore subject: "Every time I tackle Jim Brown, I hear a dice game going on inside my mouth."

"I kind of like [quarterback] Craig Morton. I think he's an overachiever. The main reason I like him, though, is because he can't run out of the pocket."

Jack Lambert, linebacker, Pittsburgh Steelers

"I have to be the only quarterback ever booed in Berlin. I have that distinction. What other quarterback's been booed there? Hitler? Did he play?"

Sonny Jurgensen, quarterback,
Philadelphia Eagles

Jack Lambert usually got his point across.

"When Larry Csonka goes on safari, the lions roll up their windows."

Monte Clark, head coach, Detroit Lions

Tight end Dave Casper, just after being traded from Oakland to Houston during the 1980 season: "I'm not sure what to say right now, other than it puts me a little bit closer to Willie Nelson."

"We had some talented players, but just not enough of them. We were a lot like an oil slick: We came from everywhere, but we weren't very deep."

Tom Franckhauser, cornerback, Dallas Cowboys

Denver Broncos punter Bill Van Heusen, explaining a weak effort in the Louisiana Superdome: "I figured I was kicking against the air conditioning."